American English File 1
Third Edition

Christina Latham-Koenig
Clive Oxenden
Jerry Lambert
Paul Seligson

Paul Seligson and Clive Oxenden
are the original co-authors of
English File 1 and *English File 2*

Contents

		GRAMMAR	VOCABULARY	PRONUNCIATION
1				
6	**A** Welcome to the class	verb *be* +, subject pronouns: *I, you*, etc.	days of the week, numbers 0–20	vowel sounds, word stress
8	**B** One world	verb *be* − and ?	countries, numbers 21–100	/ə/, consonant sounds /tʃ/, /ʃ/, /dʒ/, word stress
10	**C** What's your email?	possessive adjectives: *my, your*, etc.	classroom language	/oʊ/, /ɪ/, /ɑr/, the alphabet, sentence stress
12	**Practical English** Episode 1	checking in **V** in a hotel		
2				
14	**A** Are you neat or messy?	singular and plural nouns	things, *in, on, under*	final *-s* and *-es*
16	**B** Made in America	adjectives	colors, adjectives, modifiers: *very / really*	long and short vowel sounds
18	**C** Slow down!	imperatives, *let's*	feelings	linking
20	**Review and Check** 1&2			
3				
22	**A** America: the good and the bad	simple present + and −	verb phrases: *cook dinner*, etc.	third person *-s*
24	**B** 9 to 5	simple present ?	jobs	/ər/
26	**C** Love me, love my dog	word order in questions	question words	sentence stress
28	**Practical English** Episode 2	buying a coffee **V** telling the time		
4				
30	**A** Family photos	possessive *'s, Whose…?*	family	/ʌ/, the letter *o*
32	**B** From morning to night	prepositions of time (*at, in, on*) and place (*at, in, to*)	daily routine	linking
34	**C** Blue Zones	position of adverbs, expressions of frequency	months, adverbs and expressions of frequency	the letter *h*
36	**Review and Check** 3&4			
5				
38	**A** Vote for me!	*can / can't*	verb phrases: *buy a newspaper*, etc.	sentence stress
40	**B** A quiet life?	present continuous: *be* + verb + *-ing*	noise: verbs and verb phrases	/ŋ/
42	**C** A city for all seasons	simple present or present continuous?	the weather and seasons	places in Chicago
44	**Practical English** Episode 3	buying clothes **V** clothes		
6				
46	**A** A North African story	object pronouns: *me, you, him*, etc.	words in a story	/aɪ/, /ɪ/, and /i/
48	**B** The second Friday in July	*like* + (verb + *-ing*)	the date, ordinal numbers	/ð/ and /θ/, saying the date
50	**C** Making music	review: *be* or *do*?	music	/y/, giving opinions
52	**Review and Check** 5&6			

		GRAMMAR	VOCABULARY	PRONUNCIATION
7				
54	**A** Selfies	simple past of *be*: *was / were*	word formation: *write → writer*	sentence stress
56	**B** Wrong name, wrong place	simple past: regular verbs	past time expressions	*-ed* endings
58	**C** Happy New Year?	simple past: irregular verbs	*go, have, get*	sentence stress
60	**Practical English** Episode 4	asking for directions **V** directions		
8				
62	**A** A murder mystery	simple past: regular and irregular	irregular verbs	simple past verbs
64	**B** A house with a history	*there is / there are, some / any* + plural nouns	the house	/ɛr/ and /ɪr/
66	**C** Haunted rooms	*there was / there were*	prepositions: place and movement	silent letters
68	**Review and Check** 7&8			
9				
70	**A** #mydinnerlastnight	countable / uncountable nouns, *a / an, some / any*	food and drink	the letters *ea*
72	**B** White gold	quantifiers: *how much / how many, a lot of*, etc.	food containers	linking, /ʃ/ and /s/
74	**C** Facts and figures	comparative adjectives	high numbers	/ər/, sentence stress
76	**Practical English** Episode 5	ordering a meal **V** understanding a menu		
10				
78	**A** The most dangerous place…	superlative adjectives	places and buildings	consonant groups
80	**B** Five continents in a day	*be going to* (plans), future time expressions	city vacations	sentence stress
82	**C** The fortune-teller	*be going to* (predictions)	verb phrases	word stress
84	**Review and Check** 9&10			
11				
86	**A** Culture shock	adverbs (manner and modifiers)	common adverbs	connected speech
88	**B** Experiences or things?	verbs + infinitive	verbs that take the infinitive	weak *to*, sentence stress
90	**C** How smart is your phone?	definite article: *the* or no *the*	phones and the internet	*the*
92	**Practical English** Episode 6	getting to the airport **V** public transportation		
12				
94	**A** I've seen it ten times!	present perfect	irregular past participles	sentence stress
96	**B** He's been everywhere!	present perfect or simple past?	learning irregular verbs	irregular past participles
98	**C** The *American English File* interview	review: question formation		
100	**Review and Check** 11&12			
102	Communication	124 **Grammar Bank**	165 **Irregular verbs**	
113	Writing	148 **Vocabulary Bank**	166 **Sound Bank**	
118	Listening			

Course overview

American English File
Third Edition

Welcome to **American English File Third Edition**. This is how to use the Student Book, Online Practice, and the Workbook in and out of class.

Student Book

All the language and skills you need to improve your English, with Grammar, Vocabulary, Pronunciation, and skills work in every File.

Use your Student Book in class with your teacher.

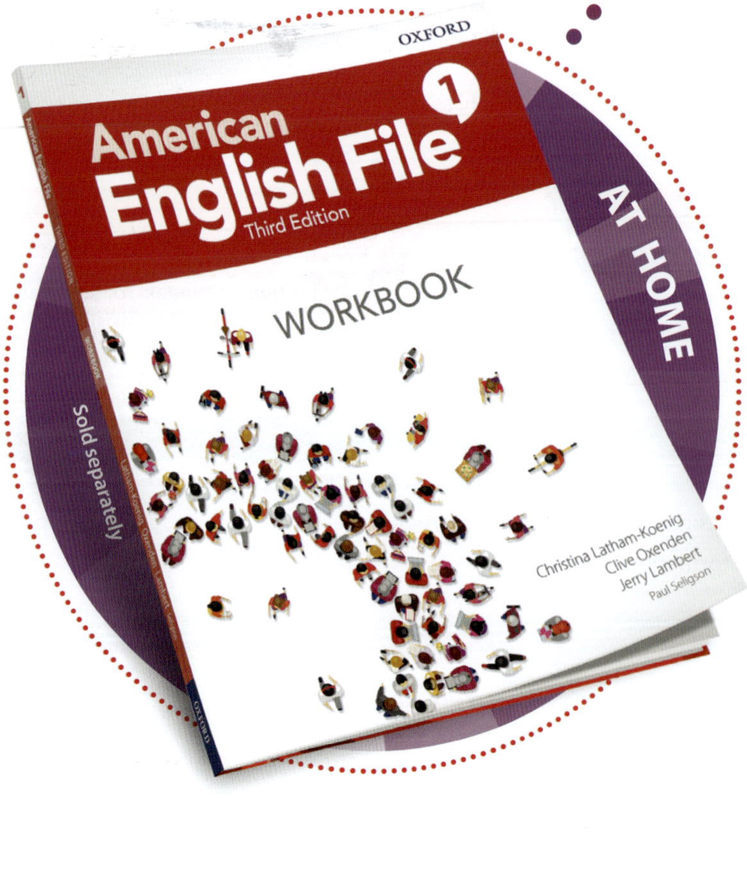

Workbook

Grammar, Vocabulary, and Pronunciation practice for every lesson.

Use your Workbook for homework or for self-study to practice language and to check your progress.

Go to americanenglishfileonline.com and use your Access Code to log into the Online Practice.

ACTIVITIES AUDIO VIDEO RESOURCES

LOOK AGAIN
- Review the language from every lesson.
- Watch the video and listen to all the class audio as many times as you like.

PRACTICE
- Improve your skills with extra Reading, Writing, Listening, and Speaking practice.
- Use the interactive video to practice Practical English.

CHECK YOUR PROGRESS
- Test yourself on the language from the File and get instant feedback.
- Try a Challenge activity.

SOUND BANK
- Use the Sound Bank video to practice and improve your pronunciation of English sounds.

Online Practice

Look again at Student Book language you want to review or that you missed in class, do extra *Practice* activities, and *Check your progress* on what you learned so far.

Use the Online Practice to learn outside the classroom and get instant feedback on your progress.

 americanenglishfileonline.com

Course overview   5

1A Welcome to the class

G verb be +, subject pronouns: I, you, etc. V days of the week, numbers 0–20 P vowel sounds, word stress

1 LISTENING & SPEAKING

a ◆ 1.2 Look at the photo story and listen to the conversations. Match the names to people A–D.

Ben   Carla   Matt   Sally

b Listen again and fill in the blanks.

1 **Teacher** Hello, everybody. Welcome to the class. I'm Carla. I'm your teacher.

2 **Matt** Hi, I'm Matt. What's your ¹_name_?
  Sally Sally.
  Matt ²_____?
  Sally Sally!

3 **Matt** What's your phone ³_____?
  Sally It's 555-413-2456.

4 **Ben** ⁴_____, Matt.
  Matt Hello. This is Sally. She's in my salsa class.
  Ben Nice to meet you. My name's Ben.
  Sally Nice to ⁵_____ you, too.
  Matt Bye, Sally.
  Sally Goodbye, Matt. Bye, Ben.

5 **Ben** Hi, Sally.
  Sally Ben! Are you in the salsa class, too?
  Ben Yes, I am. How are ⁶_____?
  Sally I'm very well, ⁷_____ you. And you?
  Ben ⁸_____, thanks. … Great! You're my partner!
  Sally Yes! See you later, Matt.

c ◆ 1.3 Listen and repeat the conversations. Copy the rhythm.

d Fill in the blanks with a word from the list.

Bye   Fine   Hi   I'm…   Thanks

Hello = _Hi_   Thank you = _____
My name's… = _____   Goodbye = _____
Very well = _____

e Introduce yourself to other students.

Hello, I'm Antonio. What's your name?

Mia. Nice to meet you.

Nice to meet you, too.

2 GRAMMAR verb be +, subject pronouns

a Complete the sentences with 'm, 's, or 're.
1. I am Carla. = I'_m_ Carla.
2. I am Matt. = I____ Matt.
3. My name is Ben. = My name____ Ben.
4. You are my partner. = You____ my partner.
5. She is in my salsa class. = She____ in my salsa class.

b **G** p.124 Grammar Bank 1A

c ◁)) 1.5 Listen and repeat the pronouns and contractions.
1)) I, I'm (I, I'm

d ◁)) 1.6 Listen. Say the contraction.
1)) I am (I'm

e In pairs, try to remember the names in your class. Say He's / She's _____.

f Stand up and speak to other students.

Hi, Mia. How are you?) (I'm fine, thanks. And you?

3 PRONUNCIATION vowel sounds, word stress

> **Vowel sounds**
> In American English, vowels (*a, e, i, o,* and *u*) and combinations of vowels (e.g., *ea, ai*) can be pronounced in different ways. Sometimes they are short sounds (e.g., *it, well*), but sometimes they are long sounds (e.g., *e = he*) or diphthongs (e.g., *i = hi*).

a ◁)) 1.7 Listen to the words and sounds. Then listen and repeat.

fish	tree	cat	egg	train	bike
it	he	am	very	they	hi
this	we	thanks	well	name	I
in	meet	Sally	welcome	later	bye

b ◁)) 1.8 Listen and write the words.

> **Word stress**
> Multisyllable words have one stressed syllable.
> good|**bye**   **so**|rry   **wel**|come

c ◁)) 1.9 Listen and underline the stressed syllable in these words.

air|port com|pu|ter e|mail ho|tel in|ter|net mu|se|um
pas|ta piz|za sa|lad sand|wich u|ni|ver|si|ty web|site

d Write the words from c in the chart.

✕ food	📶 technology	🏢 places
		airport

e In pairs, write more words that you know in each column. How do you pronounce them?

4 VOCABULARY days of the week, numbers 0–20

a ◁)) 1.10 Look at the picture. Listen and fill in the blanks.

b **V** p.148 Vocabulary Bank Days and numbers Do Parts 1 and 2.

c ◁)) 1.14 Listen and say the next day or number.
)) Monday   Tuesday (Wednesday

d Ask three students *What's your phone number?*

5 LISTENING & SPEAKING

a ◁)) 1.15 Listen. Where are they? Write 1–6 in the boxes.

	airport	Gate number _____
1	sandwich shop	_____ dollars and _____ cents
	hotel	Room _____
	museum	Closed on _____
	taxi	_____ Manchester Road
	language school	Classes on _____ and _____ mornings

b Listen again. Write a number or a day in each blank.

c ◁)) 1.16 Listen and respond.
1)) Hello. Nice to meet you. (Nice to meet you, too.
2)) What day is it today? (It's...

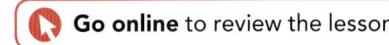

1B One world

Where are you from? I'm from Vancouver in Canada.

G verb be ⊟ and ❓ **V** countries, numbers 21–100 **P** /ə/, consonant sounds /tʃ/, /ʃ/, /dʒ/, word stress

1 VOCABULARY countries

a 🔊 1.17 Listen and match the music to the countries.
- Brazil
- China
- Mexico
- Russia

b **V** p.149 Vocabulary Bank Countries

c In groups, do The World Quiz. Answer with a continent, country, or nationality from **Vocabulary Bank** Countries.

I think it's Asia.   *I think it's Europe, but I'm not sure.*

2 PRONUNCIATION /ə/, /tʃ/, /ʃ/, /dʒ/

🔍 **The /ə/ sound**
The /ə/ sound is the most common vowel sound in English. The /ə/ sound has many different spellings, e.g., p**a**sta, M**o**rocco, **A**rgent**i**na.

a 🔊 1.20 Listen to the words and sounds. Then listen and repeat.

 computer	American Br**a**zilian
	C**a**nada Chin**a**

🔍 **Consonant sounds**
Many consonants (e.g., j) and combinations of consonants (e.g., sh) only have one pronunciation (e.g., **J**apan / **j**azz, **sh**e / Engli**sh**). Some consonants can be pronounced in different ways (e.g., g can be /g/ **E**n**g**land or /dʒ/ **G**erman).

b 🔊 1.21 Listen to the words, sounds, and sentences. Then listen and repeat. Practice with a partner.

tʃ ess	**ch**ess	**Ch**arles isn't **C**ze**ch**, he's Fren**ch**.
ʃ ower	**sh**ower	Is **sh**e Turki**sh** or Ru**ss**ian?
dʒ azz	**j**azz	We're **G**erman and they're **J**apanese.

c 🔊 1.22 Listen. Say the nationality.
1 🔊 Canada *Canadian*

THE WORLD QUIZ

1 Name the continents.
a _____ c _____ e _____
b _____ d _____ f _____

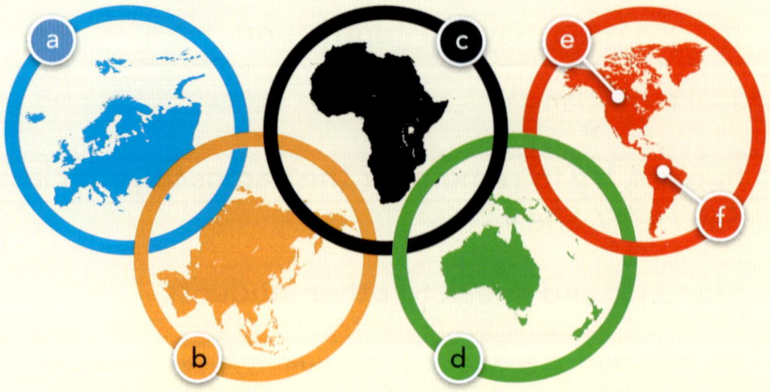

2 What country are the sports teams from?
a Toronto Maple Leafs _____
b Hanshin Tigers _____
c Galatasaray _____
d Limoges CSP _____
e Dallas Cowboys _____
f Mekong Raptors _____

3 What are the countries in English?
a Deutschland _____ d Россия _____
b España _____ e Méjico _____
c Eire _____ f Zhōngguó _____

4 What nationality are the flags?

a  _____ b  _____ c _____

d  _____ e _____

f  _____ g  _____ h _____

3 GRAMMAR verb be ⊟ and ❓

a 🔊 1.23 Read and listen to three interviews at the Olympics. Fill in the blanks with a country or a nationality.

1 A Hi. Where are you from?
   B We're from Fortaleza, in _____.
   A OK. Good luck to the _____ team!
   B Thank you!

2 A Hello. I'm Mike from *USA News*. Where are you from?
   B I'm from _____.
   A Are you from Sydney?
   B No, I'm not. I'm from Cairns.
   A Where's Cairns? Is it near Sydney?
   B No, it isn't. It's north. Am I on TV?
   A Yes, you are.
   B Wow!

3 A Hi. Are you _____?
   B No, we aren't. We're from _____.
   A Oh, sorry!

b Read the interviews again and complete the chart.

+	I'm	you're	it's
−		you aren't	
?			

c **G** p.124 Grammar Bank 1B

d 🔊 1.25 Listen and respond with a short answer.

   1 🔊 *Is Sydney the capital of Australia?* (*No, it isn't.*

e With a partner, write three questions beginning *Is…?* or *Are…?* Ask them to another pair.

   Are you from China?) (*No, we aren't.*

4 SPEAKING

a **C** Communication Where are they from? **A** p.102 **B** p.108 Ask and answer about people from different countries.

   Where's Masako from?)
      (*She's from Japan.*
   Where in Japan?)

b Imagine you're from a different country. Choose from **Vocabulary Bank** Countries **p.149** and think of a city. Ask other students *Where are you from?*

5 VOCABULARY numbers 21–100

a 🔊 1.26 Answer the questions with numbers 1–20.

   1 🔊 *What's 3 + 1?* (4.

b **V** p.148 Vocabulary Bank Days and numbers Do Part 3.

c 🔊 1.28 Listen and write the numbers.

d Write ten numbers from 21–100. Dictate them to a partner.

6 PRONUNCIATION & LISTENING
word stress

a 🔊 1.29 Listen and repeat the pairs of numbers. How is the stress different?

   1 a 13   b 30
   2 a 14   b 40
   3 a 15   b 50
   4 a 16   b 60
   5 a 17   b 70
   6 a 18   b 80
   7 a 19   b 90

b 🔊 1.30 Listen to the conversations. Which number do you hear? (Circle) a or b above.

c Play *Bingo*.

Go online to review the lesson

1C What's your email?

How do you spell your last name? V-A-Z-Q-U-E-Z.

G possessive adjectives: *my, your,* etc. **V** classroom language **P** /oʊ/, /u/, /ɑr/, the alphabet, sentence stress

1 VOCABULARY
classroom language

a Match the words and pictures.

- [ ] a board /bɔrd/
- [ ] a chair /tʃɛr/
- [ ] a computer /kəmˈpyutər/
- [ ] a desk /dɛsk/
- [1] a door /dɔr/
- [ ] a picture /ˈpɪktʃər/
- [ ] a table /ˈteɪbl/
- [ ] a wall /wɔl/
- [ ] a window /ˈwɪndoʊ/

b 🔊 1.31 Listen and check.

c With a partner, ask about things in your classroom.

What's this? — It's a chair. What's that? — It's a window.

d Match sentences 1–3 to A–C in the picture.
1 ☐ What page is it?
2 ☐ Sorry I'm late.
3 ☐ Look at the board, please.

e 🔊 1.32 Listen and check.

f **V** p.150 Vocabulary Bank Classroom language

g 🔊 1.35 Listen and follow the instructions.

2 PRONUNCIATION
/oʊ/, /u/, /ɑr/, the alphabet

a 🔊 1.36 Listen to the words and sounds. Then listen and repeat.

📞	ph**o**ne	cl**o**se g**o** Mexic**o**
👢	b**oo**t	sch**oo**l d**o** tw**o**
🚗	c**ar**	p**ar**tner **ar**e **Ar**gentina

b 🔊 1.37 Listen and repeat the alphabet.

ABC   DEF   GHI   JKL   MNO   PQR   STU   VWX   YZ

c 🔊 1.38 Complete the alphabet chart with C, D, K, N, O, S, U, and V. Listen and check.

/eɪ/	/i/	/ɛ/	/aɪ/	/oʊ/	/u/	/ɑr/
train	tree	egg	bike	phone	boot	car
A	B	F	I	___	Q	R
H	___	L	Y		___	
J	___	M			W	
___	E	___				
	G					
	P	X				
	T					
	Z					

d 🔊 1.39 Listen to the groups of letters.
1 E A I   3 K Q   5 V P B   7 V W
2 G J   4 C S   6 M N   8 Y U

e 🔊 1.40 Listen and (circle) the letter you hear.

f Practice saying the phrases below. Use abbreviations.

a **P**ersonal **C**omputer   a **V**ery **I**mportant **P**erson
the **U**nited **K**ingdom   the **U**nited **S**tates of **A**merica
the **E**uropean **U**nion   a **P**ortable **D**ocument **F**ormat
World **W**ide **W**eb   the **N**ational **B**asketball **A**ssociation

(a PC

3 LISTENING & SPEAKING

a 🔊 **1.41** Micaela is an ESL student. Listen to her Skype interview with Mark, a teacher at a language school in the United States. Complete her form.

English House Language School

Student information

First name	Micaela
Last Name	1
Age	2
Country	3
City	4
Address	Florida 5
Zip Code	6

Email address	m.vazquez@mail.com
Phone (cell)	7
Phone (landline)	8 54-

b 🔊 **1.42** Listen. Complete Mark's questions to Micaela.
1 _What's_ your first name?
2 _____ your last name?
3 _____ do you spell it?
4 _____ old are you?
5 Where are you _____?
6 _____ your address?
7 _____ your zip code?
8 What's your _____ address?
9 What's your phone _____?

> 🔍 **Sentence stress**
> In sentences we stress the important words.
> **What's** your **first name**?   It's **Mark**.

c Listen again and repeat the questions. Copy the rhythm.

d Ask your partner the questions. Write their answers.

> 🔍 **Saying emails**
> @ = at   . = dot

4 GRAMMAR possessive adjectives

a Complete the questions with *I*, *you*, *my*, or *your*.

> Where are ¹_____ from?
> ²_____ 'm from Buenos Aires.
> What's ³_____ name?
> ⁴_____ name's Micaela.

b 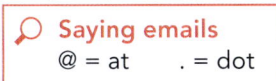 **p.124 Grammar Bank 1C**

c 🔊 **1.44** Listen. Change the sentences.
1 🔊 I'm Matt.   (My name's Matt.
2 🔊 You're Sally.   (Your name's Sally.

d 🔊 **1.45** Look at the photos. Are they their real names? Listen and check.

Shakira

Snoop Dogg

e 🅒 **Communication** What's his / her real name? **A p.102 B p.108** Complete information about some actors and singers.

5 WRITING

🅦 **p.113 Writing** Completing a form
Complete an application for a visa and write a paragraph about you.

Go online to review the lesson

EPISODE 1

Practical English Arriving in London

checking in   V in a hotel

1 VOCABULARY in a hotel

a Match the words and symbols.

- reception /rɪˈsɛpʃn/
- the elevator /ˈɛləˌveɪtər/
- a single room /ˈsɪŋɡl rum/
- a double room /ˈdʌbl rum/
- the first (second, third, etc.) floor /fɜrst flɔr/

b ◉ 1.46 Listen and check.

c Cover the words and look at the symbols. Say the words.

2 ▶ INTRODUCTION

a ◉ 1.47 Watch or listen to Jenny and Rob. Mark the sentences **T** (true) or **F** (false).
1 Rob lives and works in London.
2 He's a writer for a magazine.
3 The name of his magazine is *London 20seven*.
4 Jenny is British.
5 She's an assistant editor.
6 It's her second time in the UK.

b Watch or listen again. Say why the **F** sentences are false.

3 ▶ CHECKING IN

a ◉ 1.48 Watch or listen to Jenny checking into a hotel. Answer the questions.
1 Complete Jenny's last name: ZI__LI__SK__.
2 What's her room number? _____

b Watch or listen again. Complete the **You hear** phrases.

You hear	You say
Good evening, madam.	Hello. I have a reservation. My name's Jennifer Zielinski.
Can you ¹_____ that, please?	Z-I-E-L-I-N-S-K-I.
For five nights?	Yes, that's right.
Can I have your passport, please?	Just a second… Here you are.
Thank you. Can you sign here, ²_____ ? Thank you.	
Here's your ³_____ . It's room 306, on the third floor. The ⁴_____ is over there.	The lift? Oh, the elevator.
Yes. Enjoy your stay, Ms. Zielinski.	Thank you.

🔍 **American and British English**
elevator = American English   *lift* = British English
z = /zi/ American English   /zɛd/ British English

Greetings
Good morning = > 12:00
Good afternoon = 12:00 > 6:00
Good evening = 6:00 >
Good night = Goodbye (when you go to bed)
madam = a polite way to greet a woman
sir = a polite way to greet a man

c ▶ 1.49 Watch or listen and repeat the **You say** phrases. Copy the rhythm.

d Practice the conversation with a partner.

e Work in pairs. Read your role and look at the conversation in **3b**. What do you need to change?

A (book open) You are the receptionist.
It's 11:00 a.m.
B's room is 207 on the second floor. Begin *Good morning, sir / madam.*
B (book closed) You arrive at the hotel. Use your first name and last name.

f 👥 Role-play the conversation. Then change roles.

g ▶ 1.50 Read the information box. Listen and repeat the phrases.

> *Can you...?*
> = Please do it.
>
> *Can you spell that?*
> *Can you sign here?*
>
> *Can I have...?*
> = Please give me (my passport, etc.).
>
> *Can I have my key, please?*
> *Can I have your passport, please?*

h You are in a hotel. Ask the receptionist to give you…
- your key • your passport
- a map of London • a pen

4 ▶ JENNY TALKS TO ROB

a ▶ 1.51 Watch or listen. Mark the sentences **T** (true) or **F** (false).
1 Jenny has a coffee.
2 She is in London on business.
3 The waitress is German.
4 Jenny calls Rob Walker.
5 Jenny is tired.
6 Their meeting is at 10:00.

b Watch or listen again. Say why the **F** sentences are false.

c ▶ 1.52 Read the information box. Listen and repeat the phrases and responses.

> *Would you like...?*
> Would you like a coffee? Yes, please.
> Would you like another tea? No, thanks.
>
> We use *Would you like...?* to offer somebody something. We respond *Yes, please.* or *No, thanks.*

d With a partner, practice offering and responding with the drinks below.
- chai latte • coffee • soda • hot chocolate
- mineral water • tea

e Look at the **Social English** phrases. Who says them: **J**enny, **R**ob, or the **w**aitress?

> 💬 Social English
> 1 ☐ I'm here on business.
> 2 ☐ I'm from New York. What about you?
> 3 ☐ No problem.
> 4 ☐ This is Rob. Rob Walker.
> 5 ☐ That's perfect.
> 6 ☐ It's time for bed.

f ▶ 1.53 Watch or listen and check. Then watch or listen and repeat the phrases.

g Complete conversations A–F with **Social English** phrases 1–6. Practice with a partner.

A	Hi. Is that Jennifer? 4	Hello, Rob.
B	Oh look! It's 11:30!	Goodnight.
C	Hi. Are you here on vacation?	No,
D		I'm from London.
E	Can I have a coffee, please?	Sure.
F	Here's your coffee. Milk and sugar are on the table.	Thanks.

CAN YOU...?

☐ check into a hotel and spell your name
☐ ask somebody to do something / to give you something
☐ offer somebody a drink, and accept or refuse

Go online to watch the video, review the lesson, and check your progress

2A Are you neat or messy?

G singular and plural nouns **V** things, *in, on, under* **P** final *-s* and *-es*

What are they? They're keys.

A **neat** room

VIRGINIA WOOLF
Modernist writer (1882–1941)

B A **messy** room

IAN RANKIN
Crime writer (1960–)

1 VOCABULARY things

a Look at the photos of the two rooms. Are *you* neat or messy?

b With a partner, can you name 1–10 in the two photos?

c **V** p.151 **Vocabulary Bank** Things

2 GRAMMAR singular and plural nouns

a Complete the chart. Why is it **a** pen but **an** umbrella?

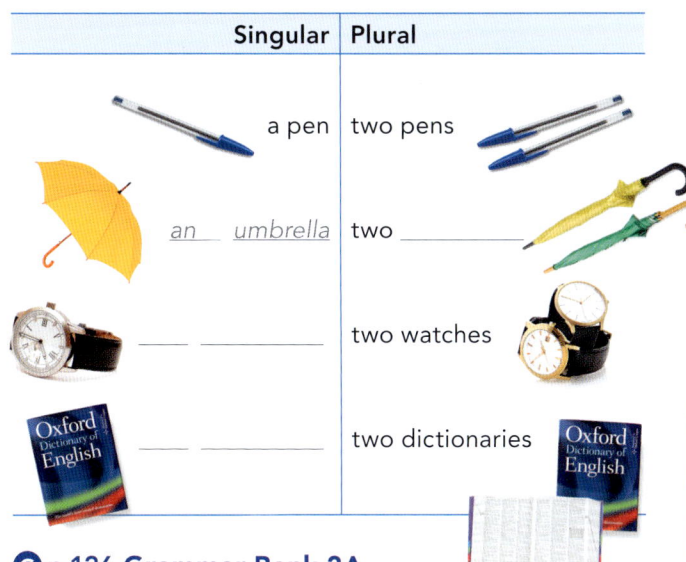

Singular	Plural
a pen	two pens
<u>an</u> umbrella	two _____
_____ _____	two watches
_____ _____	two dictionaries

b **G** p.126 **Grammar Bank** 2A

3 PRONUNCIATION final -s and -es

a 🔊 2.3 Listen to the words and sounds. Then listen and repeat.

snake	book**s** lamp**s** ticket**s**	
zebra	key**s** pen**s** photo**s**	
/ɪz/	glass**es** change purs**es** watch**es**	

> 🔍 **Final -s or -es**
> Final -s or -es after nouns ending in *ce, ch, ge, se, sh, ss,* and *x* = /ɪz/, e.g., *glasses, change purses, watches.*

b 🔊 2.4 Read the rule. Circle the words where -es is pronounced /ɪz/. Listen and check.

1 classes
2 files
3 headphones
4 boxes
5 pieces
6 tissues
7 pages
8 phones

c Look at the photos of the two rooms again. What plural things can you see?

4 VOCABULARY & SPEAKING
in, on, under

a Look at the photos. Complete the sentences with *in, on,* or *under*.

1 The glasses are _____ the notebook.
2 The credit cards are _____ the wallet.
3 The bag is _____ the desk.

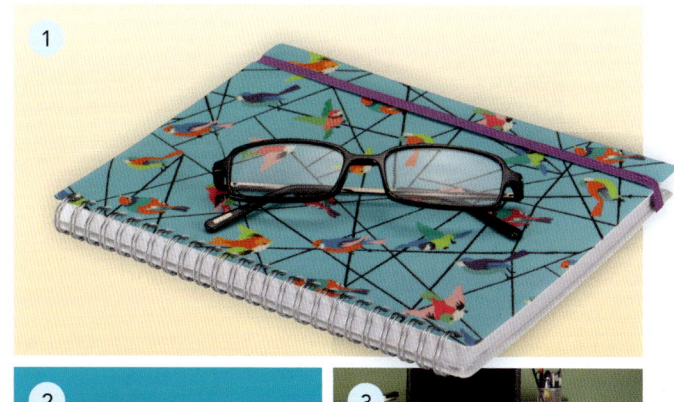

b **C** **Communication** *in, on, under* **A** p.103 **B** p.108 Where are the things?

5 LISTENING

a 🔊 2.5 Listen to three people. Number the places they talk about (1–3) in the chart.

☐ in her bag	
☐ on his desk	a computer,
☐ in her study	

b Listen again. Write what things the people have in each place.

c Talk to a partner about your bag, desk, or room. Say what things you have. Is your desk or room neat or messy?

(In my bag, I have a change purse, keys, my phone…

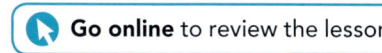

2B Made in America

G adjectives **V** colors, adjectives, modifiers: very / really **P** long and short vowel sounds

> Are taxis cheap in New York?
>
> No, they're really expensive.

1 VOCABULARY colors, adjectives

a What color is the American flag? Complete the words with vowels.

It's r__d, wh__t__, and bl____.

b 🔊 2.6 Complete the colors. Listen and check.

bl__ck   y__ll__w   gr__y   __r__ng__   br__wn
p__nk   gr____n   p__rpl__   s__lv__r   g__ld

c With a partner, practice colors with things in the classroom or in your bag.

What color is my wallet?) (It's red.
What color is that?) (It's black.

d **V** p.152 **Vocabulary Bank** Adjectives

2 GRAMMAR adjectives

a Look at the American icons. What are they? Label the photos using an adjective and a noun from each circle.

Adjectives
American New
French yellow
blue hot
fast White

Nouns
House jeans
football food
fries York
taxis dog

b (Circle) the correct word or phrase.
1 Can I have a *hot dog / dog hot*, please?
2 In New York, the taxis are *yellows / yellow*.

c **G** p.126 **Grammar Bank** 2B

d Close your books. Can you remember the eight American icons?

1 American football
2 _____
3 _____
4 _____

AMERICAN ICONS

5 the _____
6 _____
7 a _____

3 PRONUNCIATION
long and short vowel sounds

a ▶ 2.9 Listen to the words and sounds. Then listen and repeat.

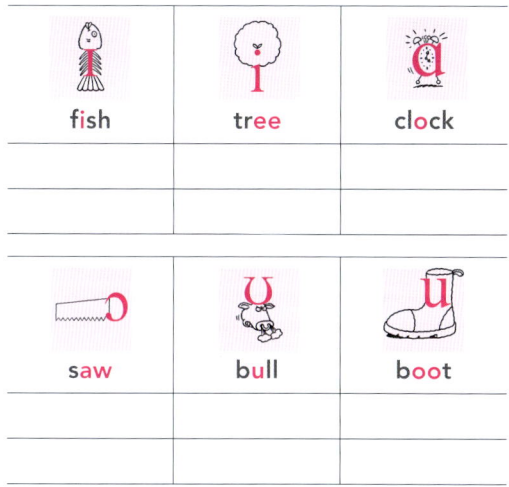

fish	tree	clock

saw	bull	boot

b ▶ 2.10 Listen and write two adjectives for each sound in the chart.

c In pairs, make phrases with an adjective and a noun with the same vowel sound. Use *a / an* with singular nouns.

Adjectives	~~big~~ black cheap good gray long new old short
Nouns	bag book boots ~~city~~ day jeans photo song story

a big city

d ▶ 2.11 Listen and check. Practice saying the phrases.

4 SPEAKING

a Tell a partner about eight things you have. Use an adjective or a color.

I have a new phone. I have a red car...

b **Communication** The same or different? **A** p.103 **B** p.109 Describe your pictures to a partner. Find the differences.

5 READING

American and British English – the same, but different

American and British people speak the same language, English, but with some small differences.

1 **Vocabulary** Some words are different in British English, for example, they say *postcode*, not *zip code*; *holiday*, not *vacation*; and *mobile phone*, not *cell phone*. Some words have different meanings, for example, in American English, a *purse* is a woman's bag. In British English, a *purse* is a thing where women have their money and credit cards.

2 _____ *Color, favor*, and other words that end in -*or* in American English end in -*our* in British English. *Center, theater*, and other words that end in -*ter* in American English end in -*tre* in British English.

3 _____ There are some small differences, especially prepositions. For example, British people say *See you on Friday*, but Americans say *See you Friday*.

4 _____ This is the really important difference between British and American English. American accents and British accents are very different. When a British person starts speaking, Americans know he or she is British, and vice versa.

a Read the article once. Complete it with the headings.

Grammar   Pronunciation   Spelling   ~~Vocabulary~~

b ▶ 2.12 Listen and read the article again. Check your answers to **a**.

c Mark the sentences **T** (true) or **F** (false).
1 American English and British English are very different.
2 *Holiday* and *postcode* are the same in British and American English.
3 *Purse* has a different meaning in American and British English.
4 *Kilometer* is the British spelling.
5 British and American grammar are not very different.
6 It's difficult to know if a person is British or American from their accent.

d Do you know any more words that are British English, not American English?

8 _____ _____

2C Slow down!

G imperatives, *let's* **V** feelings **P** linking

> I'm cold. Close the window!

1 VOCABULARY feelings

a Match the words and pictures.

☐ angry	☐ bored	☐ cold
☐ frightened	☐ happy	☐ hot
☐ hungry	☐ sad	☐ stressed
☐ thirsty	☐ tired	1 worried

b 🔊 2.13 Listen and check. Repeat the phrases.

> 🔍 **Collocation**
> Use *be* + *hungry, thirsty, hot*, etc., e.g.,
> I'm hungry. **NOT** ~~I have hungry~~.

c How do you feel? Make true sentences and tell your partner.

I'm hungry. I'm very tired.

2 LISTENING & READING

a 🔊 2.14 Lisa and John are on vacation with their baby, Henry. Listen and look at the pictures. How does each person feel?

Picture 1 Lisa *angry*   Picture 3 Lisa, John
Picture 2 John, Henry   Picture 4 Lisa, Henry

b Listen again and read the story. Check your answers to **a**.

c 🔊 2.15 Listen to the end of the story. Is it a happy ending?

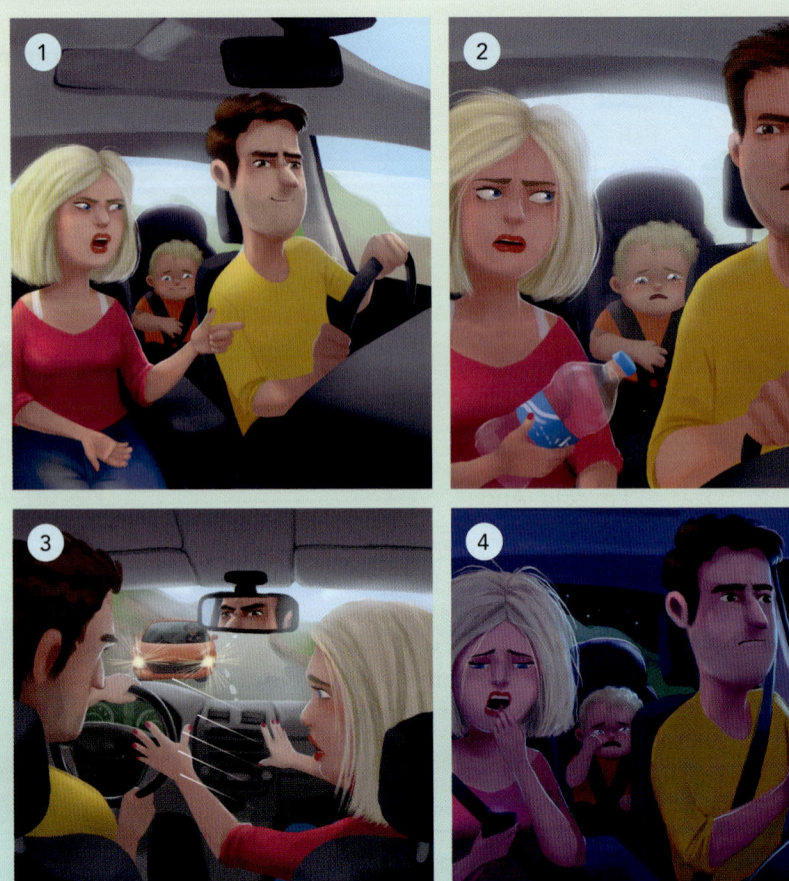

3 GRAMMAR imperatives, *let's*

a Look at the highlighted phrases in the story. Then complete the chart.

Imperatives	
➕ *Turn* right.	_____ careful!
_____ for a hotel.	
➖ _____ turn left!	_____ drive fast!
_____ worry.	

Suggestions	
➕ _____ stop for some food.	_____ go there.
➖ Let's _____ stop.	

b 🅖 p.126 **Grammar Bank 2C**

18

1　GPS　　In 100 feet turn right. Turn right.
　　Lisa　　Don't turn left! Turn right!
　　John　　It's left, I'm sure.
　　Lisa　　No, it isn't.
　　John　　Yes, it is!
　　Lisa　　No, it isn't! This is wrong!
　　John　　Oh no…

2　John　　I'm thirsty. Where's the water?
　　Lisa　　Sorry, it's empty.
　　John　　Empty?
　　Lisa　　Yes, empty. Let's stop for some food. Henry's hungry.
　　John　　OK.

3　John　　What's the matter?
　　Lisa　　I'm cold. Can you close your window?
　　John　　Cold? It's hot!
　　Lisa　　I'm cold. And Henry's cold.
　　John　　OK.
　　Lisa　　Please don't drive fast! This road's really dangerous.
　　John　　Don't worry. I'm a good driver.
　　Lisa　　Be careful!

4　Lisa　　Let's look for a hotel.
　　John　　No, let's not stop now.
　　Lisa　　But I'm tired and it's dark. And Henry's tired, too.
　　John　　OK, OK. Look for a hotel near here.
　　Lisa　　The Highland Hotel's 20 miles from here. Let's go there.
　　John　　20 miles? No problem.

c　What do signs 1–9 mean? Make ➕ or ➖ imperatives with the verb phrases.

be careful　cross the road now　eat or drink here
go in here　listen to music here　~~smoke here~~
take photos　~~turn left~~　turn off your phone

1　*Turn left.*
2　*Don't smoke here.*

d　Cover the verb phrases and look at the signs. Can you remember the phrases?

4　SPEAKING

C Communication What's the matter?
A p.103　**B** p.109　Role-play conversations.

What's the matter?　*I'm sad.*

5　PRONUNCIATION linking

🔍 **Connected speech**
When people speak, they don't separate all the words. Often, if a word ends with a consonant and the next word begins with a vowel, they link them together, e.g., *Good͜ idea.*

a　🔊 2.17　Listen and write six sentences.

b　Practice saying the sentences.

6　▶ VIDEO LISTENING

a　Watch the video *Have a safe trip!* Complete the ten tips.

1　*Plan* your trip.
2　Check your _____.
3　Listen to _____ information on the radio.
4　Take a _____ with you in the car.
5　Take bottles of _____.
6　Take books, games, and _____ with you.
7　_____ that all the passengers in the car have their seat belts on.
8　Check that you have _____.
9　After driving for two hours, stop for _____ minutes.
10　Don't use your _____.

b　Watch again. With a partner, agree your top three tips.

🔵 Go online to watch the video and review the lesson

1 & 2 Review and Check

GRAMMAR

Circle a, b, or c.

1 Hello. ____ your name?
  a What   b What are   c What's
2 Maria is German. ____ a student.
  a She's   b He's   c It's
3 A Where ____ from?   B He's from Turkey.
  a he is   b is   c is he
4 They ____ American, they're Canadian.
  a isn't   b aren't   c not are
5 A Are you from Paris?   B Yes, ____.
  a I am   b I'm   c I are
6 She's Brazilian. ____ name's Daniela.
  a His   b Her   c Your
7 We're from the US. ____ last name is Martin.
  a Your   b Their   c Our
8 A What are they?   B They're ____.
  a watches   b a watch   c watchs
9 A What is it?   B It's ____.
  a a umbrella   b an umbrella   c umbrella
10 It's an ____.
   a animal ugly   b ugly animal   c beautiful animal
11 I have a ____.
   a bag very big   b very bag big   c very big bag
12 They're very ____.
   a difficult exercises   b exercises difficult
   c difficults exercises
13 ____ careful! That dog's dangerous.
   a Have   b Be you   c Be
14 Please ____ in the library.
   a not eat   b don't eat   c no eat
15 I'm hungry. ____ stop for some food.
   a Let's   b Let   c Don't

VOCABULARY

a Complete with *at*, *from*, *in*, *off*, or *to*.

1 I'm _____ Japan.
2 Nice _____ meet you.
3 What's *bonjour* _____ English?
4 Look _____ the board.
5 Please turn _____ your phone.

b Complete the phrases with these verbs.

Answer	Open	Read	Stand	Work

1 _____ the text.   4 _____ the door.
2 _____ in pairs.   5 _____ the questions.
3 _____ up.

c Circle the word that is different.

one book six three
1 eight   file   seven   two
2 Brazil   Chinese   Vietnam   Mexico
3 France   Peruvian   Japanese   Turkish
4 Africa   Asia   Europe   Ireland
5 sixteen   forty   eighty   ninety
6 Friday   Germany   Monday   Wednesday
7 glasses   headphones   change purse   scissors
8 door   school   window   wall
9 book   magazine   newspaper   wallet
10 angry   happy   stressed   tired

d Write the opposite adjective.

1 good   _____
2 expensive _____
3 dirty   _____
4 high   _____
5 left   _____

PRONUNCIATION

a Practice the words and sounds.

Vowel sounds

f**i**sh   tr**ee**   c**a**t   c**ar**

Consonant sounds

snake   **z**ebra   **sh**ower   **j**azz

b **P** p.166–7 **Sound Bank** Say more words for each sound.

c What sound do the pink letters have in these words?
  1 **e**mail   2 f**a**st   3 p**a**ge   4 s**i**t   5 t**i**ssues

d Underline the stressed syllable.
  1 ad|dress   3 ex|pen|sive   5 thir|teen
  2 Ger|man|y   4 sun|gla|sses

CAN YOU understand this text?

a Read the article once. What kind of people is it for?

b Read the article again. Mark the sentences **T** (true) or **F** (false).
1 Rockefeller Center is very expensive.
2 It's a good place to take photos.
3 A lot of people stand and wait to get tickets for the Statue of Liberty.
4 It's a good idea to drive in New York City.
5 It's easy to walk to Coney Island from New York.
6 Good Enough to Eat is open from morning to night.

▶ CAN YOU understand these people?

🔊 2.18 Watch or listen and answer the questions.

1   2   3   4

1 Her name is ____.
  a Malini   b Mallini   c Malinni
2 Olga is from ____.
  a Mexico   b Monaco   c Moscow
3 Her name is ____.
  a Lydia   b Lisa   c Lena
  She's ____.
  a Canadian   b American   c English
4 Jake is ____.
  a very untidy   b tidy   c very tidy

CAN YOU say this in English?

Do the tasks with a partner. Check (✓) the box if you can do these things.

Can you…?
1 ☐ count from 0–20
2 ☐ count from 20–100 (20, 30, etc.)
3 ☐ say the days of the week
4 ☐ give three instructions, two ➕ and one ➖
5 ☐ introduce yourself and another person
6 ☐ answer the questions below
  • What's your first name / last name?
  • How do you spell it?
  • Where are you from?

Plan your trip to New York
with these top tips

Go to Rockefeller Center
It's cheap, and from the top floor you can see Central Park, the Empire State Building, and more. Remember to take your camera!

Buy your tickets for the Statue of Liberty online
The Statue of Liberty is an American icon, but there are always long lines for tickets. Buy them on the internet before you go.

Explore the city on foot
Don't rent a car in New York City. The best thing is to walk – but good shoes are very important! Slow down and listen to the city. Sit on the grass in Central Park on a sunny day. But if you are tired, take a bus or the subway!

Visit Coney Island
Go to Coney Island by subway (an hour) and have a delicious New York hot dog. If it's hot, go for a swim in the Atlantic!

Have a meal at Good Enough to Eat
Good Enough to Eat on 83rd Street is a great traditional American restaurant serving breakfast, lunch, and dinner. It has salads, sandwiches, steak, and more.

Go online to watch the video, review Files 1 and 2, and check your progress

3A America: the good and the bad

> It rains a lot here.
>
> Yes, b[ut it] doesn't [rain] every [day.]

G simple present + and − **V** verb phrases: *cook dinner*, etc. **P** third person -s

1 VOCABULARY verb phrases

a ◆ 3.1 Listen and match the sounds and verb phrases.

- drink water
- like animals
- watch TV
- play the guitar
- speak German

b **V p.153 Vocabulary Bank** Verb phrases

c ◆ 3.3 Listen. Say the phrases.

1))) TV (*watch TV*

2 GRAMMAR simple present + and −

a Read the article below. Complete the things Chela likes (1–8) with a word or phrase from the list.

| coffee | fast food | freeways | multiculturalism |
| sports | the freedom | the language | the weather |

b ◆ 3.4 Listen and check.

c Answer the questions with a partner.
1 Look at the highlighted phrases. How are the verbs different in phrases 7 and 8? Why?
2 Find the negative − forms in the article and complete the chart. How are they different? Why?

+	−
I have	
It rains	

d **G p.128 Grammar Bank 3A**

3 PRONUNCIATION third person -s

> 🔍 **Final -s or -es**
> The pronunciation rules for verbs ending in -s and -es are the same as for plural nouns.

a How do you pronounce these plural nouns?

books   keys   watches

b ◆ 3.6 Listen to the sounds and sentences. Then listen and repeat.

/s/ She speaks Arabic.
He drinks a lot of coffee.
She cooks every day.

/z/ It rains a lot.
He has a cat.
She does yoga.
He goes out on Friday night.

/ɪz/ He watches American shows.
The movie finishes in a minute.
The bookstore closes at ten.

c ◆ 3.7 Listen. Change the sentences.

1))) *I live in an apartment. She.*
(*She lives in an apartment.*

> My name's Chela. I'm an engineer. I like...

WHAT AMERICANS LIKE ABOUT THE US

1 <u>multiculturalism</u>. People from all over the world live in the US, and <mark>they live</mark> together happily. Usually.

2 _____. English is international. I speak English. <mark>You speak</mark> English. I don't have communication problems.

3 _____. I have a large cup of coffee every day. When I'm in a hurry, I go to the drive-thru and buy it from my car.

4 _____. I wear what I want. I say what I want. I do what I want.

5 _____. I like all kinds of sports, but I really like basketball. My favorite basketball team is the Golden State Warriors. I watch their games on TV.

6 _____. We drive a lot! The freeways are very fast and have a lot of car lanes. It's really easy to drive from one place to another.

7 _____. I love the fall weather. A good fall day is cool, but not too cold. Sometimes it rains in the fall, but it doesn't rain every day.

8 _____. My boyfriend cooks really good hamburgers, and the US is great for fast food!

d Work in pairs. Tell your partner six true things about you, three ➕ and three ➖. Choose verb phrases from **Vocabulary Bank Verb phrases p.153**.

I play tennis. I don't wear glasses…

e Change partners. Tell your new partner the six things about your old partner.

Eva plays tennis. She doesn't wear glasses…

4 READING

a Read the article on the right. Write ✓ if the person is positive about the country he or she lives in, ✗ if he or she is negative, and ✓✗ if he or she is positive and negative. Give reasons for your answers.

b Read the article again. Complete the sentences with a name.

1 _____ likes the weather.
2 _____ and _____ don't like the weather.
3 _____ likes the food.
4 _____ doesn't like the food.
5 _____ and _____ think the people are friendly.
6 _____ thinks the food costs a lot.
7 _____ thinks Americans work very hard.

c Look at two words from the article. Match them to their meanings. What do you think *everywhere* means?

everybody /ˈɛvribɑdi/
everything /ˈɛvriˌθɪŋ/

1 all things _____   2 all people _____

5 SPEAKING

a Complete the sentences under each heading in your own words. Think about why you like (or don't like) them.

Things I like about my country
My favorite thing about _____ is…
I really love…
I also like…

Things I don't like about my country
One thing that I don't like is…
I also don't like…

b Compare your sentences with a partner and say why. Do you like the same things?

My favorite thing about Italy is the food, because I love pasta and real Italian pasta is fantastic.

> 🔍 **Useful words: *Why?* and *because***
> Use *because* to answer the question *Why?*
> *I don't like the weather **because** it rains a lot.*

WHAT AMERICANS WHO LIVE ABROAD THINK ABOUT OTHER COUNTRIES

Sarah, 36, is from New York. She lives in the UK. In the US, we work really hard. Sometimes we don't take vacations because we work so hard. British people are different. They only want to finish work and go home.

Amy, 22, is from Tennessee. She lives in Thailand. I really like the weather. It's very hot and it rains a lot from June to October. Also, the people are very friendly. Everybody smiles. I love it!

Jayne, 22, is from Connecticut. She lives in Argentina. Argentina is a beautiful country, and the people are very warm and friendly. They like to talk to foreigners and they are interested in other countries. Something I don't like is the weather in winter. Sometimes it's very cold.

Gaby, 30, is from Minnesota. She lives in Mexico. My favorite thing in Mexico is the tacos al pastor. We don't have tacos al pastor in the US. Some people think Mexican food is spicy, but I love it. Everything about Mexico is great except the traffic in Mexico City. It's very slow.

Eric, 28, is from New York. He lives in Iceland. Iceland can be very cold and gray. And it rains a lot! For me, food is a problem. They eat a lot of fish and seafood here, and I don't like fish or seafood.

Christina, 21, is from California. She lives in Morocco. I love Morocco. Why? Because I like the culture, the art, the history. It's a beautiful country, too, especially the Atlas Mountains. The only thing I don't like? It's difficult for a woman to travel alone.

3B 9 to 5

> Do you work at night?
> Yes, I'm a taxi driver.

G simple present [?] **V** jobs **P** /ər/

1 GRAMMAR simple present [?]

a Look at the photo of Jess and her husband Carl. What's his job? Find the answer in the interview with Jess.

b Read the interview. Complete 1–5 with questions from the list.

Do you have time together?
Does he have free weekends?
~~What do you do, Jess?~~
What does your husband do?
Do you work long hours?

c 3.8 Listen and check.

d Cover the interview and look at the questions in **b**. How does Jess answer them?

e Do you work or study at night? What problems do you have?

f Look at the questions in **b** again. Which are…?
  1 about Jess
  2 about her husband
  3 about Jess and her husband

g **G** p.128 Grammar Bank 3B

He works at night, but she works during the day…

1 *What do you do, Jess?*
I work in an office. I'm an administrator.

2 _____
No, I don't. I work normal hours, from 9:00 to 5:00, Monday to Friday.

3 _____
He's a police officer. He works at night, from 8:00 p.m. to 6:00 in the morning.

4 _____
No, he doesn't. Well, he has two free days, but they're Wednesday and Thursday. He works Saturday and Sunday – they're busy nights for police officers.

5 _____
Not really, except when we're on vacation. I'm in bed when he comes home; he's in bed when I leave home in the morning. We don't eat together. That's awful. Sometimes I don't cook, I just have cookies for dinner.

Can you think of any good things about your different hours?
Yes, we earn more money because Carl does a lot of overtime.

Do you have any suggestions for couples like you?
Have a whiteboard in your hall or your kitchen and write down all the housework. Then check off things when you do them. That way, the dogs don't eat twice!

Glossary overtime extra hours

2 VOCABULARY jobs

a Complete the sentences with a job from the list.

> actor   administrator   police officer
> receptionist   teacher

1. A _____ works on the street, or in a police station.
2. An _____ works in a theater.
3. A _____ works in a school.
4. A _____ works in a hotel.
5. An _____ works in an office.

b **V** p.154 **Vocabulary Bank** Jobs

c What do you do? What do your parents do? Ask three other students in the class.

3 PRONUNCIATION /ɜr/

a 3.12 Listen to the words and sounds. Then listen and repeat.

| bird | nurse   thirty   her |
| | work   journalist |

> /ɜr/
> ur, ir, and er usually = /ɜr/ when they are stressed.

b 3.13 Listen to the sentences. Then practice saying them.

Doctors and lawyers earn a lot.
Journalists work all over the world.
She's a teacher. Her name's Ursula.
He's a taxi driver. He works thirty hours a week.
I'm a waiter in a burger restaurant.
I study German at the university.

4 LISTENING

a 3.14 Listen to Part 1 of a game show called *His Job, Her Job*. Three people ask Alex and Sue about their jobs. Underline the questions they ask Alex.

b Listen again. What are Alex's answers? Write ✓ (yes), ✗ (no), or **D** (it depends).

Where?	Alex	Sue
/ work outside?		
/ work inside?		
/ work in an office?	✗	
/ work at home?		
When?		
/ work in the evening?		
/ work at night?		
/ work on the weekend?		
How?		
/ work with the public?		
/ work on a team?		
/ work long hours?		
Other		
/ have special qualifications?		
/ get vacation time?		
/ speak foreign languages?		
/ travel?		
/ drive?		
/ make things?		
/ wear a uniform or special clothes?		
/ earn a lot of money?		
/ like your job?		

c 3.15 Now listen to Part 2 and do the same for Sue.

d Look at their answers and make sentences about them. What do you think their jobs are?

> *Alex doesn't work in an office.*   *He sometimes works in the evening.*

e 3.16 Listen. What do Alex and Sue do?

5 SPEAKING

a In groups of four, play *His Job, Her Job*. Choose jobs from **Vocabulary Bank** Jobs p.154. Ask questions to guess them.

> *Do you work at night?*

b Now think of a person you know who has one of the jobs. Is it a man or a woman? Play the game again.

> *Does she speak foreign languages?*

3C Love me, love my dog

What kind of music do you like? I like classical music.

G word order in questions **V** question words **P** sentence stress

1 LISTENING

a ▶ 3.17 A man and a woman meet in the park. Listen. Match the names to the people or dogs. What do you find out about the dogs?

Becca — his dog
Barry — the man
Dave — her dog
Dolly — the woman

b ▶ 3.18 Listen to their conversation at the café. What happens at the end?

c Listen again. Complete the questions.

> D It's really hot. Would you ¹_like_ a drink? Or some ice cream?
> B Yes, why not? Let's go to the café.
> D ² _____ kind of ice cream do you _____?
> B Uh, an ice-cream bar if they have it.
> D Here you are. One ice-cream bar.
> B Thanks, Dave.
> D ³ _____ do you _____?
> B I live near here, on Park Road. And you?
> D I live across town on Lake Street. ⁴ _____ do you _____, Becca?
> B I'm a journalist.
> D Really? How interesting! Do you ⁵ _____ for a newspaper?
> B No, for TV. ⁶ _____ about you?
> D I'm a teacher. I'm on vacation now.
> B Me too. Oh! My ice cream.
> D Dolly! Bad dog! I'm really sorry.
> B That's OK.
> D Do you ⁷ _____ another ice-cream bar?
> B No, thanks.
> D Are you sure? I'm really sorry. Look, let's have lunch one day. I know a great place that's dog friendly. Are you free on Saturday?
> B Oh, well, OK. Yes. Thanks.

d ▶ 3.19 Read the information box. Listen and repeat the phrases for showing interest. Copy the intonation.

> 🔎 **Showing interest**
> When you have a conversation, show interest in what the other person says. Use _Really? How interesting! What about you? Me too._, etc.

e Practice the conversation in **c** with a partner.

f ▶ 3.20 Becca meets Dave at a dog-friendly restaurant. Listen and complete the sentences with **B** (Becca), **D** (Dave), or **R** (the restaurant).

1 ____ thinks the restaurant is cute.
2 ____ has good food for people and dogs.
3 ____ doesn't really like dogs.
4 ____ doesn't have a big apartment.
5 ____ has two cats.
6 ____ serves homemade ice cream.

g Do you think the lunch is a success?

26

2 GRAMMAR word order in questions

a Put the words in order to make the questions.
1 Barry is old how
_____?
2 his name what's
_____?
3 like do it you
_____?
4 about feel do cats you how
_____?

b ◐ 3.21 Listen and check.

c Ⓖ p.128 Grammar Bank 3C

3 VOCABULARY question words

a Complete the questions with a question word or phrase.

| How many   ~~What~~   What kind of   When |
| Where   Which   Who   Why |

1 _What_____ phone do you have?
 I have a Samsung.
2 _____ brothers and sisters do you have?
 I have two sisters.
3 _____ do you prefer, cats or dogs?
 Cats, I think.
4 _____ do you work?
 In a restaurant near the river.
5 _____ do you have language classes?
 On Mondays and Wednesdays.
6 _____ music do you like?
 I like pop and reggae.
7 _____'s your favorite actor?
 Michael B. Jordan.
8 _____ do you like him?
 Because he's a really good actor.

b ◐ 3.24 Listen and check. Then answer the questions.
1 How is *Wh-* pronounced in *Who*?
2 How is *Wh-* pronounced in the other question words?
3 What's the difference between *What…?* and *Which…?*

4 PRONUNCIATION sentence stress

a ◐ 3.25 Listen to the questions. Then listen and repeat. Copy the rhythm.

Where do you **work**?

What phone do you **have**?

What kind of **music** do you **like**?

Who's your **favorite actor**?

b Work in pairs. **A** ask **B** the questions in **3a**. **B** give your own answers. Then change roles.

5 SPEAKING

a Look at the questions. What words are missing in each group?

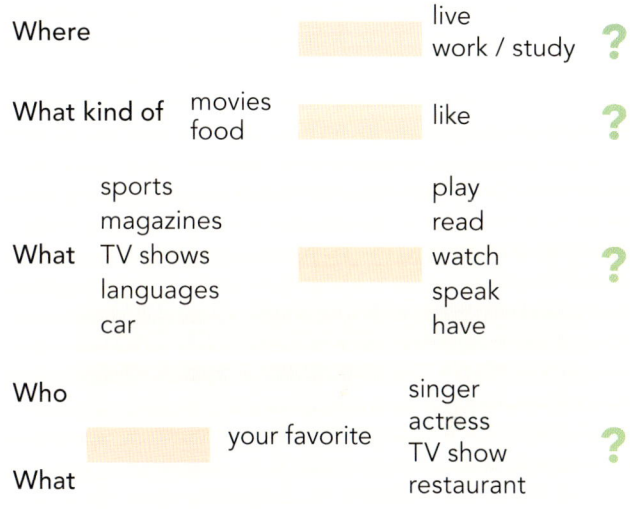

b Work in pairs. Interview a partner with the questions in a. Then change roles.
 A Ask **B** the first question.
 B Answer the question. Give more information if you can.
 A Show interest. Then ask the next question.

 A *Where do you live?*
 B *In the downtown area, near the train station.*
 A *Really? Me too.*

6 WRITING

Ⓦ p.113 Writing A personal profile Write a profile of yourself.

Go online to review the lesson

EPISODE 2

Practical English At a coffee shop

buying a coffee   V telling the time

1 VOCABULARY
telling the time

a Look at the clock. What time is it?

b **V** p.157 **Vocabulary Bank** Time Do Part 1.

c **C Communication** What's the time?
A p.104 B p.109 Practice times.

2 ▶ ROB AND JENNY MEET

a 🔊 3.27 Watch or listen to what happens when Rob and Jenny meet. What do they decide to do?

b Watch or listen again. Answer the questions. Why…?
1 is Rob late
2 doesn't Jenny like the hotel breakfast
3 is Jenny busy after 9:30
4 does Rob say "Don't worry."

3 ▶ BUYING A COFFEE

a Look at the coffee shop menu. Do you know what all these things are?

☕	ESPRESSO	single 2.45	double 2.80
☕	AMERICANO	regular 3.15	large 3.95
☕	LATTE	regular 3.45	large 3.65
☕	CAPPUCCINO	regular 3.45	large 3.65
☕	TEA	regular 2.65	large 3.10
	BROWNIE	3.00	
	CROISSANT	3.00	

b 3.28 Watch or listen to Rob and Jenny buying coffee. Answer the questions.

1 What kinds of coffee do Jenny and Rob have?
2 What do they have to eat?
3 How much is it?

c Watch or listen again. Complete the **You hear** phrases.

You hear	You say
Can I [1]_________ you?	What would you like, Jenny? An espresso, please.
[2]_________ or double?	Double. Can I have a latte, please?
[3]_________ or large?	Large.
To have [4]_________ or take away?	To take away.
Anything else?	No, thanks. A brownie for me, please...and a croissant.
OK.	How much is that?
That's £12.45, please.	Sorry, how much?
£12.45. Thank you.	
And your [5]_________.	Thanks.

d 3.29 Watch or listen and repeat the **You say** phrases. Copy the rhythm.

e In threes, practice the conversation.

f Use the coffee shop menu. Role-play the conversation in groups of three. Then change roles.

A (book open) You are the barista.
B (book closed) You invite **C** (book closed) to have a drink.
A begins *Can I help you?*
B asks **C** *What would you like?*

Glossary
barista a person who works in a coffee shop

4 FIRST DAY IN THE OFFICE

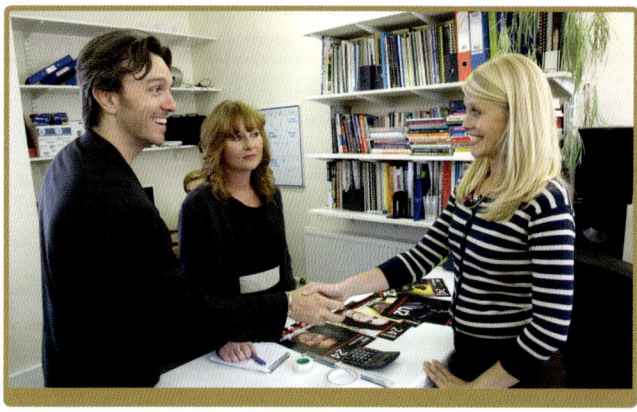

a 3.30 Watch or listen and answer the questions.

1 What's Karen's job?
2 Where in Europe does Jenny have family?
3 Where does she live in New York?
4 Does Karen have family in New York?
5 What does Daniel offer Jenny to drink?
6 What time is his next meeting?

b Look at the **Social English** phrases. Who says them: **R**ob, **K**aren, or **D**aniel?

Social English
1 ☐ Here we are.
2 ☐ Is this your first time in the UK?
3 ☐ Would you like something to drink?
4 ☐ Talk to you later.

c 3.31 Watch or listen and check. Then watch or listen and repeat the phrases.

d Complete conversations A–D with **Social English** phrases 1–4. Practice with a partner.

A	Sit down. ☐	No, thanks, I'm fine.
B	☐ Bye.	Bye.
C	Nice to meet you. ☐	No, it isn't. I know London very well.
D	OK. ☐ This is your hotel.	Oh, it's very nice.

CAN YOU...?

☐ tell the time
☐ order food and drink in a café
☐ meet and introduce people

Go online to watch the video, review the lesson, and check your progress

4A Family photos

Who's that? She's my niece – my brother's daughter.

G possessive 's, Whose...?   V family   P /ʌ/, the letter o

1 GRAMMAR possessive 's, Whose...?

a Look at the title of the article and the photo of Doug. Who do you think his brother is? Do you think it's good or bad to have a famous person in your family?

b Read the article. Now do you know who Doug's brother is? Does he like having a famous brother?

I'M NOT FAMOUS... BUT MY BROTHER IS

Doug is a businessman, and a photographer. He is also the founder of Care to Learn, an organization that helps poor children in the US do well in school. He's married with three children, and he and his family have a normal life. But for many people, he is always "_____'s brother."

Doug's life can be difficult. People follow him on the street. They ask him questions about his brother, his brother's ex-wife, who is also very famous, and their six children. The paparazzi follow Doug's children and take photographs.

But it also has advantages. "I go to movie premieres and I meet famous actors. And when I call people and ask for money for Care to Learn, it helps when I say I'm _____'s brother."

Doug is not jealous of his older brother. He is happy with his life. "I see the world of famous people from the outside. I can leave it, but my brother can't."

c Look at some photos of actors with family. With a partner, choose a or b below.

Carey Mulligan

Meryl Streep

Jake Gyllenhaal

Will Smith

Mary-Kate Olsen

		a	b
1	He's Carey Mulligan's	a husband.	b brother.
2	She's Meryl Streep's	a sister.	b daughter.
3	She's Jake Gyllenhaal's	a wife.	b sister.
4	He's Will Smith's	a son.	b brother.
5	He's Mary-Kate Olsen's	a father.	b husband.

d 🔊 4.1 Listen and check.

e G p.130 **Grammar Bank 4A**

f Look at some things from the photos. Whose are they? Ask and answer with a partner.

Whose bow tie is it?   *It's Will Smith's bow tie.*

a bow tie

a bag

glasses

a watch

a ring

2 VOCABULARY family

a **V** p.155 **Vocabulary Bank** The family

b In pairs, answer the questions.
   Who's...?
   1 your mother's mother   my _grandmother_
   2 your father's brother   my _____
   3 your brother's / sister's daughter   my _____
   4 your aunt's child   my _____
   5 your husband's / wife's brother   my _____
   6 your niece's brother   my _____

3 PRONUNCIATION /ʌ/, the letter o

a ▶ 4.4 Listen to the words and sound. Then listen and repeat.

	up	mother brother son husband uncle couple cousin

> 🔍 **Remember!**
> The same vowel in English can be pronounced in different ways, e.g., o can be /ɑ/ (n**o**t), /oʊ/ (ph**o**to), /ʌ/ (m**o**ther), and /u/ (tw**o**).

b How is the letter o pronounced in these words? Put them in the correct column.

~~come~~ ~~do~~ ~~doctor~~ ~~don't~~ go home hot job
London model money no one stop who

clock	phone	up	boot
doctor	don't	come	do

c ▶ 4.5 Listen and check. Practice saying the words.

d Practice the conversations with a partner.

   1 A Who's that?
      B My m**o**ther.
      A She's very y**ou**ng!
      B N**o**, she's sixty-**o**ne. She's a d**o**ctor.

   2 A Who are they?
      B My br**o**ther and his s**o**n.
      A D**o** they live in L**o**ndon?
      B N**o**, they d**o**n't.

   3 A What's her j**o**b?
      B She's a m**o**del. She earns a l**o**t of m**o**ney.

4 LISTENING & SPEAKING

a ▶ 4.6 Listen to Grace showing a friend photos on her phone. Who are Mark, Celia, and Miriam? Complete the first row of the chart.

	Mark	Celia	Miriam
Grace's...	boyfriend		
More information			

b Listen again. Write down more information, e.g., ages, jobs, where they live, etc.

c Work with a partner.
   A Show **B** some photos of family or friends on your phone or write their names on a piece of paper.
   B Ask three questions about each person.

   Who's that?
      That's Yolanda. She's my sister.
   How old is she?

Go online to review the lesson

4B From morning to night

> What time do you go to work? At 8:00.

G prepositions of time (*at, in, on*) and place (*at, in, to*) **V** daily routine **P** linking

1 VOCABULARY daily routine

a 🔊 **4.7** Listen to the sounds and number the phrases 1–6.

- [ ] get dressed
- [1] wake up
- [ ] have breakfast
- [ ] take a shower
- [ ] go to work / school
- [ ] have a coffee / tea

b What order do you do these things in the morning? Tell your partner.

First, I wake up, then I…

c **V** p.156 **Vocabulary Bank** Daily routine

2 PRONUNCIATION linking

> 🔍 **Connected speech**
> Remember, when people speak they usually link words together. Sometimes three linked words sound like one word, e.g., I <mark>getupat</mark> seven.

a 🔊 **4.9** Listen and write five sentences.

1 _____ (5 words)
2 _____ (5 words)
3 _____ (6 words)
4 _____ (6 words)
5 _____ (5 words)

b 🔊 **4.10** Listen and repeat the sentences. Try to link the words with ‿.

I **get**‿**up**‿at **seven**.
I **take**‿a **shower**.
I **go** to **work**.
I **have**‿a **sandwich** for **lunch**.
I **get home**‿at **six**.
I **make** the **dinner**.
I **go** to **bed**‿at **ten**.
What‿a **life**!

3 READING & LISTENING

a Read the article. Use the glossary to help you. How do you think Marjan feels at the end of a typical day? Choose from the adjectives in the list.

bored   happy   relaxed   sad   stressed   tired

Busy lives
MOTHER…

Marjan Jahangiri, originally from Iran, is one of the only women professors of cardiac surgery in Europe. She does more than 300 operations a year. She lives in London with her husband and their 17-year-old son, Darius.

Can you describe your daily routine?

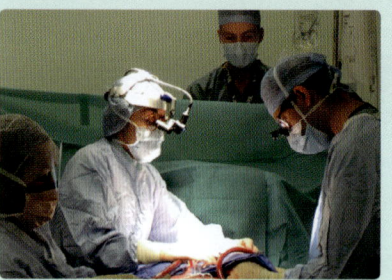

I get up between 6:00 and 6:30 a.m., I get to work at 7:00, and my meetings usually start at 7:30. After that, I don't have a break. I have lunch at my desk. I often do two operations a day, and I also have lectures and more meetings. At home, I have dinner with my son. Between 9:30 and 11:30 p.m., I do research and I watch the news on TV. One or two nights a week I'm on call, so I probably need to do operations during the night. I often work on weekends, too. But that's OK – I think I have a great life because I love my work.

How do you balance work with your family life?

I spend a lot of time with my son. I want him to learn about hard work and good values, and I want to be an example for him. My husband is away a lot, but we talk on the phone every day. I think one reason why I am successful in my professional life is because he isn't at home all the time!

What do you do to relax?

I play the piano for an hour every day, late at night. I think it helps me with my operations – it's technical in the same way. I also go to the hair stylist twice a week. I do a lot of my research there! They turn the music off for me, and I use the time to read all my academic papers.

> **Glossary**
> **cardiac surgery** an operation to repair somebody's heart
> **a lecture** a talk to a group of people to teach them about something, e.g., at a university
> **be on call** be available for work if necessary
> **do research** study something to learn more about it

b Read the article again. In pairs, answer the questions from memory.
1 What time does Marjan get up?
2 What does she do when she's at work?
3 Where does she have lunch?
4 What does she do in the evening?
5 Is her job a 9–5 job? Why (not)?
6 Does she see her family a lot?
7 How does she relax?
8 Does she like her job?

...AND SON

MORNING

[1] **7:30**	He gets up. He has breakfast and then he goes to school by Tube.
8:20	[2] He _____ to school.
9:00	Classes start. [3] He has _____ or _____ classes before lunch.

AFTERNOON

1:00	He has lunch at [4] _____.
[5] _____	His classes start again.
4:15	He finishes school. He doesn't [6] _____ _____ then. He studies in the library or plays music. On Tuesdays, he [7] _____ in the school choir and on [8] _____ he [9] _____ percussion in the school orchestra.

EVENING

6:00	He gets home. [10] He _____ a _____ and then has dinner. After dinner, he does homework for [11] _____ or _____ hours.
[12] _____	He goes to bed.

Glossary
the Tube the London subway
choir a group of people who sing together
percussion musical instruments, e.g., drums
A levels exams that UK students take in the final year of school

c ▶ 4.11 Listen to Darius, Marjan's 17-year-old son, talking about his day. Complete blanks 1–12.

d What do Marjan and Darius have in common? Who do you think is more tired in the evening?

4 GRAMMAR prepositions of time and place

a Look at some sentences from Darius's day. Complete them with *at*, *in*, *on*, or *to*.
1 I get up ____ 7:30.
2 I usually go ____ school by Tube.
3 I have lunch ____ school.
4 I usually have two or three classes ____ the afternoon.
5 I sing in the school choir ____ Tuesdays.

b ▶ 4.12 Listen and check.

c G p.130 Grammar Bank 4B

d ▶ 4.15 Listen and say the time phrases with the correct preposition.
1 ▶) the weekend (on the weekend

5 SPEAKING & WRITING

a Look at the questions to ask your partner. What two words are missing?

What time / get up?
/ have breakfast in the morning? What / have?
How / go to work or school?
What time / start work or school?
What time / have lunch? Where?
/ have a long lunch break? How long?
What time / finish work or school?
What / do after work or school?
/ go out during the week? Where / go?
/ relax in the evening? What / do?
When / do English homework?
What time / go to bed?
How / feel at the end of the day?

b Work in pairs. Use the questions to interview your partner about a typical weekday. What do you have in common?

(We both get up at 7:00.

c W p.114 Writing An article Write about your favorite day of the week.

4C Blue Zones

G position of adverbs, expressions of frequency   V months, adverbs, and expressions of frequency   P the letter h

How often do you eat fish?

Hardly ever. Maybe once a month.

1 VOCABULARY months, adverbs, and expressions of frequency

a ◆ 4.16 Complete the months in the phone calendar. Listen and check.

b Listen again and repeat the months. Which five are stressed on the second syllable?

c Say the month of your birthday around the class.

d V p.157 **Vocabulary Bank** Time Do Parts 2 and 3.

2 GRAMMAR position of adverbs, expressions of frequency

a Read the text about teenagers in the US. Are teenagers in your country similar?

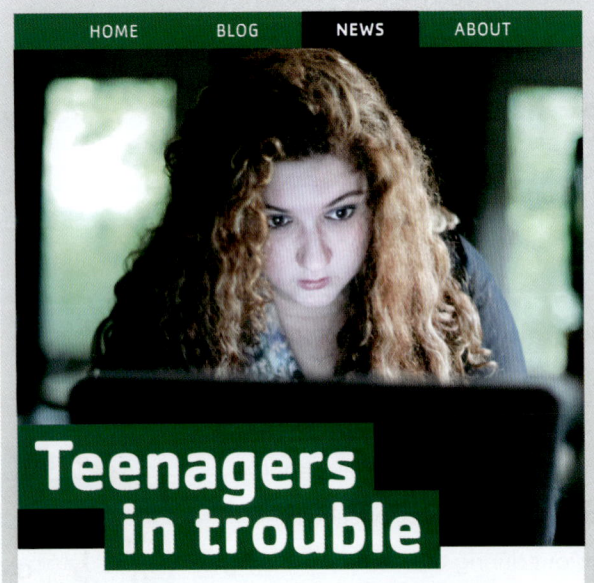

HOME   BLOG   NEWS   ABOUT

Teenagers in trouble

American teenagers may, for the first time in the nation's history, live shorter lives than their parents because of their unhealthy lifestyles. According to recent research:
- 96% **spend** more than five hours looking at a screen **every day**.
- 86% **hardly ever eat** fruit or green vegetables.
- 75% **don't usually sleep** for eight hours a day – the average is seven hours.
- 34% **eat** fast food at least **once a day**.
- 33% **drink** more than four sugary drinks **every day**.
- 31% **are often** very stressed.
- 25% **never play** sports or exercise.

b Look at the position of the highlighted words and expressions. Circle the correct rule.
  1 Adverbs of frequency (e.g., *usually*) go:
     before / after a main verb.
     before / after the verb *be*.
  2 Expressions of frequency (e.g., *every week*) go *at the beginning / at the end* of a phrase or sentence.

c G p.130 **Grammar Bank** 4C

d C **Communication** Short Life, Long Life? p.104 Do the questionnaire.

3 PRONUNCIATION the letter h

a ◆ 4.21 Listen to the words and sound. Then listen and repeat.

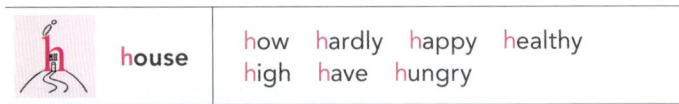

| house | how   hardly   happy   healthy |
| | high   have   hungry |

b ◆ 4.22 Listen. Circle one word where *h* is **not** pronounced. Then practice saying the sentences.
Harry's a hair stylist.
He hardly ever has breakfast.
He's often in a hurry.
He usually has half an hour for lunch.
He often has a hamburger for dinner.
Harry isn't very healthy.

c In pairs, make true sentences about you with the verb phrases and an adverb or expression of frequency.

be at home on Saturday night   be in a hurry
do housework   go to the hair stylist   have a healthy lunch
take a hot bath   sleep for eight hours

(*I'm not usually at home on Saturday night.*

4 READING & SPEAKING

a Look at the photos and read the text. What are the "Blue Zones"? How old do you think Alexis and María are?

b **⊙ Communication A** Ikaria p.104 **B** Nicoya p.110
Read and tell your partner about the place.

c What words and phrases can you remember from the articles? With a partner, write words in each category.

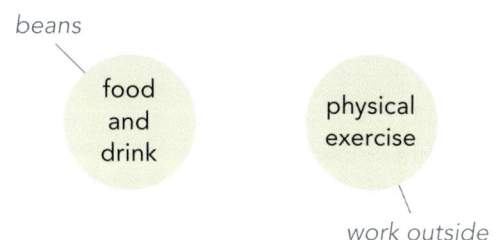

5 ▶ VIDEO LISTENING

a Watch the documentary *The island of Okinawa*. Mark the sentences **T** (true) or **F** (false).

1 The island of Okinawa is north of Japan.
2 70-year-old Okinawans have the bodies of 50-year-olds.
3 *Hara hachi* means stop eating before you're full.
4 The Okinawans don't eat meat or fish.
5 They eat a lot of seaweed.
6 They do yoga every day.
7 The Okinawans are often in a hurry.
8 When Okinawans reach 100, they have a ceremony called *kajimaya*.

b Watch again and correct the **F** sentences.

c What does Okinawa have in common with Ikaria and Nicoya? Are there people in your country who live like this? In what ways is your lifestyle similar to or different from life in the "Blue Zones"? Would you like to live in one of the "Blue Zones"?

What are their secrets?

What do the Greek island of Ikaria, the Nicoya peninsula in Costa Rica, and the island of Okinawa in Japan have in common? The answer is that, together with Loma Linda in California and Sardinia in Italy, they are the five so-called "Blue Zones," the best places in the world to live if you want to have a long and healthy life. Many people there live until they are 100 or more. So what are their secrets?

Alexis is a construction worker from Ikaria.

María from Nicoya cooks and goes to the market every day.

▶ Go online to watch the video and review the lesson

3 & 4 Review and Check

GRAMMAR

Circle a, b, or c.

1 I ____ live near here.
   a not   b don't   c doesn't
2 My sister ____ three children.
   a has   b have   c haves
3 ____ English?
   a Are they speak
   b Speak they
   c Do they speak
4 ____ your sister work?
   a Does   b Is   c Do
5 A Do you work here?   B Yes, I ____.
   a work   b do   c am
6 A What ____?   B He's an engineer.
   a he does   b does he   c does he do
7 What languages ____?
   a speak you
   b do you speak
   c you speak
8 Bill is ____.
   a Carla's husband
   b husband's Carla
   c the Carla's husband
9 This is my ____ house.
   a parent's   b parents'   c parents
10 ____ book is this?
    a Who's   b Who   c Whose
11 We usually have lunch ____ two o'clock.
    a in   b on   c at
12 What time do you go ____ bed?
    a in   b to   c at
13 She ____ late for class.
    a never is   b is never   c isn't never
14 I ____ early.
    a usually get up   b get usually up
    c get up usually
15 I have an English class ____.
    a one a week
    b one the week
    c once a week

VOCABULARY

a Complete with *at, in, on, to,* or *up*.

1 ____ Saturday night, I go to the movies.
2 I work ____ a fast-food restaurant.
3 What time do you usually wake ____?
4 My brother lives ____ an apartment.
5 What time do you go ____ work?

b Complete the phrases with these verbs.

| do | get | go | have | listen | play | read | see | take | wear |

1 ____ dressed
2 ____ the dog for a walk
3 ____ lunch
4 ____ your homework
5 ____ shopping
6 ____ the guitar
7 ____ to music
8 ____ friends
9 ____ the newspaper
10 ____ glasses

c Circle the word that is different.

1 brother   grandfather   niece   uncle
2 aunt   husband   mother-in-law   stepsister
3 chef   cleaner   factory   pilot
4 always   early   often   never
5 April   August   July   Monday

d Complete with *How many, Who, Why, What,* or *Where*.

1 ____ do you live?
2 ____ does your father do?
3 ____ is your favorite family member?
4 ____ hours do you work?
5 ____ do you want to learn English?

PRONUNCIATION

a Practice the words and sounds.

Vowel sounds

bird   computer   up   clock

Consonant sounds

house   flower   chess   witch

b p.166–167 **Sound Bank** Say more words for each sound.

c What sound do the pink letters have in these words?

1 br**o**ther   2 n**e**phew   3 **C**zech   4 **wh**ich   5 **w**ork

d Underline the stressed syllable.

1 be|cause   3 un|em|ployed   5 grand|moth|er
2 den|tist   4 re|cep|tion|ist

CAN YOU understand this text?

a Read the article once. What is unusual about David Guetta's life?

A DAY IN THE LIFE

THE SUPERSTAR DJ DAVID GUETTA

I wake up at about 1:00 p.m., and the first thing I do is go outside. I live in Ibiza, and I like having breakfast in the sun. I usually have fruit juice, eggs, fruit, and tea. I never drink coffee. After breakfast, I answer my emails for an hour. Then I go to the gym.

I never listen to music in the house, or even in the car, because music is my job. On a typical day, I spend two or three hours in my studio, and then another four hours at a nightclub. My work starts in the evening. I usually have dinner in a restaurant, and then I go to the club. I try to have a normal life, but my job isn't normal. I arrive at a club like a secret agent – I go in through the back door and security takes me to the stage.

I finish work at 4:00 in the morning. Security takes me out, and then I go home. After about four hours playing music, I'm very excited. My manager says, "Go home and sleep," but that's impossible. First I need to calm down. When I get home, I have a cup of tea, brush my teeth, and say, "Thank you for this wonderful life." I am 47 now, but I want to do this when I'm 60 or 80. I want to do this forever.

b Read the article again. Mark the sentences **T** (true) or **F** (false).

1 He gets up in the afternoon.
2 He only eats fruit for breakfast.
3 He exercises every day.
4 He works six to seven hours a day.
5 He eats out in the evening.
6 When he finishes work, he goes home and sleeps.
7 He doesn't want to change his life.

▶ CAN YOU understand these people?

🔊 4.23 Watch or listen and answer the questions.

1 Talitha   2 Joelle   3 Sophie   4 Jake   5 Tom

1 Talitha works ____.
   a 27 hours a week
   b in a market
   c 37 hours a week
2 Joelle has ____.
   a a 13-year-old sister
   b a 30-year-old sister
   c three sisters
3 Sophie usually gets up at ____ on weekends.
   a 7:30
   b 9:00
   c 9:30
4 Jake ____.
   a goes to the gym and walks
   b exercises at the school gym
   c walks to the gym every day
5 Tom likes ____ in New York.
   a the taxis
   b the people
   c the food

CAN YOU say this in English?

Do the tasks with a partner. Check (✓) the box if you can do these things.

Can you…?

1 ☐ say where you live and what you do
2 ☐ say what time you usually get up and go to bed
3 ☐ say what you do on a typical Monday morning
4 ☐ ask questions with the words below
   • What sports…?   • What languages…?
   • What kind of music…? • What TV shows…?

Go online to watch the video, review Files 3 and 4, and check your progress

5A Vote for me!

Can you sing? — Yes, but I can't dance.

G can / can't **V** verb phrases: *buy a newspaper*, etc. **P** sentence stress

1 VOCABULARY verb phrases

a Can you remember these verb phrases for things people do in their free time? Match the words.

go play do yoga
watch to music
TV a coffee
have listen the guitar
to the gym

b **V** p.158 **Vocabulary Bank** More verb phrases

2 LISTENING

a In your country, do you have TV competitions for people who do things well, e.g., sing, dance, or cook? Do you watch them? Why (not)?

b 🔊 5.2 Amy goes to an audition for a TV singing competition. Look at the pictures. Then listen and answer questions 1–9.

c 🔊 5.3 Now listen to Amy, Justin, and Naomi sing. Vote for the person you want to be in the show.

d 🔊 5.4 Listen to what the judges say. Do they agree with you? How does Amy feel?

12:30 In a long line outside the Conference Center in Portland.

1 What does Amy need to go into the Conference Center?
2 What does she show the man?

12:45 In the waiting area with 350 other singers!

3 Where does Amy's friend wait?
4 How many people does the woman call?

4:00 Three hours later! My turn at last!

5 What does Amy's friend say to her before she goes to the audition?
6 What does Amy do with her bag?

4:15 In the audition, with three judges. Really nervous!

7 What's Amy's song?
8 What's her problem with the microphone?
9 What does Amy say when they ask her to start her song?

3 GRAMMAR can / can't

a Look at four can / can't sentences (1–4) from Amy's story. Match them to their meanings (a–d).

1 ☐ You can't sing!
2 ☐ You can't come in if you don't have ID.
3 ☐ Can you come with me, please?
4 ☐ She can wait there.

a It isn't OK.
b It's possible.
c Please do it.
d You don't know how.

b ⓖ **p.132 Grammar Bank 5A**

4 PRONUNCIATION
sentence stress

a 🔊 5.6 Listen to the conversations. Then listen and repeat. Copy the <u>rhythm</u>.

1 A Can you **play** a **musical instrument**?
   B **Yes**, I **can**.
   A **What** can you **play**?
   B I can **play** the **guitar**.

2 A **Where** can I **sit**?
   B You can **sit over there**.

3 A Can I **park here**?
   B **No**, you **can't**. You **can't park here**.

b 🔊 5.7 Listen. Can you hear the difference?

1 a I can sing.
  b I can't sing.
2 a She can dance very well.
  b She can't dance very well.
3 a He can cook.
  b He can't cook.
4 a I can come to the meeting.
  b I can't come to the meeting.
5 a You can park here.
  b You can't park here.
6 a I can drive.
  b I can't drive.

c 🔊 5.8 Listen. (Circle) a or b.

5 SPEAKING

a Work in pairs. Interview each other with the questionnaire. Ask *Can you…?* If the answer is *Yes, I can*, ask *How well?* and write 1 (= not very well), 2 (= well), or 3 (= very well).

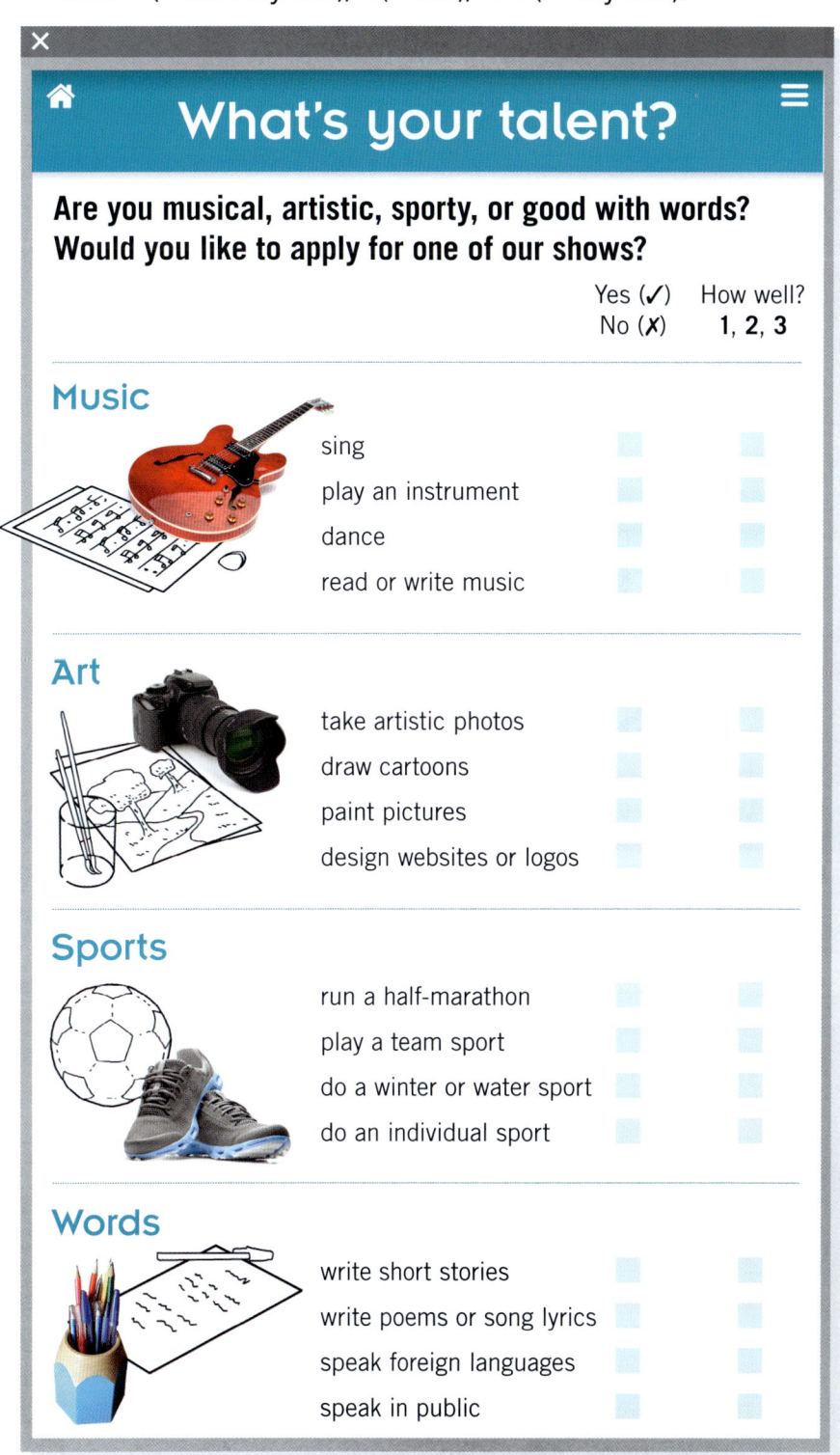

What's your talent?

Are you musical, artistic, sporty, or good with words? Would you like to apply for one of our shows?

Yes (✓)   How well?
No (✗)   1, 2, 3

Music
- sing
- play an instrument
- dance
- read or write music

Art
- take artistic photos
- draw cartoons
- paint pictures
- design websites or logos

Sports
- run a half-marathon
- play a team sport
- do a winter or water sport
- do an individual sport

Words
- write short stories
- write poems or song lyrics
- speak foreign languages
- speak in public

b Look at your partner's answers. What can he or she do? Can you think of any competitions or TV shows he or she can enter?

c Change partners and tell your new partner what your first partner can or can't do.

Go online to review the lesson

39

5B A quiet life?

G present continuous: be + verb + -ing   V noise: verbs and verb phrases   P /ŋ/

> What are you doing?
> I'm trying to study.

1 VOCABULARY & SPEAKING noise: verbs and verb phrases

a Are your family or neighbors noisy? Answer questions 1–4 with a partner.

1 How many family members do you live with?
2 Are they…?
   a very noisy   b noisy   c not very noisy
3 Do you have neighbors…?
   a upstairs   b downstairs   c next door
4 Are they…?
   a very noisy   b noisy   c not very noisy

b ◆ 5.9 Read part of an online forum. Guess the meaning of the highlighted verbs and verb phrases. Then listen to eight sounds and write 1–8 in the boxes.

NOISY FAMILY? NOISY NEIGHBORS?

Do you have a problem with noise, for example, when you want to study, or at night when you want to sleep? Tell us about your problems.

- ☐ The baby in the apartment upstairs cries all the time.
- ☐ My sister practices the piano for hours.
- ☐ The neighbors' dog barks all day – and all night!
- ☐ The people next door often have noisy parties until 3:00 a.m.
- ☐ My son plays loud music in his room – awful music, too.
- ☐ The couple next door argues a lot.
- ☐ The old people in the apartment next door have the TV on very loud – and their living room is next to my bedroom!
- ☐ The people next door have young children who make a lot of noise.

c Now answer questions 5–7.

5 What noises do your family or neighbors make? Are the noises a problem for you?
6 Are you noisy? Do you do any of the things in **b**?
7 Are people in your country noisy? Is this a problem?

2 GRAMMAR present continuous

a ◆ 5.10 Look at the picture of the houses and listen. Why are Max and his mother unhappy?

b Listen again and complete the conversations with verbs from the list.

barking   cooking   happening   having   listening
making   playing   practicing   trying

1 **Max** Hey, Lucy. I'm ¹_____ to study, and you're ²_____ too much noise.
Lucy It isn't noise, it's Beethoven. I'm ³_____ – I have a school concert tomorrow. You can study downstairs.
Max I can't, Jake's ⁴_____ a video game.
Lucy What about the kitchen?
Max No, Mom's ⁵_____ dinner, and she's ⁶_____ to the radio. It's impossible to work in this house!

2 **Isabel** Paul! Come here.
Paul Yes, dear? What's the matter?
Isabel What's ⁷_____ next door? Why's their dog ⁸_____? I can't hear the radio.
Paul They're ⁹_____ a party in the yard.
Isabel Not again! Can you go and talk to them?
Paul Yeah, OK. It's their second party in three weeks!

c 🔊 **5.11** Listen. What happens when Paul goes next door?

d Complete the sentences with the correct form of the verb *be*.

➕ They	_____ having a party next door.
❓	_____ they playing music?
➖ No, they	_____ playing music. They're talking.

e Read the rule and ⓒircle the correct option.

> We use the present continuous (*be* + verb + *-ing*) to talk about *now* / *every day*.

f **G** p.132 **Grammar Bank 5B**

g 🔊 **5.13** Listen to the sounds. What's happening? Write eight sentences.

1 *Somebody's cooking.*

3 PRONUNCIATION & SPEAKING /ŋ/

a 🔊 **5.14** Listen to the words and sounds. Then listen and repeat.

si**ng**er	si**ng**ing goi**ng** doi**ng** studyi**ng**
	la**n**guage wro**ng** you**ng**
	thi**n**k ba**n**k pi**n**k tha**n**ks

b In pairs, point and ask and answer about the people in the picture of the houses.

What's she doing?

She's playing the piano. What are they doing?

c **C Communication** Spot the differences **A** p.105 **B** p.110 Describe the pictures and find eight differences.

4 LISTENING

a 🔊 **5.15** Listen to a short conversation. What's the woman doing?

She's checking in...

b Listen again. What words help you to understand the situation?

c 🔊 **5.16** Now listen to five more conversations. What are the people doing?

d Listen again. For each conversation, write two words or phrases that help you to understand what's happening.

Go online to review the lesson

5C A city for all seasons

> Look! It's snowing!
> It doesn't often snow here.

G simple present or present continuous? **V** the weather and seasons **P** places in Chicago

1 VOCABULARY & LISTENING
the weather and seasons

a Look at the weather forecast for the week and answer the questions.
  1 What's the maximum temperature? What's the minimum?
  2 What time of year do you think it is?
  3 Do you think it's typical weather for Chicago?

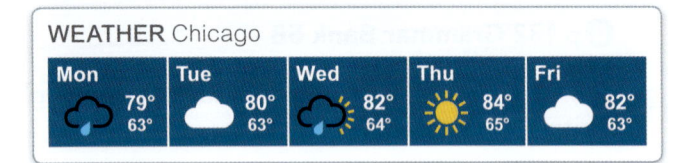

WEATHER Chicago

Mon	Tue	Wed	Thu	Fri
79° / 63°	80° / 63°	82° / 64°	84° / 65°	82° / 63°

b **V** p.159 Vocabulary Bank The weather and dates Do Part 1.

c 🔊 5.19 Listen to a travel guide talking about the weather in Chicago. Mark the sentences **T** (true) or **F** (false). Then listen again and say why.
  1 It's often very hot or very cold.
  2 The normal temperature in the summer is 84°F.
  3 It's often above freezing for weeks at a time in the winter.
  4 In the spring and the fall, the weather changes a lot.
  5 It's often windy in downtown Chicago.

d What's the weather like where you live in different seasons?

2 GRAMMAR simple present or present continuous?

a Look at the photos and the messages. Why are Tim and Jane sad?

> **Mike** FRI 7:01
> View from my window this morning. It's snowing. Hooray! I love winter!

> **Tim** FRI 8:04
> Lucky you! I love the snow. It never snows here in Miami. ☹

> **Jane** MON 11:30
> We're in Mexico – Cancún – but it's raining! ☹

> **Lizzie** MON 5:35
> Poor you! Does it often rain there in March? I'm walking home, and it's a beautiful evening – the sun's shining. Sorry!

b Read the messages again, and focus on the highlighted verbs. When do we use the simple present? When do we use the present continuous?

c **G** p.132 Grammar Bank 5C

d **C** Communication What do you do? What are you doing now? **A** p.105 **B** p.111 Ask and answer questions.

What to do in Chicago at different times of the year

In the spring
Go to the Chicago Riverwalk. This is one of the highlights of Chicago. It's open all year round, and it's
05 beautiful in the spring with all the trees and flowers. The Riverwalk is 3.4 miles long, and you can see tall buildings, boats on the river, outdoor
10 art, and famous bridges, including the Michigan Avenue Bridge. If you don't want to walk, you can sit and "people watch" or enjoy a
15 meal at a café. Remember to bring a jacket—the weather can be cool and windy in the spring.

In the summer
**Go to the open air theater
20 in Millennium Park.** Open from April to November, this is a great place to listen to music, including classical, Broadway, and rock. Come
25 prepared with a blanket or chair and an umbrella or a plastic raincoat. Concerts at this open air theater usually take place in all kinds of
30 weather! You can buy a boxed meal or bring your own food. It's very popular, so get there early.

3 READING & SPEAKING

a Read the questions about things to do in Chicago. Then read the online guide and find the answers. Answer with **CR** (Chicago Riverwalk), **OAT** (open air theater), **CM** (Chicago Marathon), or **AIC** (Art Institute of Chicago).

Where can you…?
1 ____ watch people while you rest
2 ____ buy food to eat outside
3 ____ see art by the water
4 ____ see works by famous artists
5 ____ watch what's happening from different places
6 ____ sit on a blanket
7 ____ see famous people doing a sport
8 ____ have lunch, but not dinner

In the fall
Watch (or run) the
35 **Chicago Marathon.** One of the biggest marathons in the US takes place in the fall every year, usually in October. About 40,000
40 people, including top runners and celebrities, run 26.2 miles through the city. There's a fantastic atmosphere. You can watch
45 anywhere along the route, but the Chicago Theater and the finish, near Grant Park, are my favorite places. The fall in Chicago usually
50 means good weather, but be prepared for rain or sun—just in case!

In the winter
Visit the Art Institute of Chicago. Chicago is full of
55 wonderful museums, where you can happily spend a cold winter's day. My favorite is the Art Institute of Chicago. It's one of the world's top
60 museums. It has more than 300,000 works of art, including amazing collections of paintings, sculptures, ceramics, and glass.
65 Collections include works by artists Grant Wood, Edward Hopper, Georges Seurat, and Marc Chagall. It has special activities for children, and
70 several great cafés, open until 4:00. There is an entrance fee for adult visitors, but children under 13 are free.

b Look back at the guide. Complete the nouns for these adjectives.
1 famous *bridge*
2 great _____, _____
3 a fantastic _____
4 my favorite _____
5 good (or bad) _____
6 wonderful _____
7 amazing _____

c Talk to a partner.
• Which of the four things would you like to do? Why?
• What are good things to do at different times of the year where you live?

4 PRONUNCIATION places in Chicago

a 🔊 5.21 Place names in Chicago are sometimes difficult for visitors to pronounce and understand. Listen and underline the stressed syllable in the **bold** words.

Wrig|ley Field
the Mag|nif|i|cent Mile
Bu|cking|ham Foun|tain
Tha|lia Hall
Sol|dier Field

Mil|len|ni|um Park
Ad|ler Plan|e|tar|i|um
Na|vy Pier
Hum|boldt Park
Sky|deck Chi|ca|go

b Listen again and repeat the names.

c 👥 Role-play with a partner. Imagine you are in a taxi. **A** is the driver, **B** is the passenger. Have a short conversation. Use the phrases below.

A	B
Where do you want to go?	Is it far?
Where are you from?	Can you stop here, please?
Are you on vacation?	How much is it?
Do you like Chicago?	Can I pay by credit card?

Where do you want to go?
Skydeck Chicago, please. Is it far?

5 WRITING

a What social media do you use, e.g., Twitter or Facebook? Do your family and friends use the same ones as you?

b 🅦 **p.115 Writing** Posting on social media Write posts to say what you're doing on vacation.

Go online to review the lesson

Practical English In a clothing store

EPISODE 3

buying clothes   V clothes

1 VOCABULARY clothes

a Match the words and photos.

☐ a jacket /ˈdʒækət/
☐ jeans /dʒinz/
☐ a shirt /ʃərt/
☐ a T-shirt /ˈtiʃərt/
☐ a skirt /skərt/
☐ shoes /ʃuz/
☐ a sweater /ˈswɛtər/
☐ pants /pænts/

b 🔊 5.22 Listen and check.

c Cover the words and look at the photos. Say the words.

2 ▶ MEETING ON THE STREET

a 🔊 5.23 Watch or listen to Jenny and Rob. What problem does Rob have?

b Watch or listen again. Complete the sentences.
1 Rob has a _____ for Jenny.
2 Jenny has another meeting with _____.
3 Rob has an interview in _____ minutes.
4 Jenny's meeting is at nine _____.
5 Rob needs to buy a new _____.
6 They go to a clothing _____.
7 Jenny needs to answer her _____.

c 🔊 5.24 Read the information box. Listen and repeat the phrases.

> 🔍 **Apologizing**
> I'm sorry.   That's OK.
> I'm so sorry.   Don't worry.
> I'm really sorry.   No problem.

d Cover the box. In pairs, practice apologizing and responding.

3 ▶ BUYING CLOTHES

> 🔍 **Saying prices in the US**   **Saying prices in the UK**
> $5.00 = five dollars   £5.00 = five pounds
> $5.50 = five dollars and   £5.50 = five pounds fifty
>   fifty cents,
>   five-fifty
> 50¢ = fifty cents   50p = fifty pence
>
> **Sizes**
> S = small, M = medium, L = large, XL = extra large

a 🔊 5.25 Watch or listen to Rob buying a shirt. Answer the questions.
1 What size does Rob want?
2 Does he try it on?
3 How much is the shirt?

b Watch or listen again. Complete the **You hear** phrases.

You hear	You say
Can I ¹_____ you?	Yes, what size is this shirt?
Let's see. It's a small. What ²_____ do you need?	A medium.
This is a ³_____.	Thanks. Where can I try it on?
The changing ⁴_____ are over there.	Thank you.
⁵_____ is it?	It's fine. How much is it?
	It's £44.99.

c ▶ 5.26 Watch or listen and repeat the **You say** phrases. Copy the rhythm.

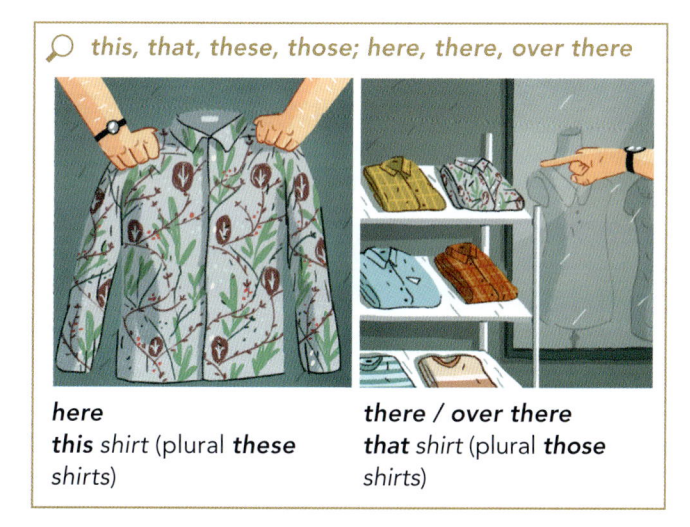

> *this, that, these, those; here, there, over there*
>
> **here**
> **this** shirt (plural **these** shirts)
>
> **there / over there**
> **that** shirt (plural **those** shirts)

d Read the information box. Then practice the conversation in **b** with a partner.

e Use the photos. In pairs, role-play buying clothes. Then change roles.
  A (book open) You are the sales assistant. Begin *Can I help you?*
  B (book closed) You are the customer. Buy a T-shirt, a jacket, or jeans.

$24.50
$82.99
$75

4 ▶ **JENNY'S ON THE PHONE**

a ▶ 5.27 Watch or listen and mark the sentences **T** (true) or **F** (false).
  1 Jenny is talking to Eddie.
  2 She says she doesn't like London.
  3 She says she likes the people in the office.
  4 Jenny is standing outside the store.
  5 Eddie thinks that Rob is her boss.
  6 Jenny loves Rob's new shirt.

b Watch or listen again. Say why the **F** sentences are false.

c Look at the **Social English** phrases. Who says them: **J**enny, **R**ob, or **E**ddie?

> **Social English**
> 1 ☐ It's so cool!   5 ☐ Have fun!
> 2 ☐ Right now?   6 ☐ What's wrong?
> 3 ☐ Wait a minute.   7 ☐ No way!
> 4 ☐ I have to go.

> **American and British English**
> store = American English
> shop = British English
> (nine)-thirty = American English
> half past (nine) = British English

d ▶ 5.28 Watch or listen and check. Then watch or listen and repeat the phrases.

e Complete conversations A–G with **Social English** phrases 1–7. Practice with a partner.

A		I can't find my phone. I don't know where it is.
B	What are you doing?	I'm talking to you!
C	What do you think of New York?	I love it!
D	I can't talk now. I'm at a party.	OK.
E	Let's go – come on!	I'm just finishing an email.
F	Would you like a coffee?	I never drink coffee in the evening.
G		Bye.	Bye. See you later.

CAN YOU...?

☐ apologize   ☐ buy clothes   ☐ say prices

6A A North African story

G object pronouns: me, you, him, etc. V words in a story P /aɪ/, /ɪ/, and /i/

Do you know him?
Yes, but I don't like him.

The Glass Bottle

PART 1

Hassan and Walid are brothers. They live in a small house in the desert, near the mountains, a long way from a town or village. They're very poor. They have no money and they have no animals. Their house only has two rooms. Every day is the same. They get up, and they have sweet black coffee for breakfast. Then Hassan works in the fields – but Walid just sits and looks at the hot, empty desert and the hot, empty sky. They live with their mother. She takes care of them, but she's old and tired.

One day she says, "We're poor and hungry. Why don't you leave here and find work? We need money for food and clothes."

"If you want some money, you have your silver ring – you can sell that," answers Walid.

"I can't sell it," she says. "It's your father's. Every night I look at it and remember him."

Hassan wants to help his mother, and he decides to leave home. His mother gives him bread, and water in a glass bottle. He kisses her, and he walks towards the mountains.

1 SPEAKING

a How do you usually read, on paper or on screen? Which do you prefer? Why?

b **C Communication** Reading in English p.105 What are your reading habits?

2 READING

a ◆)) 6.1 Read and listen to Part 1 of a traditional story. Answer the questions.

1 Who are Hassan and Walid? Where do they live?
2 What kind of life do they have?
3 In what way are Hassan and Walid different?
4 What valuable thing does their mother have? Why doesn't she want to sell it?
5 Why does Hassan decide to leave home?

b Match the words and pictures.

☐ a desert ☐ a field ☐ mountains ☐ the sky

1 2 3 4

c Read Part 1 again. Then look at the picture. What can you see?

3 GRAMMAR object pronouns

a Look at the highlighted words in Part 1 of the story. Who or what do they refer to?

them = *Hassan and Walid*

b **G** p.134 Grammar Bank 6A

c ◆)) 6.3 Listen and say the sentences with a pronoun instead of the name(s).

1 ◆)) I like Anna. (I like her.

4 READING & LISTENING

a ◆)) 6.4 Read and listen to Part 2 of the story. Answer the questions.

1 Where does Hassan go?
2 What happens when he finds the palace?
3 Why is the palace unusual?
4 What does he give the prince?
5 Why is the prince surprised?
6 What does the prince give Hassan?
7 Why is Hassan's mother happy when he comes home?
8 What is Walid's plan?

PART 2

Hassan walks for five days through the mountains. The sun shines. At night, it's very cold. Then one evening, he arrives at a rich and beautiful palace. The prince in the palace welcomes ¹him. He gives him food and drink, and Hassan sleeps in a comfortable bed. There is one strange thing – the windows have no glass.

The next day, Hassan says goodbye. ²He wants to thank the prince and give him something, but he only has ³his empty water bottle. He gives ⁴it to ⁵him. The prince is very surprised.

"What's this?" he says. "I can see through it! It's beautiful! It's wonderful!"

⁶He is very happy, and in return, he gives Hassan a box.

"Don't open ⁷it until you get home," he says. "And be careful with it. It's very valuable."

Hassan walks through the mountains again, and after five days, he arrives home. Walid and ⁸their mother watch ⁹him open the box. He finds 100 gold coins inside. His mother is very happy! "Hassan, you clever boy!" she says. "Now ¹⁰we can buy food and clothes!"

The next night, Walid makes a plan.

"100 gold coins in return for a glass bottle," ¹¹he thinks. "If I give the prince my mother's silver ring, perhaps I can get 1,000 gold coins!"

So Walid gets up, goes very quietly into his mother's room, and takes ¹²her ring from a box under her bed. The next morning, he asks his brother where the palace is, and he leaves.

🔍 **Pronouns and possessive adjectives**
When you read, be careful with pronouns and possessive adjectives, e.g., *he, his, him*. Make sure you know who (or what) they refer to.

b Read Part 2 of the story again. With a partner, say who or what the highlighted pronouns and possessive adjectives refer to.

The prince in the palace welcomes ¹him.
him = Hassan

c ▶ 6.5 What do you think happens in Part 3 of the story? Listen and check.

(I think Walid goes to the palace and…)

5 VOCABULARY words in a story

a Look at these words from the story. Put them in the correct column.

arrive comfortable decide desert inside into
leave mountain palace sell strange surprised
through towards valuable village

adjectives	verbs	nouns	prepositions
comfortable	arrive		

b ▶ 6.6 Listen and check. Listen again and repeat.

6 PRONUNCIATION /aɪ/, /ɪ/, and /i/

a ▶ 6.7 Say the three groups of words and match them to a sound picture. Then listen and check.

bike	fish	tree

1 him it his ring sit kiss
2 he she me meet read leave
3 my I buy sky nice high

b ▶ 6.8 Listen. Can you hear the difference?

1 a he's	b his	4 a leave	b live
2 a me	b my	5 a kiss	b keys
3 a it	b eat	6 a we	b why

c ▶ 6.9 Listen and check (✓) the word you hear.

d Practice saying the sentences.
1 His mother has a silver ring.
2 She looks at it and thinks of him.
3 That night he decides to leave home.
4 The prince gives him food and drink.
5 After five days, he arrives home.

7 SPEAKING

Work in pairs. A, you are Hassan. Tell the story to B until you get home from your trip.

(I'm Hassan. I live with my mother and brother in the desert. We're very poor. One day, I decide to leave home…)

B, you are Walid. Continue the story.

(I'm Walid, Hassan's brother. When I see the 100 gold coins, I make a plan. At night, I take my mother's ring…)

Go online to review the lesson

6B The second Friday in July

> I like getting up early.
> I hate it!

G like + (verb + -ing) **V** the date, ordinal numbers **P** /ð/ and /θ/, saying the date

1 VOCABULARY & PRONUNCIATION
the date, /ð/ and /θ/

a Can you remember the months of the year? Say them around the class.

b **V** p.159 **Vocabulary Bank** The weather and dates Do Part 2.

c 🔊 6.11 Listen to the words and sounds. Then listen and repeat.

mother	this the that they
thumb	Thursday third thirteenth thirtieth

> 🔍 **Ordinal numbers** *first, fourth,* etc.
> Some ordinal numbers can be difficult to say because they end in two or more consonant sounds, e.g., *sixth* /sɪksθ/.

d 🔊 6.12 Listen and repeat the ordinal numbers. Then practice saying them.

fifth   sixth   eighth   twelfth

e 🔊 6.13 How do you say these dates? Listen and check.

3/1   11/2   5/3   6/4   1/5   7/6   9/12
10/17   8/20   2/23   4/28   12/31

f Listen again and repeat the dates. Copy the <u>rhythm</u>.

🔊 March first

g What days are holidays in your country? What do people do on these days?

2 LISTENING

a 🔊 6.14 Listen to five conversations. (Circle) the ordinal number you hear.

1	15th	21st	26th	
2	3rd	13th	30th	
3	5th	6th	7th	
4	50th	51st	53rd	
5	6th	9th	16th	

b Listen again. Match the ordinal numbers to these things. Write them in the chart in **a**.

a street   a drink   a birthday   a floor   a date

3 READING

a Read the introduction on the forum. What's special about the second Friday in July and the third Monday in January?

Home   **News**   **Top stories**   **For you**   **Account**

Good times, bad times

Psychologist Dr. Cliff Arnall says the happiest day of the year is the second Friday in July. It's easy to see why — it's summer, it's ==warm== outside, the evenings are light, and it's the day before a weekend! And the third Monday in January is the most ==depressing== day of the year. Why? Because it's winter, the weather is usually ==gray== and cold, the days are ==dark==, and Monday is the first day of the working week. People are also often short of money after Christmas, and some people feel bad after breaking their New Year's resolutions.

Do you agree? What's your favorite month, day, and time? And what's your least favorite?   12 answers

---

b Read the forum comments on p.49. Complete them with these months, days, and times.

February	June	October	December
Monday	Friday	Saturday	Sunday
6:30 a.m.	9:00 a.m.	5:30 p.m.	7:45 p.m.

c Look at all the ==highlighted== adjectives. What do they mean?

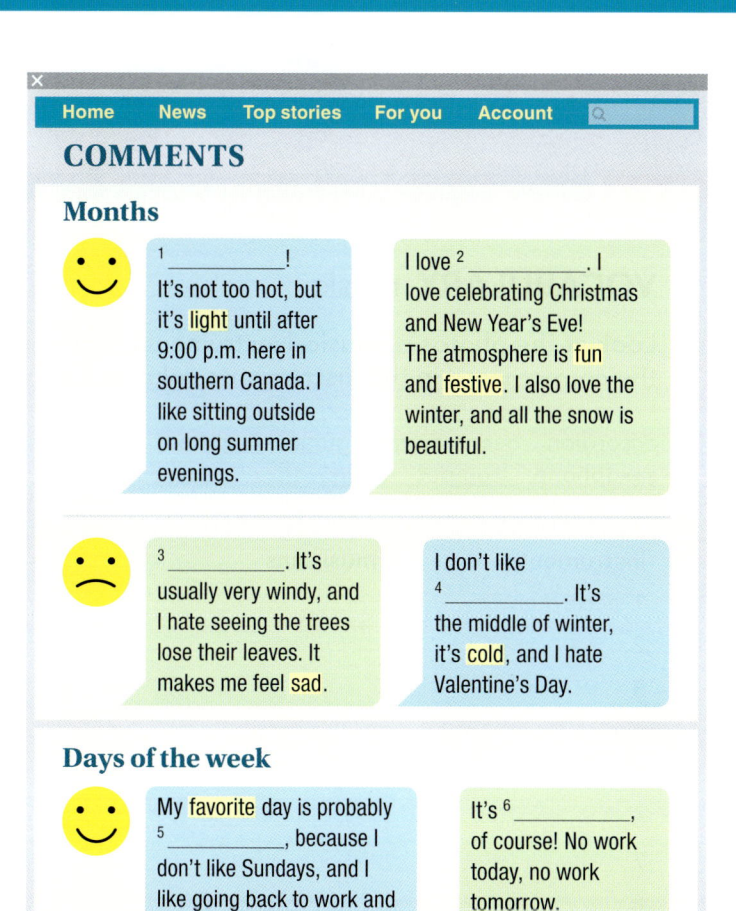

COMMENTS

Months

😊 1 _____! It's not too hot, but it's light until after 9:00 p.m. here in southern Canada. I like sitting outside on long summer evenings.

😊 I love 2 _____. I love celebrating Christmas and New Year's Eve! The atmosphere is fun and festive. I also love the winter, and all the snow is beautiful.

☹ 3 _____. It's usually very windy, and I hate seeing the trees lose their leaves. It makes me feel sad.

☹ I don't like 4 _____. It's the middle of winter, it's cold, and I hate Valentine's Day.

Days of the week

😊 My favorite day is probably 5 _____, because I don't like Sundays, and I like going back to work and seeing my friends!

😊 It's 6 _____, of course! No work today, no work tomorrow.

☹ 7 _____ is my least favorite day of the week, especially the evening. I don't mind working – I like my job – but I don't like thinking about going back to work.

☹ I really hate 8 _____. I'm always tired because it's the end of the week, and I want to go home and rest. But it's when my friends want to go out, so in the end, I usually go out with them, but I never enjoy it.

Times of day

😊 My favorite time is 9 _____, because my roommates leave the house early and then I'm all alone. I can enjoy my breakfast coffee in silence, and then go to school.

😊 I like 10 _____ on Tuesdays and Wednesdays. It's when my exercise class at the gym finishes, and it's when I start to relax and think about what to eat.

☹ My least favorite time is 11 _____. That's when I set my alarm in the morning so I can take a shower and have a quick breakfast. I hate getting up early. I'm absolutely not a morning person.

☹ Surprisingly, my least favorite time of the day is 12 _____, when I finish work. I hate the ride home on the subway. It's dirty, and you can't sit anywhere. It's not so bad in the morning.

4 GRAMMAR *like* + (verb + -ing)

a Complete the chart with a verb phrase from the list.

I don't like   I don't mind   I hate   I like   I love

😃	
🙂	
😐	
🙁	
😠	

b Complete the sentences from the forum comments.
1 **I love** c_____ Christmas and New Year's Eve!
2 **I like** s_____ outside on long summer evenings.
3 **I don't mind** w_____ – I like my job.
4 **I don't like** th_____ about going back to work.
5 **I hate** g_____ up early.

What is the form of a verb after *love*, *like*, etc.?

c 🅖 p.134 **Grammar Bank 6B**

d In pairs, make true sentences beginning *I like*, *I hate*, etc., and the verb phrases below.

get up early
have eggs for breakfast
take selfies
listen to music when I'm studying
do housework on the weekend

drive at night
swim in a cold ocean
watch soccer on TV
play games on my phone
shop online

5 SPEAKING & WRITING

a In pairs, interview your partner with the questions. Say why when you answer. Are you similar or different?

What's your favorite / least favorite month?
What's your favorite / least favorite day of the week?
What's your favorite / least favorite time of day?

> My favorite month is July because I usually go on vacation then, and I love traveling...

b Write one positive and one negative comment for each section of the forum in **3**.

Go online to review the lesson

49

6C Making music

> What kind of music do you like?
>
> I like classical music, and I love jazz.

G review: *be* or *do*? V music P /y/, giving opinions

1 VOCABULARY music

a Look at the photos of musical instruments. Write the correct word in the **instruments** column.

a<u>cc</u>ordion   bass   drums   guitar   <u>key</u>board   p<u>i</u>ano   s<u>a</u>xophone   <u>tru</u>mpet   vio<u>lin</u>

instruments	musicians
1 *accordion*	
2	
3	
4	
5	
6	
7	
8	
9	

b 🔊 6.16 Listen and check.

c 🔊 6.17 Listen and complete the **musicians** column.

d Listen again. Focus on the musicians and <u>un</u>derline the stressed syllable. Then compare the two columns. When is the stress different?

e 🔊 6.18 Cover the chart. Listen to the music and say the name of the instrument and the musician.

f Do you play a musical instrument? How good are you?

2 GRAMMAR review: *be* or *do*?

a (Circle) the correct words.
1. What kind of music *are you* / *do you* listen to?
2. *I'm not* / *I don't* like hip hop.
3. She *isn't* / *doesn't* listening to you.
4. *Are you* / *Do you* play in a band?
5. Where *is* / *does* Adele from?

b G p.134 Grammar Bank 6C

c 🔊 6.21 Listen and make the question.
1. 🔊 *She's American.* (*Is she American?*
2. 🔊 *He plays the piano.* (*Does he play the piano?*

3 SPEAKING

Read the questionnaire and think about your answers. Then interview a partner with the questionnaire. Ask for more information. Do you have similar musical tastes and habits?

MY MUSIC

1 What kinds of music do you like?
classical music   folk   hip hop
jazz   pop   reggae   other

2 How often do you...?
go to concerts   go dancing
watch music videos online   download music
look for song lyrics on the internet

3 How do you usually listen to music?
on the radio   online   on my phone   on CDs

4 When you're in a car, what do you prefer listening to?
the radio (which station?)   my own music   nothing

5 When do you listen to music?
When I'm exercising.
When I'm traveling on public transportation.
When I'm walking around town.
When I'm working or studying.
When I'm relaxing.

6 What kind of music do you like listening to when you are...?
sad   happy

7 Are you listening to a particular song or piece of music a lot right now?

8 Do you sing or play in a group, e.g., a choir or band? What kind of music do you sing or play?

4 PRONUNCIATION /y/, giving opinions

a ▶ 6.22 Listen to the words and sounds. Then listen and repeat.

| y | yacht | you   yellow   young |
| | | your   yoga   year |

🔍 **Hidden /y/ sound**
Some words with the /u/ sound (spelled with u or ew) also have a /y/ sound before the /u/, e.g., *music* /ˈmyuzɪk/ **NOT** ~~/ˈmuzɪk/~~.

b ▶ 6.23 Listen and write five phrases.

c ▶ 6.24 Listen and repeat the opinions. Then practice saying them. Copy the stress and intonation.
I **like** him. He's great.
I **really** like her. She's fan**tas**tic.
I **don't like** them. They're **aw**ful.
I **don't like** it. It's **ter**rible.

d Write the names of six musicians and bands: three you love and three you hate. Then in pairs, ask your partner *What do you think of...?*

Male musicians   _____ _____
Female musicians   _____ _____
Bands   _____ _____

5 ▶ VIDEO LISTENING

a Do you have street performers where you live? Do you give them money? Why (not)?

> **street performer** [N AmE /strit pərˈfɔrmər/]/
> **busker** [BrE /ˈbʌskər/] *noun* a person who performs in public places and asks for money

b Watch the documentary *A street performer*. Do you think Charlotte likes her job?

c Watch again and mark the sentences **T** (true) or **F** (false). Correct the **F** sentences.
1 Charlotte only performs in the morning.
2 Street performers usually play pop or folk songs.
3 Street performers can't play anywhere they want to.
4 Charlotte always plays in the same area of the city.
5 She only plays other people's songs.
6 Charlotte prefers performing in the summer to performing in the winter.

d Do you think Charlotte is a good musician? Would you give her money?

6 WRITING

W p.115 **Writing** An informal email Write an email to a friend.

> Go online to watch the video and review the lesson

5 & 6 Review and Check

GRAMMAR

Circle a, b, or c.

1 She ____ the piano.
 a can play b can to play c cans play
2 ____ come tonight?
 a Do you can b You can c Can you
3 A What's that noise? B ____ a party upstairs.
 a They having b They're having c They're have
4 The weather is cold, but ____ raining.
 a it doesn't b it isn't c it not
5 A What ____ doing? B I'm studying for an exam.
 a are you b do you c you are
6 The sun ____! Let's go for a walk.
 a shine b shines c is shining
7 The museum ____ at 2:00 on Mondays.
 a closes b is closing c close
8 A What ____? B I'm a nurse.
 a are you doing b do you do c do you
9 Our son always calls ____ every day.
 a we b us c our
10 Is your sister at home? I need to speak to ____.
 a him b she c her
11 Do you like ____ housework?
 a doing b do c making
12 I don't mind ____ early.
 a get up b getting up c to get up
13 A ____ hungry? B Yes. What's for dinner?
 a Do you b Have you c Are you
14 What song ____ listening to?
 a are you b do you c you are
15 What time ____ she usually go to bed?
 a do b is c does

VOCABULARY

a Complete the phrases with these verbs.

| buy call dance forget have hear play |
| run take tell |

1 ____ a noise
2 ____ a musical instrument
3 ____ somebody's birthday
4 ____ a present for your mother
5 ____ somebody a secret
6 ____ a party
7 ____ a photo
8 ____ a marathon
9 ____ a taxi
10 ____ the tango

b Complete the sentences with *at*, *for*, *in*, *on*, or *to*.

1 She goes to bed ____ about 11 o'clock.
2 They have their TV ____ very loud.
3 I can't find the keys. Can you look ____ them?
4 I need to talk ____ the doctor.
5 I'm coming! Wait ____ me!
6 My birthday's ____ July.
7 Their wedding is ____ March 2nd.

c **Circle** the word that is different.

1 cloudy fog sunny windy
2 cold shine snow rain
3 fall season spring winter
4 first seven third twelfth
5 twenty-second twenty-five twenty-one twenty-three
6 desert field mountain ring
7 accordion drummer guitar violin
8 street performer concert singer trumpeter

PRONUNCIATION

a Practice the words and sounds.

Vowel sounds

| bull | boot | train | bike |

Consonant sounds

| singer | thumb | mother | yacht | nose |

b p.166–7 **Sound Bank** Say more words for each sound.

c What sound do the pink letters have in these words?
 1 cook 2 sitting 3 tenth 4 there 5 violin

d Underline the stressed syllable.
 1 neigh|bor 3 fif|ti|eth 5 pi|a|nist
 2 re|mem|ber 4 sax|o|phone

CAN YOU understand this text?

a Read the article once. What is *your* perfect "wake-up song"?

b Read the article again. Circle a, b, or c.
1. Dr. Greenberg's list comes from information from ____.
   a the internet   b his friends   c his students
2. One of the things Dr. Greenberg *doesn't* say is important in the song is ____.
   a the words   b the instruments   c the singer
3. He says that waking up ____ can help most people feel good all day.
   a to Coldplay   b to the right music   c early in the morning
4. ____ doesn't have a wake-up song.
   a Sandy   b Martha   c Martin

▶ CAN YOU understand these people?

🔊 6.25 Watch or listen and answer the questions.

1. Duncan 2. Alice 3. Tiffany 4. Stephen 5. Dasha

1. Duncan ____.
   a can't play the violin very well
   b can't play the violin
   c can play the violin very well
2. Alice's neighbors ____ make a noise.
   a always   b sometimes   c never
3. Tiffany's favorite month is ____.
   a October   b November   c December
4. Stephen doesn't like ____.
   a opera   b country music   c the band Wye Oak
5. Right now, Dasha is reading ____.
   a a modern novel
   b a book about French history
   c a book about the Russian Revolution

CAN YOU say this in English?

Do the tasks with a partner. Check (✓) the box if you can do these things.

Can you...?
1. ☐ say two things you can do well, and two things you can't do (e.g., cook)
2. ☐ say three things you can or can't do in class (e.g., use your cell phone)
3. ☐ say what kind of books you usually read, and what you are reading right now
4. ☐ ask questions with the words below
   • ...tired?
   • ...like watching sports on TV?
   • ...enjoying your English classes?
   • ...play a musical instrument?

THE MOMENT I WAKE UP...

Getting up in the morning is hard, but for many people, music seems to help them start the day. There is actually a list of perfect "wake-up songs" compiled by a psychologist, David M. Greenberg, using data from the music download website, Spotify.

When choosing the perfect "wake-up songs," Greenberg considered things like how the music builds up, positive lyrics, and strong rhythm. He says that the music needs to start gently, and then slowly build up to help people to wake up. It must have positive lyrics to change people's mood from bad to good. The rhythm also needs to be strong, with a lot of bass and drums.

Greenberg's top choice of song is *Viva La Vida*, by Coldplay, which has all the three necessary elements. "Science shows that music affects us in all kinds of ways, including emotionally, physiologically, and in the brain," he says. "The right music – like *Viva La Vida*, with its positive energy and strong momentum – can help you wake up and feel energetic for the rest of your day."

What's your favorite "wake-up song"? Leave your comments below.

Comments:

S — Mine is definitely *Say a Little Prayer* by Aretha Franklin. I always play it first thing in the morning. *Sandy*

M — I like getting up to a song by Imagine Dragons, called *On Top of the World*. I think it fits Dr. Greenberg's criteria because it's really positive! *Martha*

M — I hate listening to music when I wake up. I prefer listening to the early morning news. Then I can start the day knowing what's happening in the world. *Martin*

Adapted from a website

Go online to watch the video, review Files 5 and 6, and check your progress

7A Selfies

Who was he? **He was a famous painter.**

G simple past of *be*: was / were   V word formation: write → writer   P sentence stress

1 GRAMMAR simple past of *be*

a Look at a self-portrait by a famous painter. Answer the questions.
1 Do you know who he is?
2 How old do you think he is in this painting?
3 Do you know any of his paintings? Do you like them?

b ◆)) 7.1 Listen to an audio guide. Check your answers to 1 and 2 in **a**.

c Listen again. Choose a, b, or c.
1 He was born in ____ in 1853.
   a Belgium   b the Netherlands   c Germany
2 His parents weren't ____.
   a artists   b married   c poor
3 Before he was a painter, he was a ____.
   a teacher   b doctor   c lawyer
4 There are ____ photos of him when he was young.
   a no   b a lot of   c not many
5 This self-portrait was a present for the painter ____.
   a Monet   b Picasso   c Gauguin
6 The relationship between the two painters wasn't ____.
   a bad   b easy   c complicated
7 He was only ____ when he died.
   a 27   b 37   c 47
8 During his life, his paintings were ____.
   a unpopular   b valuable   c famous

d Look at the highlighted verbs in **c**. Complete the chart.

Present	is	are	isn't	aren't
Past				

e **G** p.136 Grammar Bank 7A

2 PRONUNCIATION sentence stress

a ◆)) 7.3 Listen and repeat. Copy the rhythm.

> ➕ He was a **painter**. I was **born** in **Mexico**.
> They were **good friends**.
> ➖ He **wasn't married**. They **weren't** very **happy**.
> ❓ **Where** were you **born**? **Where** was the **hotel**?
> Was it **expensive**? **No**, it **wasn't**.
> Were they at the **concert**? **Yes**, they **were**.

b ◆)) 7.4 Listen. Say the sentences in the simple past.
1))) *I'm at home.*   (*I was at home.*

3 READING

a Look at three self-portraits on p.55. Do you think the self-portraits look like the people in the photos?

b Read the three biographies and number the events in the correct order, 1–3.

Kurt Vonnegut
☐ *Slaughterhouse-Five* was a bestseller.
☐ He was a soldier.
☐ He was a painter.

Billy Dee Williams
☐ He was in his first movie.
☐ He was very successful as an actor.
☐ He was an art student.

Adele
☐ She wasn't very interested in schoolwork.
☐ *19* was a bestseller.
☐ She was a student with singer Jessie J.

c Read the biographies again. Then cover them. What can you remember about each person?

d Which of the four self-portraits in this lesson do you like the most? Why?

Kurt Vonnegut

Kurt Vonnegut was an American writer. He was born in 1922 in Indianapolis. He was a soldier during World War II, and was in
05 a prison camp in Germany from 1944 to 1945. His first novel was *Player Piano*, published in 1952, but it wasn't a success. However, his novel *Slaughterhouse-Five*, an anti-
10 war book, was a best-seller, and was made into a movie in 1972. In his later life, he was interested in politics and painting. His art was an escape from the "work"
15 of writing.

Billy Dee Williams

Billy Dee Williams is an American actor. He was born in New York in 1937. His father was a caretaker and his mother was an elevator operator. He was a
20 student at the High School of Music & Art. He was a theater actor for 15 years, and in 1959, he was in his first movie. He was very successful in the 1980s, when he was in two Star Wars movies,
25 *The Empire Strikes Back* and *Return of the Jedi*. Before he was an actor, Williams was at a fine arts academy in New York, and this self-portrait is in the National Portrait Gallery in
30 Washington, D.C.

Adele

Adele is a British singer and songwriter. She was born Adele Laurie Blue Adkins in London in 1988. When she was a child, she
35 was much more interested in music than in schoolwork. When she was 14, her musical tastes were very different from most teenagers – she was a big fan of
40 Billie Holiday and Eminem. She was a performing arts student at the BRIT School in London, where she was a classmate of singers Leona Lewis and Jessie J.
45 Her first album, *19*, in 2008, was an immediate success, and she is now a major star. Adele isn't a painter; this self-portrait was for an online art project called *Face Britain*.

4 VOCABULARY word formation

a Find words in the biographies for people's jobs made from these verbs.

1 write _____   3 sing _____
2 act _____   4 paint _____

> 🔍 **Word building: professions**
> We often add *-er* or *-or* to a verb, e.g., *writer*, *actor*.
>
> We often add *-ian* or *-ist* to a noun, e.g., *musician*, *pianist*.

b Look at the two groups below. Are the words verbs or nouns? Can you make the words for the jobs?

1 compose   dance   direct   invent
2 art   novel   politics   science

c 🔊 **7.5** Listen and check. Underline the stressed syllable. Practice saying the words.

d Write the names of four famous people in each circle. Then change circles. Ask a partner about the people in his / her circles.

Who's Sia? *She's an Australian singer.*

Who was Alexander Graham Bell?
He was an American scientist.

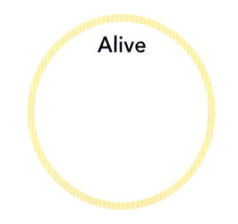

(Alive)   (Dead)

5 SPEAKING

Talk to a partner.
Do you ever take selfies?

YES
Do you have any on your phone?
Where were you?
When was it?
Who were you with?

NO
Why don't you take them?
Why do you think other people take them?
Do any of your friends and family take them?
Do you have any photos of you on your phone that are not selfies? Where were you?

Go online to review the lesson

7B Wrong name, wrong place

> Where did they want to go?
> They wanted to go to Granada.

G simple past: regular verbs **V** past time expressions **P** -ed endings

1 READING & LISTENING

a Read the beginning of a true story about a problem with a flight. Answer the questions.
1. Where did Adam and India want to travel?
2. Who booked the tickets?
3. What problem do you think there was with the booking?

Last March, Adam and his girlfriend India, who live in Manchester, decided to go to Ibiza on vacation. India's stepfather booked the tickets for them with Ryanair. He needed Adam's last name. He wasn't sure what it was, so he looked on Facebook. The name on Adam's page was Adam West, and he booked the tickets in that name, to fly on June 11th.

b Read the rest of the story. Put the parts in the correct order, 1–6.

A ☐ …to pay $288, so he decided to change his last name to West. It was free to change his name, but then he needed a new passport with his new name. The new passport…

B ☐ 1 Unfortunately it wasn't the right name – "Adam West" is the name of an actor who played Batman in the 1960s. Adam…

C ☐ …that it was possible, but he needed to pay $288 – double the cost of the flight. He didn't want…

D ☐ …used the name on his Facebook page as a joke. His real name is Adam Armstrong. When Adam…

E ☐ …realized the mistake, he called Ryanair. He asked them to change the last name on his booking. Ryanair replied…

F ☐ …was $135 – so Adam saved $153. And he and India traveled to Ibiza on June 11th.

c Do you think Adam's solution was a good one? Why (not)?

d You're going to listen to another true story. Before you listen, read sentences A–G and put them in a logical order, 1–7.

☐ A They asked the flight attendant a question.
☐ B Edward booked the flights.
☐ 1 C Edward and Lowell wanted to go on vacation to Spain.
☐ D They parked their car.
☐ E They changed planes at Heathrow Airport.
☐ F They looked for flights online.
☐ G They checked into their first flight.

e 🔊 7.6 Now listen to the first part of the story. Was your order in **d** correct?

f 🔊 7.7 Listen to the end of the story. What was the problem?

g Whose fault was the problem in each story?

2 GRAMMAR simple past: regular verbs

a Find the past tense of these verbs in **1b**. Write them in the chart.

	Present	Past
1	ask	
2	decide	
3	reply	
4	don't want	

b ▶ 7.8 Listen to an extract from the second story. What's the missing word?

Edward, _____ you check the airport when you booked?

c **G** p.136 Grammar Bank 7B

d Stand up and move around the class. Ask *Did you…?* questions about yesterday with the verb phrases below. When somebody answers *Yes, I did.*, write their name.

YESTERDAY
Find a person who…

_____ watched soccer on TV
_____ called a taxi
_____ studied for an exam
_____ cooked dinner
_____ arrived at work / school late
_____ listened to the radio
_____ started a new book
_____ worked / studied until late
_____ played a computer or video game

Did you watch soccer on TV yesterday?

No, I didn't. Did you call a taxi…?

3 PRONUNCIATION -ed endings

Simple past regular verbs
The *e* in *-ed* is not usually pronounced, and *-ed* is pronounced /d/ or /t/, e.g., *closed* /kloʊzd/, *stopped* /stɑpt/.

The *-ed* is pronounced /ɪd/ **only** in verbs that end with the sound /t/ or /d/, e.g., *wait – waited* /ˈweɪtɪd/, *decide – decided* /dɪˈsaɪdɪd/.

a ▶ 7.10 Listen and repeat the sentences.

1 /d/ I call**ed** a taxi. I us**ed** an app. It arriv**ed** in five minutes.

2 /t/ We talk**ed** about a vacation. We look**ed** online. We book**ed** a hotel.

3 /ɪd/ He need**ed** a passport. He want**ed** it fast. He wait**ed** a long time.

b ▶ 7.11 Look at the verbs in the list. (Circle) the ones that belong to group 3 (/ɪd/). Listen and check.

asked   cooked   ended   finished   liked   lived   painted
played   started   stopped   traveled   watched   worked

c ▶ 7.12 Listen to some verb phrases. Make true + or − sentences about yesterday.

1 ▶ play tennis   *I didn't play tennis yesterday.*

4 VOCABULARY & SPEAKING
past time expressions

a Number the past time expressions 1–10.

____ yesterday morning   ____ last week
____ last night   ____ last summer
____ last month   ____ the day before yesterday
____ three days ago   ____ a year ago
 1   five minutes ago   10   in 2017

Past time expressions
We say *last week*, *last month*
NOT *the last week*, *the last month*.

b ▶ 7.13 Listen and check. Then listen and repeat.

c Complete the sentence for each activity with a past time expression.

When was the last time?

I traveled by bus…	I booked some tickets…
I posted a photo online…	I downloaded a song…
I walked more than 5 miles…	I played a sport…
I watched a really good movie…	I danced at a party…
I arrived late for something…	

d Work in pairs. **A** tell your partner your first sentence. **B** ask for more information.

I traveled by bus this morning.   *Where to?*

Go online to review the lesson

57

7C Happy New Year?

> What did you do? — We went to a party.

G simple past: irregular verbs **V** go, have, get **P** sentence stress

1 READING

a When is New Year's Eve? Is it an important celebration in your country?

b Read three stories. Who had…?
- a great evening
- an OK evening
- a terrible evening

c Read the stories again. Complete the sentences with **A** (Andy), **J** (Jenny), or **M** (Mina).

1. ____ was outside at midnight.
2. ____ didn't know exactly when midnight was.
3. ____ was alone at midnight.
4. ____ was at work at midnight.
5. ____ heard the celebrations, but didn't see them.
6. ____ was surprised by something people did.

d How do people celebrate New Year's Eve in your country? Do you think most people enjoy it? Why (not)?

2 GRAMMAR simple past: irregular verbs

a With a partner, find the past tense of these irregular verbs in the stories.

buy	bought	/bɔt/
can	_____	/kʊd/
come	_____	/keɪm/
feel	_____	/fɛlt/
find	_____	/faʊnd/
get	_____	/gɑt/
go	_____	/wɛnt/
have	_____	/hæd/
know	_____	/nu/
put on	_____	/pʊt ɑn/
say	_____	/sɛd/
sing	_____	/sæŋ/
take	_____	/tʊk/
think	_____	/θɔt/
wear	_____	/wɔr/

b 🔊 7.14 Listen and check. Practice saying the verbs.

c **G** p.136 Grammar Bank 7C

NEW YEAR'S EVE – ONE TO REMEMBER OR ONE TO FORGET?

MINA This was last year, and I went to a hotel with some friends. It had a restaurant on the top floor, and that's where the party was. We got there at
05 about 11:00. About half an hour before midnight I realized I didn't have my phone – it was in my car. So I took the elevator down to the parking lot. I found my phone, and then I got back into the
10 elevator – I was the only person in it. But then, between the third and fourth floors, the elevator stopped completely and I couldn't get out. I pressed the button and asked for help, but a guy said there
15 was an electrical problem and I needed to wait. Then a few minutes later, I could hear people outside celebrating. It was awful – I didn't get out until almost 1:00 in the morning. And on top of it all, my
20 friends didn't realize that I wasn't there!

JENNY I had a fantastic New Year's Eve in Iceland in 2013. First, we went to a really expensive restaurant for dinner. It was early, about 6:00, because that's when people have dinner in Iceland. I wore a fantastic dress, but after dinner we got a taxi back to the hotel and I put on boots and a warm
25 jacket. Then we went out and watched the amazing fireworks. Suddenly, at about 10:00, everyone went home to watch TV – there's this famous TV show they always watch on New Year's Eve! It was really strange – the streets were empty for a little bit. But then just before midnight, people came out again and danced and sang till about 5:00 in the morning. It was incredible.

3 VOCABULARY go, have, get

a Can you remember these phrases? Write *went*, *had*, or *got*.
1 I _____ to a hotel with some friends.
2 It _____ a restaurant on the top floor.
3 We _____ there at about 11:00.
4 I _____ a fantastic New Year's Eve.
5 We _____ to a really expensive restaurant.
6 We _____ a taxi back to the hotel.

b ⓥ p.160 **Vocabulary Bank** *go, have, get*

ANDY I'm a DJ, and this happened to me a few years ago. It was my first time at a New Year's Eve party, and I planned all the music really carefully. I knew exactly which tracks I was going to play. The first part of the night was fine, but just when I thought it was time to start the countdown to midnight, I saw that people were all at the bar, not on the dance floor, and the TVs were on. On the screens I could see fireworks! I looked at my watch and I realized it was about two minutes slow! I felt really stupid. I bought a new watch the next day!

4 LISTENING

a 🔊 7.17 Listen to Denisa from Slovakia talk about a memorable New Year's Eve. Where was Denisa at midnight?

b Can you remember what she says about these people and things?
1 Marcelo
2 white clothes
3 Marcelo's mother
4 dinner
5 Copacabana
6 a show
7 almost midnight
8 a swim at Praia do Arpoador

c Listen again and check.

d Would you like to spend New Year's Eve in Rio? Is there anywhere else in the world you'd like to spend it?

5 PRONUNCIATION sentence stress

a Look at the questions. What words are missing?

A memorable New Year's Eve
1 What year _____ it?
2 Where _____ you?
3 Who _____ _____ with?
4 Where _____ _____ have dinner?
5 What _____ _____ wear?
6 What _____ _____ do before midnight?
7 What _____ _____ do at midnight?
8 What _____ _____ do after midnight?
9 How _____ the weather?
10 What time _____ _____ go to bed?
11 _____ _____ have a good time?

b 🔊 7.18 Listen and repeat the questions. Copy the rhythm.

6 SPEAKING & WRITING

a Think about a time when you had a memorable New Year's Eve. Look at the questions in **5a** and plan your answers. Add all the extra information you can.

b Interview each other about your New Year's Eve.

c Write about your New Year's Eve. Answer the questions in **5a**, and use the stories in **1** to help you.

Go online to review the lesson

Practical English Getting lost

EPISODE 4

asking for directions V directions

1 ▶ A FREE MORNING

a ◉ 7.19 Watch or listen to Rob and Jenny planning their free morning. What's the problem?

b Watch or listen again. Complete the sentences with a word, a name, or a number.
1 Rob suggests that they go _____.
2 He says that they can _____ bikes.
3 _____ calls _____.
4 Rob needs to interview an _____.
5 Rob asks if he can do the interview on _____.
6 Rob and Jenny arrange to meet at _____ o'clock outside the Tate Modern.

Glossary
(the) Tate Modern a famous art gallery in London

2 VOCABULARY directions

a Match the phrases and pictures.

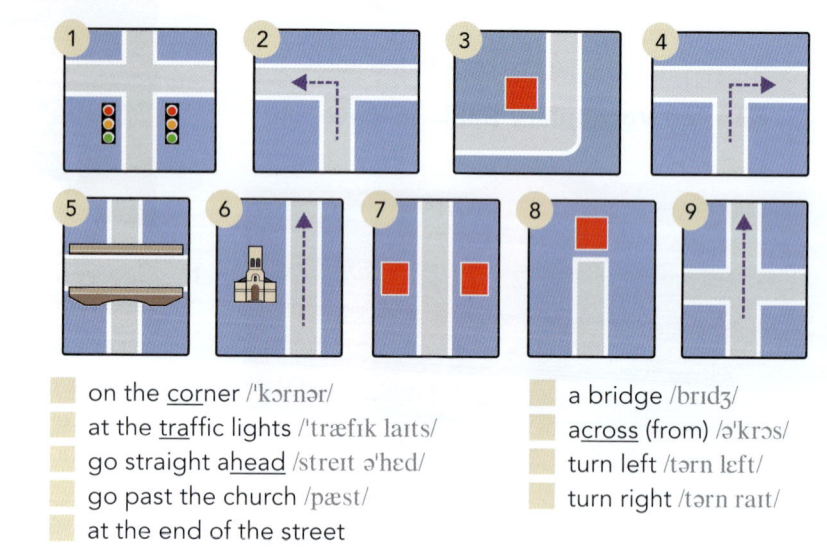

☐ on the corner /ˈkɔrnər/
☐ at the traffic lights /ˈtræfɪk laɪts/
☐ go straight ahead /streɪt əˈhɛd/
☐ go past the church /pæst/
☐ at the end of the street
☐ a bridge /brɪdʒ/
☐ across (from) /əˈkrɔs/
☐ turn left /tɜrn lɛft/
☐ turn right /tɜrn raɪt/

b ◉ 7.20 Listen and check.

c Cover the phrases and look at the pictures. Say the phrases.

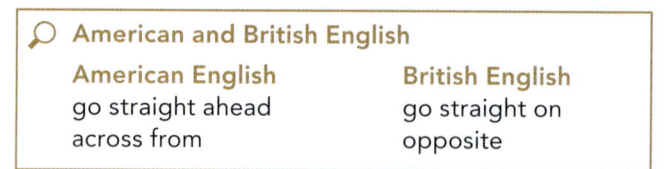

🔍 **American and British English**
American English	British English
go straight ahead	go straight on
across from	opposite

3 ▶ ASKING FOR DIRECTIONS

a ◉ 7.21 Jenny is trying to find the Tate Modern. Watch or listen. Is it A, B, C, or D? How many people does she ask?

b Watch or listen again. Complete the **You hear** phrases.

You say	You hear
Excuse me, please. Where's the Tate Modern?	¹_____, I don't live here.
Excuse me. Is the Tate Modern near here?	The Tate Modern? It's near here, but I don't know exactly ²_____. Sorry.
Thank you.	
Excuse me. Can you tell me the way to the Tate Modern, please?	Yes, of course. Go straight on. Go ³_____ the church. Then turn ⁴_____ at the traffic lights. And it's at the end of the street.
Sorry, could you say that again, please?	Yes, go straight on. …You can't ⁵_____ it!
Thank you.	

c ▶ 7.22 Watch or listen and repeat the **You say** phrases. Copy the rhythm.

d Practice the conversation with a partner.

> 🔍 **Can you…? or Could you…?**
> Can you tell me the way to the Tate Modern?
> Could you say that again, please?
>
> We can use *Can you…?* or *Could you…?* when we want to ask another person to do something. *Could you…?* is more polite.

e 👥 In pairs, role-play the conversation.
You are where Jenny is.
A Ask for directions to building A (the library). Begin *Excuse me, where's…*.
B Give directions. Then change roles. **B** ask for directions to building C (the post office).

4 ▶ JENNY AND ROB GO SIGHTSEEING

a ▶ 7.23 Watch or listen to Rob and Jenny. (Circle) the correct option.
1 The *Millennium / London* Bridge is only for people.
2 It was the first new bridge over the Thames in *100 / 200* years.
3 Jenny doesn't like *the theater. / Shakespeare*.
4 Jenny *can / can't* meet Daniel for lunch.
5 There's a great *gift shop / restaurant* on the top floor of the Tate Modern.
6 The Tate Modern was a *power / train* station until 1981.

b Look at the **Social English** phrases. Who says them: **J**enny, **R**ob, or **D**aniel?

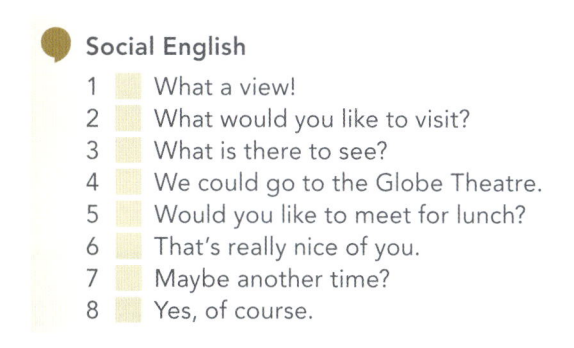

> 💬 **Social English**
> 1 ☐ What a view!
> 2 ☐ What would you like to visit?
> 3 ☐ What is there to see?
> 4 ☐ We could go to the Globe Theatre.
> 5 ☐ Would you like to meet for lunch?
> 6 ☐ That's really nice of you.
> 7 ☐ Maybe another time?
> 8 ☐ Yes, of course.

c ▶ 7.24 Watch or listen and check. Then watch or listen and repeat.

d Complete conversations A–H with **Social English** phrases 1–8. Practice with a partner.

A	What can we do this afternoon?	☐	I love Shakespeare!
B	We have all day in Oxford. ☐		I'd like to see the colleges and the High Street.
C	Let's go to the Tate Modern.		It's closed today. ☐
D	What are you doing at noon? ☐		Yes, I'd love to.
E	☐ I can see St. Paul's cathedral.		Yes, and the London Eye's over there.
F	Can you tell me the way to Victoria Station?	☐	Go straight down there and turn left.
G	I hear the British Museum is great. ☐		Right now, there's a new exhibition about the Greeks.
H	Would you like to go out tonight?	☐	But I'm afraid I'm busy tonight.

CAN YOU…?

☐ ask for and understand directions
☐ give simple directions
☐ ask somebody to do something in a polite way

Go online to watch the video, review the lesson, and check your progress

8A A murder mystery

G simple past: regular and irregular **V** irregular verbs **P** simple past verbs

> Did you love your husband?
>
> No. But I didn't kill him.

1 READING

a Read about the Travers murder and look at the photos of the victim and the suspects. Then cover the text and look at the photos. Can you remember who the people are?

Who's Amanda?) (*She's Jeremy's wife.*

b 🔊 8.1 Read and listen to the story. Mark the sentences **T** (true) or **F** (false). Correct the **F** sentences.

1 Somebody killed Jeremy between 11:00 p.m. and 7:00 a.m.
2 The detective questioned Amanda in the living room.
3 Jeremy went to bed before Amanda.
4 Amanda and Jeremy slept in the same room.
5 Somebody opened and closed Amanda's door.
6 Amanda got up at 7:00.
7 Amanda didn't love Jeremy.

The Travers murder

- June 22, 1965 – Jeremy Travers's 60th birthday
- He had dinner at his country house with:
  – Amanda, his wife
  – Barbara, his daughter
  – Gordon, his business partner
  – Claudia, his secretary.
- The next morning, Amanda Travers went to her husband's bedroom. She found him dead.

The victim, Jeremy Travers

Detective Granger arrived at about 9:00. He [1] was a tall man with a big mustache. Amanda, Barbara, Claudia, and Gordon [2] were in the living room. The detective [3] came in.

"Mr. Travers died between midnight last night and 7:00 this morning," he [4] said. "Somebody in this room killed him." He looked at them one by one, but nobody [5] spoke.

"Mrs. Travers, I want to talk to you first. Come into the library with me, please."

Amanda followed the detective into the library and they [6] sat down.

"What did your husband do after dinner last night?"

"We finished dinner at about 9:30. Then Jeremy said he was tired and he [7] went to bed."

"Did you go to bed then?"

"No, I didn't. I went for a walk in the yard."

"What time did you go to bed?"

"At about a quarter to twelve."

"Was your husband asleep?"

"I don't know, Dectective. We…we [8] slept in different rooms. But I [9] saw that his door was closed."

"Did you hear anything when you were in your room?"

"Yes, I [10] heard Jeremy's bedroom door. It opened. I [11] thought it was Jeremy. Then it closed again. I [12] read in bed for half an hour and then I went to sleep."

"What time did you get up this morning?"

"I [13] got up at about 7:15. I [14] had breakfast and at 8:00 I [15] took a cup of tea to my husband. I [16] found him in bed. He was…dead."

"Tell me, Mrs. Travers, did you love your husband?"

"Jeremy is…was a difficult man."

"But did you love him, Mrs. Travers?"

"No, Detective. I hated him."

2 PRONUNCIATION simple past verbs

a Look at the **highlighted** irregular verbs in the story. What are the base forms?

1 *be – was*   2 *be – were*
3 *come – came*

b 🔊 8.2 Listen and check. Then listen and repeat.

c 🔊 8.3 Find and underline nine simple past ⊞ **regular** verbs in the story. How do you pronounce them? Listen and check. Then listen and repeat the verbs and phrases.

🔊 arrived (*Detective Granger arrived.*

Amanda Travers

Barbara Travers

Gordon Summers

Claudia Pasquale

b   Compare your chart with a partner. Who do you think was the murderer: Amanda, Barbara, Gordon, or Claudia? Why?

c   🔊 8.7 Now listen to what happened. Who was the murderer? Why did he / she kill Mr. Travers? Were you right?

4 GRAMMAR & VOCABULARY
simple past: regular and irregular

a   Cover the story and look at these verbs. Are they regular or irregular in the simple past? Write the simple past form ➕ and ➖ for each verb.

arrive   close   come   hate   kill   sit   sleep   speak

arrive   arrived   didn't arrive

b   🔊 8.8 Listen and check.

c   **G** p.138 **Grammar Bank 8A**

d   p.165 **Irregular verbs** Check (✓) the irregular verbs you know. Choose three new ones and learn them.

5 SPEAKING

What time did you get home?

At about 11:30.

C Communication Police interview **A** p.106 **B** p.111 Interview robbery suspects. Are they telling the truth?

3 LISTENING

a   🔊 8.4, 8.5, 8.6 Listen to part of the TV adaptation. The detective questions Barbara. Write the information in the chart. Listen again and check. Then do the same for Gordon and Claudia.

	Amanda	Barbara	Gordon	Claudia
What did he / she do after dinner?	She went for a walk.			
What time did he / she go to bed?	11:45.			
Did he / she hear anything?	Jeremy's door opened and closed.			
Did he / she have a motive?	She hated him.			

Go online to review the lesson

63

8B A house with a history

Is there a dishwasher? No, there isn't.

G there is / there are, some / any + plural nouns **V** the house **P** /eɪ/ and /ɪr/

1 VOCABULARY the house

a Read the advertisement. Would you like to rent this house? Why (not)?

b Cover the advertisement. What can you remember about the house?

c With a partner, think of three things you usually find in a bedroom, a bathroom, and a living room.

d **V** p.161 **Vocabulary Bank** The house

FOR RENT

Beautiful country house. Very quiet. Six bedrooms, four bathrooms, large yard. Five miles from town. Perfect family house. Low price.

2 LISTENING

a 🔊 8.11 Kim and Leo are a young couple. They want to rent the house in **1**. Cover the conversation and listen. Which three rooms in the house do they go into?

b Listen again and complete the conversation.

K The yard's wonderful, I love it.
L Is there a ¹ *garage*?
B Oh yes, there's a big garage over there.
K You lived in this house, is that right, Mrs. …?
B Miss Travers. But call me Barbara, dear. Yes, I lived here. A long time ago. Now I live in town. Let's go inside the house…
   This is the ² _____ _____. It's a lovely room, very bright. And this is the library…
L Wow! There's a library, Kim!
K I love the furniture, the old sofa, the armchairs, the ³ _____ …
B And this is the ⁴ _____. As you can see, it's very big.
K Is there a dishwasher?
B No, there isn't. It's an old house.
L Never mind. I think it's nice. Is there a ⁵ _____ downstairs?
B Yes, there's one ⁶ _____ and there are three upstairs.
K Are there any ⁷ _____ with children?
B No, there aren't any neighbors near here. But there are some families with children in town.
K That's great. We have two children.
B Very nice, dear. Now, let's go ⁸ _____ …

c 🔊 8.12 Listen. What does Kim say about one of the bedrooms? Whose bedroom was it? Do they decide to rent the house?

d 🔊 8.13 Kim and Leo go to a local restaurant. Listen and complete extracts 1–6 from their conversation. What do you think they find out?

Leo	Well, here's to our new ¹_____.
Leo	Is something ²_____?
Waiter	Some people ³_____ that she was the one who did it.
Waiter	Didn't she ⁴_____ you?
Kim	Tell us ⁵_____?
Kim	Oh, how ⁶_____!

e 🔊 8.14 Now listen to the whole conversation. What do Kim and Leo decide to do in the end? Why?

3 GRAMMAR *there is / there are, some / any* + plural nouns

a In groups of three, practice the conversation in **2b**. Then complete the chart.

singular	plural
➕ There's a library.	There _____ some families in town.
➖ There _____ a dishwasher.	There aren't any neighbors.
❓ _____ _____ a garage?	_____ _____ any neighbors?

b What's the difference between…?
 1 There are **three** families in town.
 2 There are **some** families in town.

c 🅖 p.138 Grammar Bank 8B

d 🅒 Communication *Is there…? Are there…?*
 A p.106 B p.111 Ask and answer questions.

4 PRONUNCIATION /ɛr/ and /ɪr/

a 🔊 8.16 Listen to the words and sounds. Then listen and repeat.

| ɛr | ch**air** |
| ɪr | **ear** |

b Put the words in the correct row.

th**ere**   h**ere**   c**are**ful   d**ear**   w**ear**
th**ey're**   n**ear**   st**airs**   w**e're**   h**ear**   wh**ere**

c 🔊 8.17 Listen and check. Then listen and repeat. Which three pairs are pronounced the same?

d 🔊 8.18 Listen and write six sentences or questions.

5 SPEAKING

a Imagine you want to rent a house or an apartment. Interview a partner. Ask for and give more information if you can.

> Is it a house or an apartment?
> How old is it?
> How big is it?
>
> How many | bedrooms / bathrooms | are there?
>
> Is there | a study?
> | a yard or a balcony?
> | a garage?
> | heat or central air conditioning?

b Draw a simple plan of one room. Show the plan to your partner and describe the room.

> This is the living room. It's big and it's very bright. There are two sofas and an armchair.

6 WRITING

🅦 p.116 Writing Describing your home Write a description of your house or apartment for a website.

Go online to review the lesson

8C Haunted rooms

> Were there any ghosts?
> No, but there was a strange noise.

G there was / there were **V** prepositions: place and movement **P** silent letters

1 READING & LISTENING

a Do you believe in ghosts? Are there buildings in your town / city that people think are haunted?

b Read a newspaper article about The Roosevelt Hollywood, a hotel in Los Angeles. With a partner, answer questions 1–5.
1 What famous people stayed in The Roosevelt Hollywood?
2 Which movie did the hotel appear in?
3 Who lived in the hotel in the 1950s?
4 What does Montgomery Clift do to guests in room 924?
5 What happened to a partygoer in the hotel's ballroom?

c 🔊 8.19 Listen to two guests at the hotel. Did they see a ghost?

d Listen again. Who did these things happen to? Check (✓) the correct column(s).

The man   The woman
1   knew about the ghosts in the hotel.
2   woke up during the night.
3   heard strange noises.
4   felt frightened when he / she heard the noises.
5   complained to reception.
6   wrote to the hotel after getting home.
7   only stayed at the hotel for one night.
8   doesn't want to stay at the hotel again.

e Complete the sentences from the article and the listening. What do the verb phrases mean?
1 She got _____ to open the window.
2 We woke _____ at about 3:30 in the morning.
3 The noises stopped and we went _____ to sleep.
4 We checked _____ of the hotel the same morning.

f Would you like to stay in one of the haunted rooms at the Roosevelt Hollywood? Why (not)?

WOULD YOU LIKE TO STAY IN A HAUNTED ROOM?

The US is well-known for having houses and hotels with ghosts, but did you know there was one in downtown Hollywood?

The Hollywood Roosevelt is a famous Los Angeles hotel situated near the Chinese Theater. The hotel was built in 1927 and has 300 rooms. In the past, many famous people stayed at the hotel, including
05 Marilyn Monroe, F. Scott Fitzgerald, and Prince. Montgomery Clift, who starred in *From Here to Eternity*, also stayed there while filming the movie. More recently, the hotel appeared in the movie *Catch Me if You Can* and the TV show *Curb Your*
10 *Enthusiasm*.

The Hollywood Roosevelt has the reputation of being haunted, especially rooms 1200 and 924. People say the hotel has several ghosts, including Marilyn Monroe who haunts room 1200. She lived
15 there during happier times in the 1950s. Guests say they see Marilyn in the room's mirror. Montgomery Clift appears in room 924. A recent guest in that room reported she got up to open the window and
20 felt someone pat her back. Others say Clift plays the trumpet in the room. In addition, other guests claim to see a young girl in a blue dress walk through the hotel's halls.

When a partygoer went to the hotel's ballroom for an
25 Oscars Viewing Party last March, he reported that a strange thing happened during the event. He posted on Twitter, "Fabulous party, but it was very cold in one part of the ballroom—like ten degrees colder. Weird!" The hotel hosted the first Academy Awards
30 in 1929. Some psychics say there is a ghost anxiously waiting in this cold spot. Perhaps he is waiting for his Academy Award!

2 GRAMMAR there was / there were

a ▶ 8.20 Complete the sentences from the listening with *was*, *wasn't*, *were*, or *weren't*. Then listen and check.
1. There _____ a strange noise outside our door.
2. There _____ any more strange noises.
3. We knew that people said there _____ ghosts.
4. There _____ anybody in that room last night.

b **p.138 Grammar Bank 8C**

3 VOCABULARY prepositions: place and movement

a Read two sentences from the text. Complete with the correct prepositions.
1. Montgomery Clift appears _____ room 924.
2. A young girl in a blue dress walks _____ the hotel's halls.

b **p.162 Vocabulary Bank Prepositions**

4 PRONUNCIATION silent letters

> **Silent letters**
> Some English words have a silent letter, e.g., in *ghost* /goʊst/ you don't pronounce the *h*.

a ▶ 8.24 Listen and cross out the silent letter in these words.

| could | cupboard | friend | guest | half | hour | island |
| know | listen | talk | what | write | | |

b Practice saying the words.

5 SPEAKING

Was there a TV? *No, there wasn't.*

Communication A haunted room **A** p.106 **B** p.111 Look at a photo of a haunted hotel room in the UK. Remember what there was in the room.

6 ▶ VIDEO LISTENING

a Watch the documentary *A haunted castle* about the four ghosts of Portchester Castle. How many of them are frightening?

b Watch again and complete the sentences.
1. Portchester Castle is more than _____ years old.
2. The castle is part of a charity called _____ Heritage.
3. Some workers at the castle leave their jobs because of the _____.
4. The ghost of a Roman _____ guards the walls of the castle.
5. The ghost of a monk disappears when people _____ at him.
6. The White Lady is the ghost of a woman who died when she tried to save her _____.
7. One of the staff members who saw the ghost of the man on a horse screamed and ran _____.
8. One visitor to the castle heard the sound of _____ on the video that he filmed.

c Would you like to visit Portchester Castle and see a ghost?

> **Go online** to watch the video and review the lesson

7 & 8 Review and Check

GRAMMAR

Circle a, b, or c.

1 Van Gogh and Gauguin ____ both painters.
   a was   b were   c is
2 Where ____ Shakespeare born?
   a was   b were   c is
3 ____ the tickets expensive?
   a Was   b Were   c Did
4 I ____ a good movie on TV last night.
   a watched   b watch   c watches
5 They ____ at the right airport.
   a didn't arrived   b don't arrived   c didn't arrive
6 ____ you see the soccer game last night?
   a Did   b Do   c Were
7 We ____ to Istanbul three years ago.
   a go   b were   c went
8 When ____ in Los Angeles?
   a you lived   b did you lived   c did you live
9 I ____ you at the party last night.
   a didn't saw   b didn't see   c don't saw
10 What time ____ home?
   a did you get   b you did get   c you got
11 ____ a big table in the living room.
   a There are   b There is   c It is
12 How many bedrooms ____?
   a there are   b are there   c are they
13 There aren't ____ pictures on the walls.
   a any   b some   c a
14 ____ only three guests in the dining room.
   a There was   b There were   c There is
15 How many people ____ in the hotel?
   a there were   b was there   c were there

VOCABULARY

a Complete the professions with -er, -or, -ian, or -ist.

1 act____
2 art____
3 paint____
4 music____
5 scient____

b Complete the phrases with go, have, or get.

1 _____ a good time
2 _____ an email
3 _____ away for the weekend
4 _____ a taxi
5 _____ on vacation

c Complete the sentences with back, by, in, out, or to.

1 I went _____ with my friends on Saturday night.
2 They went home _____ car.
3 What time did you get _____ the restaurant?
4 I was born _____ 1995.
5 After lunch, I went _____ to work.

d Label the pictures.

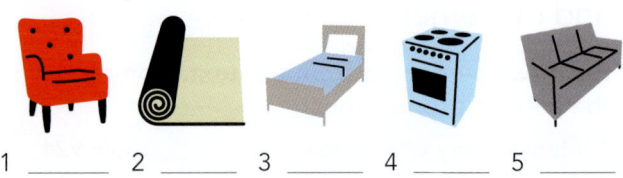

1 _____   2 _____   3 _____   4 _____   5 _____

e Write the prepositions.

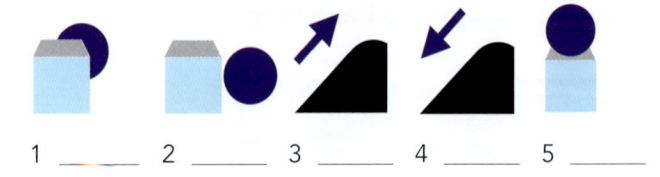

1 _____   2 _____   3 _____   4 _____   5 _____

PRONUNCIATION

a Practice the words and sounds.

Vowel sounds

ear   chair   phone   saw

Consonant sounds

dog   tie   vase   bag   parrot

b p.166–7 Sound Bank Say more words for each sound.

c What sound do the pink letters have in these words?

1 hall   2 here   3 lived   4 looked   5 there

d Underline the stressed syllable.

1 sci|en|tist   3 yes|ter|day   5 fire|place
2 a|go   4 be|tween

CAN YOU understand this text?

a Read the article once. Do you have any favorite detectives or detective writers?

b Read the article again. Mark the sentences **T** (true) or **F** (false).
 1 Gillian Flynn and Lee Child are modern crime writers.
 2 Sherlock Holmes only appeared in short stories.
 3 Agatha Christie's novels were similar to older crime fiction.
 4 She wanted her readers to try to solve the crimes themselves.
 5 If you read detective fiction from the 19th and early 20th century, you can learn about how people thought and behaved.
 6 Not many people now enjoy Dorothy Sayers's books.

How the modern detective novel was born

Millions of readers, like me, love the books of Gillian Flynn and Ruth Rendell, of Lee Child and Laura Lippman. But most fans of modern crime fiction know very little about the writers who invented the modern detective novel.

Many of the best early detective stories were short stories. Edgar Allan Poe (1809–1849) was probably the author of the first detective story. Arthur Conan Doyle (1859–1930) created perhaps the most famous detective, Sherlock Holmes. Father Brown was also a detective who was nearly as popular as Holmes; he was created by G.K. Chesterton (1874–1936). Father Brown only appeared in short stories, and Sherlock Holmes appeared in over 50 short stories and only four novels, including *The Hound of the Baskervilles*, where he solves the mystery of an enormous ghost dog.

In 1916, in her book *The Mysterious Affair at Styles*, Agatha Christie introduced a new type of detective novel, and a new detective, Hercule Poirot. This book was a little bit different because the plot was more important than the characters and the writer asked readers to guess the name of the murderer. Later, in the 1930s and 40s, Dorothy Sayers wrote detective novels where the relationships between the characters were sometimes more interesting than the plot.

Reading can give us a fascinating view of the past, and when we read these detective stories and novels, we can also learn something about how people lived and thought in the 19th and 20th centuries. These authors are still very popular. They influence present-day authors, such as J.K. Rowling, and they are probably going to inspire crime fiction for decades to come.

Adapted from the British press

CAN YOU understand these people?

8.25 Watch or listen and answer the questions.

1 Joelle 2 Katie 3 Maura 4 Asya 5 Jake

1 Joelle's family lives in ____.
 a New York   b North Carolina   c Canada
2 Last weekend, Katie ____.
 a went out with friends   c watched a movie
 b went to a friend's house
3 In Maura's bedroom, there's ____.
 a a TV and a cupboard   c a bed and a desk
 b a wardrobe and a bed
4 Yesterday, Asya ____.
 a went to bed late   c had lunch with her brother
 b went out with her sister
5 Last New Year's Eve, Jake celebrated ____.
 a at home   b at a club   c at a restaurant

CAN YOU say this in English?

Do the tasks with a partner. Check (✓) the box if you can do these things.

Can you…?
1 ☐ say three things about a famous (dead) person from your country
2 ☐ say five things you did last week, using past time expressions, e.g., *last night*, *yesterday*, *(three) days ago*, etc.
3 ☐ say where and when you were born
4 ☐ ask five questions about the past with *was / were* or *did*

Go online to watch the video, review Files 7 and 8, and check your progress

9A #mydinnerlastnight

What did you have for dinner? A pizza and some salad.

G countable / uncountable nouns, a / an, some / any **V** food and drink **P** the letters ea

1 VOCABULARY food and drink

a Take the quiz with a partner. Add vowels to make the words.

FOOD & DRINK QUIZ

1. two kinds of Italian food
   pzz _pizza_   pst _____
2. two things you can add to coffee
   mlk _____   sgr _____
3. a kind of food that vegetarians don't eat
   mt _____
4. a drink you buy in a bottle
   wtr _____
5. something cold, sweet, and delicious
   c crm _____ _____
6. a vegetable you can make French fries from
   ptt _____
7. something you use to make an omelet
   ggs _____
8. a lot of people are addicted to this sweet food
   chclt _____
9. a snack made with two pieces of bread
   sndwch _____
10. the three meals we usually have every day
    brkfst _____   lnch _____   dnnr _____

b **V** p.163 **Vocabulary Bank** Food and drink

c What's your favorite…?

| breakfast | dessert | fruit | snack | vegetable |

Is there any food or drink you don't like?

2 GRAMMAR countable / uncountable nouns, a / an, some / any

a Look at the photo of blogger Nathan Wiebe's lunch. Can you name any of the things in the photo? Do you think it's a healthy lunch?

b Look at the title. Why do you think he eats the same thing every day? Read his blog and check.

c Read the blog again. Answer the questions with a partner.

1. What do Jobs, Zuckerberg, and Einstein have in common?
2. What are two positive things about Nathan's diet?
3. Does he ever get bored of it? Why (not)?
4. Do *you* think Nathan's diet is healthy?
5. Is there a meal where you eat the same thing every day? What?
6. Would you like to try wearing the same clothes or eating the same food every day? How long do you think you could do it for?

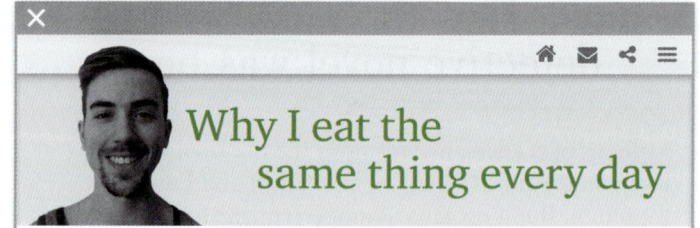

Why I eat the same thing every day

Steve Jobs, Mark Zuckerberg, and Albert Einstein have one thing in common. They all wear, or wore, more or less the same clothes every day. Why? Because if you wear the same clothes every day, you don't waste time choosing what to wear. I decided to copy them, but with my diet, so I eat the same food every day. This is what I have:

– breakfast: a cup of black coffee
– lunch: some smoked salmon, an avocado, and some cream cheese on a piece of bread
– dinner: some bacon, two eggs, some cheese, and some green vegetables

The good thing about this plan for me is that I spend less time and money buying food, and I also never need to worry if my diet is healthy or not (because I know it is). Now, you're probably thinking, "he's sure to get tired of eating the same food every day." Well, after about a year, I can promise you that I'm not. I change my meals a bit by having different kinds of cheese and using different herbs and spices. I also change the vegetables that I have for dinner.

d   Complete the sentences with *a*, *an*, or *some*.
   1 Nathan has _____ cup of coffee for breakfast.
   2 He has _____ smoked salmon and _____ avocado for lunch.
   3 He has _____ cheese and _____ vegetables for dinner.

e   **G** p.140 **Grammar Bank 9A**

f   **9.3** Listen to a couple talking about what food they need to buy. Write their shopping list.
   some coffee, some milk,…

3 LISTENING

a   Look at the photos posted with the hashtag #mydinnerlastnight. With a partner, which photo do you think shows…
   1 ☐ something that the person cooked
   2 ☐ take-out food that the person ordered
   3 ☐ something that the person ate in a restaurant
   4 ☐ something that the person's mother cooked

b   **9.4** Listen to the people talking about their photos and check your answers to **a**.

   Glossary
   Thanksgiving a US holiday in November

c   Listen again. Who (1–4) talks about…?
   ☐ a good restaurant near their house
   ☐ ways of preparing something
   ☐ a dish with two main ingredients
   ☐ a meal for a special occasion

d   Which of the four dishes or meals would you like to eat? Which wouldn't you like?

4 PRONUNCIATION the letters *ea*

a   How is *ea* pronounced in these words? Put them in the correct column.

   | bread   breakfast   eat   healthy |
   | ice cream   meat   peas   steak   tea |

tree	egg	train

b   **9.5** Listen and check. Practice saying them. Which is the most common pronunciation of *ea*?

#mydinnerlastnight

A
B
C
D

5 SPEAKING

a   Make a food journal for yesterday. Write what food and drink you had.
   Breakfast – a cup of coffee, some cereal

b   Work in pairs. Tell each other what you had yesterday. Say where you had it and who made it.

   I had breakfast at home, and I made it.
   I had a cup of coffee and some cereal.

c   Answer the questions in pairs.

   What do you usually have…?
   • for a quick lunch when you don't have time to cook
   • for dessert at home or in a restaurant
   • when you're hungry between meals
   • for breakfast on the weekend
   • for a special occasion
   • when you order to go

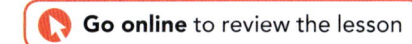

Go online to review the lesson

9B White gold

How much sugar do you eat? A lot.

G quantifiers: *how much / how many, a lot of*, etc. **V** food containers **P** linking, /ʃ/ and /s/

1 VOCABULARY & PRONUNCIATION
food containers; linking

a ◉ 9.6 Match the words and photos. Listen and check.

- a bag
- a <u>bo</u>ttle
- a box
- a can
- a <u>car</u>ton
- a jar
- a <u>pa</u>ckage

b ◉ 9.7 Listen to five people asking for things in a store. Write the things they want to buy.

c Make phrases with the containers in **a** and the words below.

<u>ce</u>real   coffee   cookies   jam   milk   potato chips   soda   sugar   tuna

a box of cereal

2 GRAMMAR quantifiers

a Look at the photos of food and drink. Number the photos 0, 1, or 2 (0 = no sugar / salt; 2 = a lot of sugar / salt).

How much sugar?

How much salt?

b Ask and answer questions about the things in **a**.

none | a little / not much | a lot

How much sugar is there in dark chocolate?
I'm not sure. I think there's a lot.

c ⓒ **Communication** Sugar and salt p.106 Check your answers to **a**.

d Complete the sentences with a food or drink from **a**.
1. There **isn't any** salt in _____.
2. There's **a little** sugar in _____.
3. There's **not much** salt in _____.
4. There's **a lot of** sugar in _____.

e **G** p.140 Grammar Bank 9B

f Work in pairs. **A** say how much you eat of the first thing in the list below. Give more information if you can. Then ask *How about you?* **B** do the same for the second thing, etc.

fish   meat   potatoes   vegetables
chocolate   fast food   eggs   pasta
olive oil   butter   cheese

I eat a lot of fish. I eat it maybe three or four times a week. How about you?

3 PRONUNCIATION /ʃ/ and /s/

a ◉ 9.9 Listen to the words and sounds. Then listen and repeat.

/ʃ/	**sh**ower	**s**ugar fi**sh**
/s/	**s**nake	**s**alt chocolate**s**

b ◉ 9.10 Put the words in the correct row. Listen and check.

center   **c**ereal   deli**c**ious   fre**sh**   gla**ss**
information   re**c**eption   ri**c**e   **s**alad
science   **sh**opping   spe**c**ial   **sp**i**c**e   **s**ure

c ◉ 9.11 Listen and repeat the conversation. Then practice it with a partner.

A Are you **s**ure thi**s** is **s**alt? I think it's **s**ugar.
B No, I'm **s**ure it's **s**alt. I put **s**ome in the ri**c**e **s**alad.
A Let's ta**s**te the **s**alad. Aargh. It wa**s s**ugar. I told you.
B Sorry!

Fascinating facts about...
sugar and salt

At different times in history, both sugar and salt were called "white gold" because they were so expensive and difficult to get. But there are many more interesting facts about sugar and salt...

- [1] _____ is used to make glass, laundry detergent, and paper.
- [2] _____ really helps the medicine go down! It's an important ingredient of many modern medicines.
- Christopher Columbus introduced [3] _____ to the New World in 1493 on his second voyage.
- If you put [4] _____ into a vase of flowers, the flowers last longer.
- If you want to check if an egg is fresh, put it in a cup with water and [5] _____. If the egg floats, it isn't very fresh.
- In the UK, there's a club for people who collect the little packets of [6] _____ you get when you order tea or coffee in a café or restaurant.
- If your dog or cat has fleas, and they are now living in your rugs, put some [7] _____ on the rugs and leave it for 12 hours. This kills all the fleas.
- Only 6% of the [8] _____ used in the US is used in food; another 17% is used for de-icing roads in the winter months.
- *Sure* and [9] _____ are the only two words in the English language that begin with "su" and are pronounced "sh."
- Scientists use [10] _____ to make different kinds of plastic, e.g., for food packaging.
- [11] _____ kills some bacteria, and so helps food to last longer, which is why cheese contains a lot.
- If you eat too much [12] _____ (about one gram per kilogram of weight), you can die. This was a method of ritual suicide in ancient China.

Glossary
flea a very small insect that can jump and that lives on and bites animals and people

4 READING

a Read the magazine article. With a partner, complete the facts with *sugar* or *salt*.

b ⏵9.12 Listen and check.

c Find these verbs in the article. What do they mean? How do you pronounce them?

introduce   float   collect   order   de-ice   contain

d How many of the facts did you know? Which ones?

5 SPEAKING

a Read the questionnaire and complete the questions with *How much* or *How many*.

b In pairs, interview your partner. Do you think he / she needs to eat less sugar and salt?

How much sugar and salt do YOU have a day?

Sugar

1 _____ spoonfuls of sugar do you have in your tea or coffee?
   a two or more   **b** one   **c** none
2 _____ bottles or cans of soda (or other carbonated drinks) do you drink a day?
   a two or more   **b** one   **c** none
3 _____ fruit or fruit juice do you have a day?
   a a lot   **b** not much   **c** none
4 _____ cookies do you eat a week?
   a a lot   **b** not many   **c** none

Salt

5 How often do you add salt to your food at the table?
   a always   **b** sometimes   **c** never
6 _____ take-out food do you eat?
   a a lot   **b** not much   **c** none
7 _____ bread do you eat a day?
   a a lot   **b** a little   **c** none
8 _____ bags of potato chips do you eat a week?
   a a lot   **b** a few   **c** none

Go online to review the lesson

9C Facts and figures

G comparative adjectives **V** high numbers **P** /ər/, sentence stress

> Is the US bigger than China?
> No, China is bigger.

1 VOCABULARY high numbers

a Read three questions from a radio quiz show. Choose a, b, or c.

1 What is the population of Canada?
  a 27,000,000
  b 37,000,000
  c 57,000,000
2 How far is it from New York City to Los Angeles?
  a about 1,500 miles
  b about 2,500 miles
  c about 3,100 miles
3 How many politicians are there in the British Parliament?
  a 450
  b 650
  c 750

b ◉ 9.13 Listen and check. Were you right? How do you say the three answers?

c **V** p.148 **Vocabulary Bank** Days and numbers Do Part 4.

d ◉ 9.15 Listen and write the ten numbers you hear.

1 *199*

e Answer the questions with a partner.

1 What's the population of your town or city?
2 What's the population of your country?
3 How far is it from your town or city to…?
  a New York
  b London
4 How many politicians are there in your country's government?

2 LISTENING

a ◉ 9.16 Listen to the introduction to a show called *Quiz Night*. Answer the questions.

1 How long do the contestants have to say if the sentences are true or false?
2 How much do they win if they get…?
  a the first answer right
  b the second answer right
  c the third answer right
  d all eight answers right
3 If they get an answer wrong, how much do they lose?
4 What can a contestant do if they are not sure of the answer?

b In pairs, look at sentences 1–8 from *Quiz Night*. Write **T** (true) or **F** (false).

QUIZ NIGHT

1 ___ A **whale** can make a louder noise than a **lion**.
2 ___ **World War I** was shorter than **World War II**.
3 ___ The **American** movie industry is bigger than the **Indian** movie industry.
4 ___ In July, **Seattle** is hotter than **Sydney**.
5 ___ **Silver** is heavier than **gold**.
6 ___ The mountain **K2** is more difficult to climb than **Mount Everest**.
7 ___ Driving in **Italy** is more dangerous than driving in **the US**.
8 ___ It's better to exercise in the **morning** than in the **afternoon**.

c ◉ 9.17 Listen to a contestant on *Quiz Night*. Check your answers to **b**. How much money does he win?

d Listen again for why the answers are true or false. Write down all the important numbers in each answer.

3 GRAMMAR comparative adjectives

a Look at the adjectives in the *Quiz Night* sentences. In pairs, answer the questions.

Using adjectives to compare two things:
1 What two letters do you put at the end of one-syllable adjectives, e.g., *loud*?
2 Why is *big* different?
3 What happens when an adjective ends in consonant + *y*, e.g., *heavy*?
4 What word do you put in front of long adjectives, e.g., *dangerous*?
5 What's the comparative form of *good*?
6 What's the missing word?
China is bigger _____ Japan.

b ⓖ **p.140 Grammar Bank 9C**

4 PRONUNCIATION & SPEAKING
/ər/, sentence stress

a 🔊 9.19 Listen to the sentence. How is *-er* pronounced at the end of a comparative adjective? How is *than* pronounced?

A whale can make a loud**er** noise **than** a lion.

b 🔊 9.20 Listen and write six comparative sentences.

c Listen again and <u>copy</u> the <u>rhy</u>thm. Are the sentences true or false?

d ⓒ **Communication** *Quiz Night* **A p.107 B p.112** Play *Quiz Night*.

5 READING

a Read the first part of the article about trivia night. Do you have something similar in your country?

b Now read the **Tips for how to win** and complete them with A–G.

A Choose your team carefully.
B Don't be a sore loser.
C Don't cheat!
D ~~Enjoy yourself!~~
E Keep your eyes open.
F Know about current affairs.
G Learn the big names.

c Look at these words from the article to do with quizzes. What do they mean? How do you pronounce them?

a team   an M.C.   an expert   to cheat
to memorize   to be a sore loser   to win

d Answer the questions with a partner.
1 Do you play any games or take quizzes with general knowledge questions, e.g., *Trivial Pursuit*?
2 Are you a good or sore loser? Do you ever cheat?
3 What TV quiz shows are popular in your country? Do you watch any of them? Why (not)?
4 Do you know anyone who loves a particular quiz show? Which one? Why?
5 Would you like to be a contestant on a quiz show? Which one?

TRIVIA NIGHT QUIZ

Round 1 *(Culture)*

1	Madonna	✓
2	?	✗
3	the 1812 Overture	✗
4	Denzel Washington	✓
5	Guillermo del Toro	✓
6	Prince	✓
7	??	✗
8	Amy Adams	✓

Round 2 *(Sports)*

1	Derek Jeter	✓
2	Chloe Kim	✗
3	?	✗
4	Usain Bolt	✓
5	The Stanley Cup	✓
6	the Denver Broncos	✓
7	4 minutes	✓
8	??	✗

Round 3

1	
2	
3	
4	
5	
6	
7	
8	

TRIVIA NIGHT!

A trivia quiz is a general knowledge quiz held in a bar or a restaurant. They started in the UK in the 1970s and have become very popular in the US in the last ten years. Friends form teams, usually of about five or six people, and they decide on a name for their team. The person who asks the questions is called the "M.C." (or the master of ceremonies), and the teams write their answers of a piece of paper. You can't use your phone to look for the answers! In some trivia night competitions, teams pay to be part of the event – from about $5 to $25 person – and the winning team gets the money. But a lot of trivia nights are free because restaurants and bars want people to come on nights that aren't usually busy, like Mondays and Tuesdays.

Tips for how to win

1 **D** That's really what it's all about. And don't take it too seriously.
2 ☐ Make sure you have friends who are experts at different subjects.
3 ☐ Cell phones, reference books, newspapers, etc., are not permitted.
4 ☐ Find out about events in the news, especially politics.
5 ☐ Memorize the winners of recent and past sporting events, Academy Awards, Grammys, reality TV shows, political elections, etc., as well as the latest singles and album charts.
6 ☐ Always look out for new facts, wherever you are.
7 ☐ If you don't win, remember, there is always next time.

▶ **Go online** to review the lesson

Practical English At a restaurant

EPISODE 5

ordering a meal   **V** understanding a menu

1 ▶ AN INVITATION TO DINNER

a 🔊 **9.21** Watch or listen. Mark the sentences **T** (true) or **F** (false).
1 Jenny and Rob worked last night.
2 Jenny wants to read Rob's article.
3 It's Eddie's birthday today.
4 Rob and Daniel invite Jenny to dinner.
5 Jenny says yes to Rob.

b Watch or listen again. Say why the **F** sentences are false.

c 🔊 **9.22** Read the information box. Listen and repeat **B**'s phrases.

> 🔍 **Responding to what somebody says**
> 1 **A** It's my birthday today.
>   **B** Happy Birthday!
> 2 **A** We won the game!
>   **B** Congratulations!
> 3 **A** I have my driving test tomorrow.
>   **B** Good luck!
> 4 **A** I got all my English homework right.
>   **B** Good job!
> 5 **A** I didn't get the job.
>   **B** Better luck next time.

d 🔊 **9.23** Listen and respond with phrases from the box.

1 ▶) *I got two goals this afternoon.*   (*Good job!*

2 VOCABULARY understanding a menu

a Complete the menu with **Main courses**, **Desserts**, or **Appetizers**.

Luigi's

2 courses $20.00   3 courses $29.00

1 _____

Onion soup ⓥ Ⓖ
Mozzarella and tomato salad ⓥ Ⓖ

2 _____

Grilled chicken breast with vegetables
Mushroom ravioli ⓥ
Seafood risotto Ⓖ

3 _____

Homemade vanilla ice cream with hot chocolate sauce ⓥ Ⓖ
Fresh fruit salad ⓥ Ⓖ
Tiramisu ⓥ

ⓥ Vegetarian Ⓖ Gluten-free   If you have any other dietary requirements, please let us know and we will try our best to accommodate your needs.
Tables of 8 or more are subject to a discretionary service charge of 18%.

b 🔊 **9.24** What do the highlighted words mean? How do you pronounce them? Listen and check.

c Cover the menu. In pairs, try to remember what's on it.

3 ▶ ORDERING A MEAL

a 🔊 **9.25** Watch or listen to Jenny and Daniel having dinner. Check the things they order on the menu.

b Watch or listen again. Complete the **You hear** phrases.

You hear	You say
Good evening. Do you have a ¹_____?	Yes, a table for two. My name's Daniel O'Connor.
Come this ²_____, please.	
Are you ready to ³_____?	Yes. The soup and the mushroom ravioli, please.
	I'd like the mozzarella salad and then the chicken, please.
What would you ⁴_____ to drink?	Just water for me.
	A bottle of mineral water, please.
⁵_____ or sparkling?	Is sparkling OK?
	Yes, sparkling.
Thank you, sir.	Thank you.

c 🔊 **9.26** Watch or listen again and repeat the **You say** phrases. Copy the rhythm.

d In threes, practice the conversation.

e 👥 Role-play the conversation in groups of three. Then change roles.

A you are the waiter.
B and C go to *Luigi's*.
A begin *Good evening. Do you have a reservation?*

4 ▶ THE END OF THE MEAL

a 🔊 **9.27** Watch or listen and answer the questions.
1 How does Jenny usually celebrate her birthday?
2 Do they order dessert or coffee?
3 What does Daniel say to Jenny after the meal?
4 How does Jenny answer?
5 Does Barbara give Jenny good news or bad news?
6 Where does Jenny want to go after the meal?

b Look at the **Social English** phrases. Who says them: **J**enny, **D**aniel, the **w**aiter, or **B**arbara?

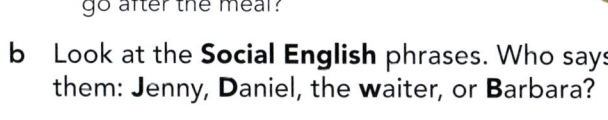

💬 Social English
1 ☐ Nothing special.
2 ☐ Would you like a dessert?
3 ☐ Not for me, thanks.
4 ☐ A decaf espresso.
5 ☐ The same for me, please.
6 ☐ Go ahead.
7 ☐ Good news?
8 ☐ Could I have the bill, please?

🔍 **American and British English**
check = American English   bill = British English

c 🔊 **9.28** Watch or listen and check. Then watch or listen and repeat the phrases.

d Complete conversations A–G with **Social English** phrases 1–8. Practice with a partner.

A		Yes! I have a new job!
B	Two soups, one chicken, and one fish.	Just coffee.
C	Excuse me.	Yes, of course, sir.
D	What do you usually do on New Year's Eve?	We don't really celebrate it.
E	What coffee would you like?	
F	I'd like the ravioli.	I love pasta!
G	So, can I ask him?	

CAN YOU…?

☐ use common phrases, e.g., *Good luck, Congratulations*, etc.
☐ understand a menu
☐ order a meal

10A The most dangerous place...

G superlative adjectives **V** places and buildings **P** consonant groups

> What's the oldest building in your town?
>
> I'm not sure. Probably the cathedral.

1 VOCABULARY places and buildings

a Complete these famous tourist sights in the US and the UK with a word from the list.

> Bridge   Castle   Gallery   Park   Square   Street

1. **The Brooklyn** _____ connects Manhattan and Brooklyn.
2. **Downing** _____ is where the British prime minister lives.
3. **Windsor** _____ is the royal family's weekend home and the largest inhabited castle in the world.
4. **Central** _____ is a green space in the middle of New York.
5. **The National** _____ is London's most famous art museum.
6. **Times** _____ is the center of New York's theater district.

b ◆) 10.1 Listen and check.

c **V** p.164 Vocabulary Bank Places and buildings

2 GRAMMAR superlative adjectives

a Look at the photos. What countries do you think they are in?

b With a partner, complete 1–6 with a phrase from the list.

> The biggest   The busiest   The longest
> The most dangerous   The tallest   The widest

c ◆) 10.3 Listen and check your answers to **a** and **b**.

d Complete the chart with the correct form.

Adjective	Comparative	Superlative
wide	wider	*the widest*
	taller	the tallest
long		the longest
big	bigger	
	busier	the busiest
dangerous	more dangerous	

e How are superlative adjectives different in form from comparative adjectives?

f **G** p.142 Grammar Bank 10A

g ◆) 10.5 Listen and write six superlative questions.

h In groups, ask and answer the questions in **g**. Choose from the cities below.

> Atlanta   Brussels   La Paz
> Las Vegas   New York   Tokyo

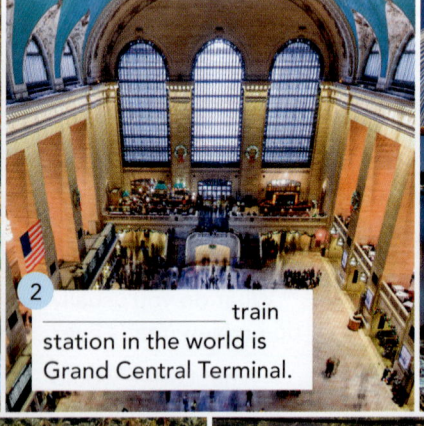

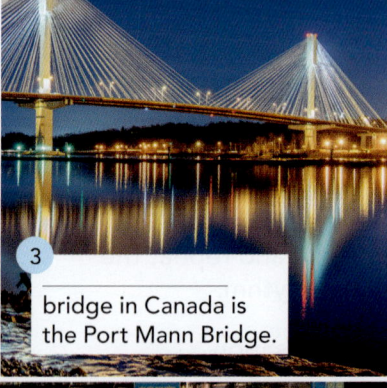

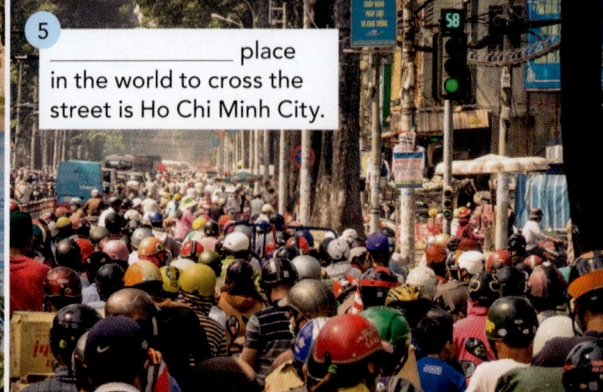

1. _____ street in Mexico is Madero Avenue.
2. _____ train station in the world is Grand Central Terminal.
3. _____ bridge in Canada is the Port Mann Bridge.
4. _____ river in the world is the Nile.
5. _____ place in the world to cross the street is Ho Chi Minh City.
6. _____ building in the world is the Burj Khalifa.

78

3 PRONUNCIATION & SPEAKING
consonant groups

> 🔍 **Consonant groups**
> Two or three consonants together can be difficult to pronounce, e.g., fas**t**est, mos**t d**angerous.

a 🔊 **10.6** Listen and repeat.

> beautiful
> the most beautiful
> the most beautiful square
> What's the most beautiful square?

b 🔊 **10.7** Now listen and repeat the same pattern with 1–4.
1 old (building)
2 interesting (museum)
3 good (shopping mall)
4 nice (place)

c **ⓒ Communication** I'm a tourist. Help!
A p.107 **B** p.112 Role-play being a tourist.

4 READING

a Read the article. Which suggestion do you think is the most useful?

b Read the article again. Complete the paragraphs with sentences A–E.
A All you need to do is smile and wave to them.
B The only thing that saved me was a student who shouted, "Don't stop, keep walking!"
C So, if you really can't cross the road, you can get a taxi to take you to the other side.
D When I heard this I thought, "Maybe it's better to just stay in my hotel and read!"
E The second time I chose a woman selling vegetables with baskets full of sweet potatoes, and again I survived.

c Cover the article. Can you remember seven words for vehicles?

d Work in groups and answer the questions.
1 What's the most popular form of transportation in your town or city?
2 In what part of town and at what time of day is the traffic the worst?
3 How do you usually get around?
4 Do cars always stop at crosswalks?
5 Are there any streets that are really difficult to cross?
6 Is there any town or city you visited where you had problems crossing the street, or where you found the traffic really frightening?

5 WRITING

Imagine you want to advertise your town or city for tourists. Write an advertisement using superlative adjectives. Add photos if you can.

Come to Eagle Rock! It isn't the cleanest or the most beautiful part of Los Angeles, but it has the nicest people and the best tacos…

The most dangerous place in the world to cross the street ❗

If you want to cross the street in most countries, you wait for a gap in the traffic, and then you cross. But not in Ho Chi Minh City, where there's never a gap in the traffic. Apart from the cars, trucks, bikes, and buses, there are millions of motorcycles and scooters, which are the most popular form of transportation in Vietnam. Crossing the road is an adventure, and many tourists find it impossible. So, what can you do?

Keep walking. The receptionist at my hotel told me, "When it feels right, walk into the road. The most important thing to remember is to keep walking. Don't stop. Don't run. Don't look left or right. And don't walk in front of a bus, because they can't stop easily."

Cross with a local person. They know what they're doing, and this is the safest way for beginners. I looked for a middle-aged local man and I crossed the road with him. I made sure that he was between me and the traffic, and I prayed as I walked next to him. And I got to the other side!

Cross in a group. I met some students who were happy to walk across the street with me. But this time, when I saw a car coming straight at me, I stopped and put up my arm (like a traffic police officer). This was a big mistake.

Find a police officer. There are really nice police officers in green uniforms, and their job is to help frightened tourists cross the road.

Take a taxi. For one or two dollars, they take you anywhere you want to go.

Go online to review the lesson

10B Five continents in a day

> Where are you going to stay?
> We're going to rent an apartment.

G be going to (plans), future time expressions **V** city vacations **P** sentence stress

1 GRAMMAR be going to (plans)

a Look at the map. Where are the cities? Say the country and continent for each city.

Caracas is in Venezuela, South America.

b 🔊 10.8 Gunnar Garfors and Adrian Butterworth are planning to break a world record by visiting five continents in one day. Listen and draw their route on the map.

c Listen again and fill in the blanks with a verb from the list.

| arrive | be | celebrate | fly | get | go out | start | visit |

d Look at the highlighted sentence in the interview. Then answer the questions.
   1 What form is the verb after *going to*?
   2 Do we use *going to* to talk about the past, the present, or the future?

e **G** p.142 Grammar Bank 10B

f 🔊 10.10 Do you think Gunnar and Adrian succeeded? Listen to Gunnar and find out.

g What do you think about Gunnar and Adrian's trip? Do you think it was a) a waste of money, b) bad for the environment, or c) an exciting thing to do?

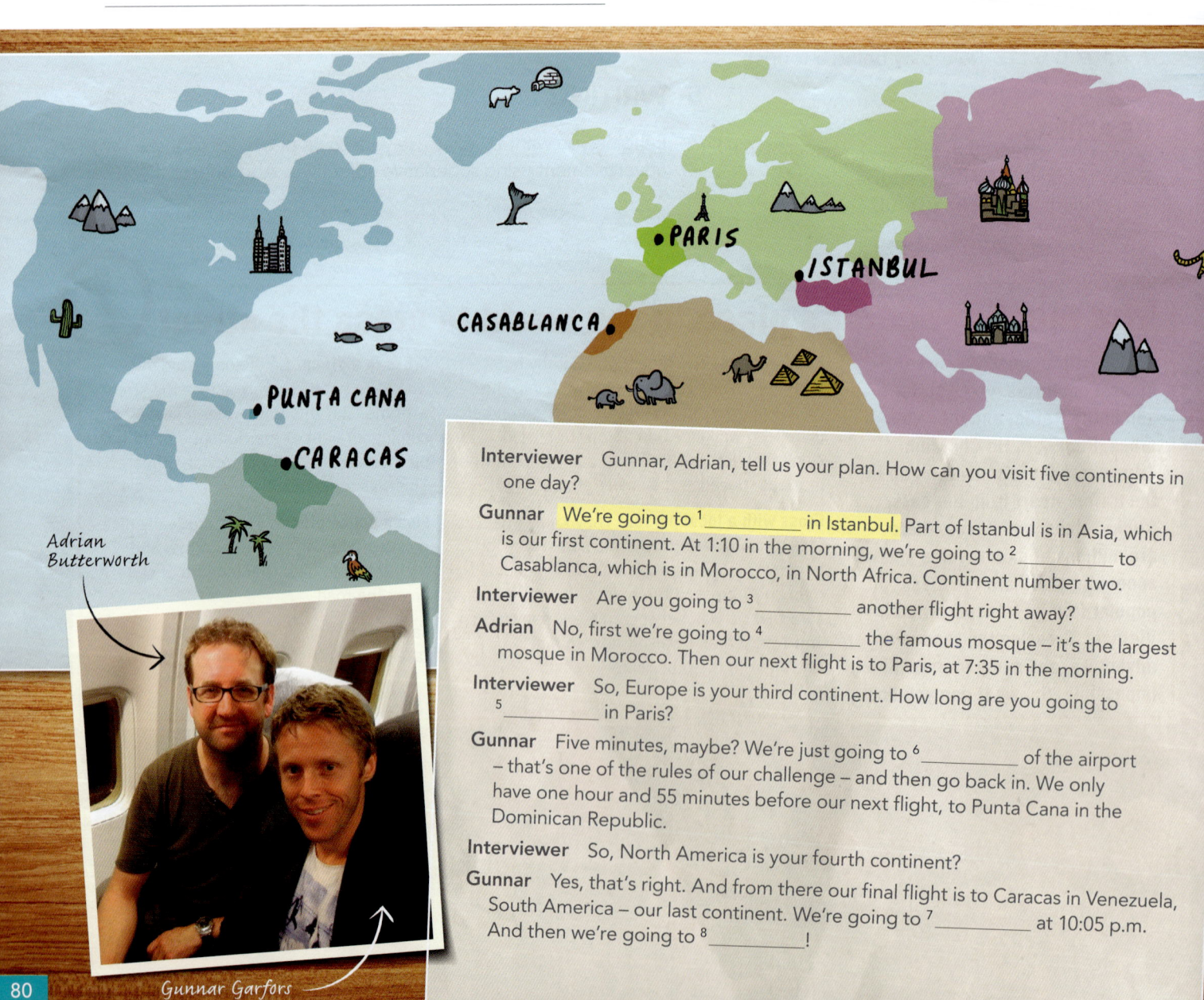

Adrian Butterworth

Gunnar Garfors

Interviewer Gunnar, Adrian, tell us your plan. How can you visit five continents in one day?

Gunnar We're going to ¹_____ in Istanbul. Part of Istanbul is in Asia, which is our first continent. At 1:10 in the morning, we're going to ²_____ to Casablanca, which is in Morocco, in North Africa. Continent number two.

Interviewer Are you going to ³_____ another flight right away?

Adrian No, first we're going to ⁴_____ the famous mosque – it's the largest mosque in Morocco. Then our next flight is to Paris, at 7:35 in the morning.

Interviewer So, Europe is your third continent. How long are you going to ⁵_____ in Paris?

Gunnar Five minutes, maybe? We're just going to ⁶_____ of the airport – that's one of the rules of our challenge – and then go back in. We only have one hour and 55 minutes before our next flight, to Punta Cana in the Dominican Republic.

Interviewer So, North America is your fourth continent?

Gunnar Yes, that's right. And from there our final flight is to Caracas in Venezuela, South America – our last continent. We're going to ⁷_____ at 10:05 p.m. And then we're going to ⁸_____!

2 PRONUNCIATION & SPEAKING
sentence stress

a **◉ 10.11** Listen and repeat the conversations. Copy the rhythm.

1 A **What** are you going to **do** this **summer**?
  B I'm going to **go** to **Thailand**.

2 A Are you going to **go out** on **Friday night**?
  B **Yes**, I'm going to **see** a **movie**.

b **◉ Communication** What are you going to do? **A p.107 B p.112** Interview a partner about his / her plans.

3 LISTENING

a Imagine you are planning a vacation. What do you think about first? Number the following 1–4.

☐ Where am I going to go?
☐ What am I going to do?
☐ Who am I going to go with?
☐ What previous vacations did I really enjoy?

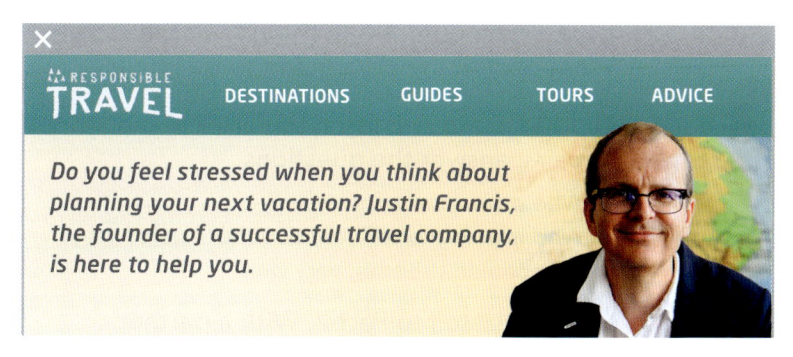

b **◉ 10.12** Listen to Justin Francis from Responsible Travel. Does he agree with your order?

c Listen again and make notes to answer the questions.
1 What examples does Justin give if you want to…?
  • relax
  • go somewhere different
  • go on an adventure
  • learn a new skill
2 If you are going to go on vacation with other people, what do you need to make sure of?
3 What does he recommend if you want to meet new people on vacation?
4 What three examples does he give of things that can make you happy on vacation?
5 What are you ready to start thinking about after following steps 1–3?

d Answer the questions.
  • What do you think of Justin's ideas? What do you usually want to do on vacation?
  • Can you remember a vacation that made you very happy? Why was it special?

4 VOCABULARY & SPEAKING
city vacations

a Complete the vacation phrases with a verb from the list.

book buy eat go have meet rent stay visit

1 _____ a flight, a train, a room
2 _____ by train / bus / plane
3 _____ a car / an apartment
4 _____ in a hotel / hostel
5 _____ out (in local restaurants)
6 _____ museums and art galleries
7 _____ souvenirs
8 _____ a good time
9 _____ new people

b Talk to a partner. What do you like doing on vacation? Try to find some things you have in common.

c With your partner, plan a dream trip. You are going to visit three cities on the same continent. Your vacation can be a maximum of ten days. Answer the questions.

What cities are you going to visit?
How long are you going to stay in each city?
How are you going to get there?
Where are you going to stay?
What are you going do in each place?

> 🔍 **Making suggestions**
> Let's (go to…).
> Why don't we (go to…)?
> That's a good idea.

d Change partners. Tell each other about your vacation plans.

> We're going to go to South America – to Buenos Aires, Rio, and Montevideo. We're going to stay in hostels because we don't have much money…

e Do you prefer your new partner's plans? Would you like to change partners and go with him / her?

5 WRITING

W p.117 Writing A formal email Make a reservation at a bed and breakfast.

10C The fortune-teller

> Am I going to fall in love?
>
> Yes, and you're going to be very happy.

G be going to (predictions) **V** verb phrases **P** word stress

1 VOCABULARY verb phrases

a Do people in your country go to fortune-tellers, or use fortune-telling sites on the internet? Why do you think they do this? Do *you* believe in fortune-telling?

b What pictures can you see on the fortune-teller's cards? Match the cards and verb phrases.

- become famous
- get a new job
- get married
- meet somebody new
- fall in love
- get a lot of money
- have a surprise
- A be lucky
- travel
- move to a new house

2 PRONUNCIATION word stress

> 🔍 **Word stress in two-syllable words**
> Approximately 80% of two-syllable words are stressed on the first syllable, e.g., *argue*.

a Look at the words from a story. Which four are stressed on the second syllable?

ar|gue   be|lieve   boy|friend   fa|mous   for|tune
fu|ture   i|dea   lu|cky   mar|ried   mon|ey   prob|lem
ques|tion   sur|prise   to|day   trav|el   wor|ry

b 🔊 10.13 Listen and check. Practice saying the words.

3 READING & LISTENING

a Look at the photos and the title of the story. What do you think it's going to be about?

b 🔊 10.14 Read and listen to Part 1 of the story. In pairs, answer the questions.
1 Who does Jane want to see?
2 Who is going to tell her about her future? Why?
3 Why couldn't she see very well?

c 🔊 10.15 Listen to Part 2. With a partner, complete the information.
1 Jane has a problem with her _____.
2 She chooses _____ cards.
3 Her first card means she's going to be _____.
4 Jane asks the fortune-teller if she's going to _____ with her boyfriend.

d 🔊 10.16 Read and listen to Part 3. In pairs, answer the questions.
1 What's the second card? What does it mean?
2 Why is this a problem for Jane?
3 What's her third card? What does it mean?
4 Who's Jim? Where did Jane meet him?
5 What do you think the fourth card is going to be?

e 🔊 10.17 Listen to Part 4. With a partner, complete the information.
1 Her fourth card means she is going to _____ her boyfriend and go to _____ with Jim.
2 Very soon they are going to _____.
3 Jane asks if she is going to be _____ and the fortune-teller says _____.
4 She pays the fortune-teller £_____.

IT'S WRITTEN IN THE CARDS

Part 1

"Come in," said a voice. Jane Ross opened the door and went into a small room. There was a man sitting behind a table.

"Good afternoon," said Jane. "I want to see Madame Yolanda, the fortune-teller."

"Madame Yolanda is not here today," said the man. "But don't worry. I'm going to tell you about your future. What questions do you want to ask?"

Jane looked at the fortune-teller. She couldn't see him very well because the room was very dark.

Part 3

He turned over the second card.

"Mm, a house. A new house. You're going to move, very soon, to another country."

"But my boyfriend works here. He can't move to another country."

"Let's look at the next card," said the fortune-teller. He turned over the third card.

"A heart. You're going to fall in love."

"Who with?" asked Jane.

"Let me concentrate. I can see a tall, dark man. He's very attractive."

"Oh, that's Jim," said Jane.

"Who's Jim? Your boyfriend?"

"No. Jim is a man I met at a party last month. He's an actor, from New York. He says he's in love with me. It was his idea for me to come to Madame Yolanda."

"Well, the card says that you're going to fall in love with him."

"Are you sure?" asked Jane. "But what about my boyfriend?"

"Let's look at the fourth card," said the fortune-teller.

4 ▶ VIDEO LISTENING

a ⏺ 10.18 Watch or listen to Parts 1–4 of *It's written in the cards* again. What do you think is going to happen?

b ⏺ 10.19 Now watch or listen to Part 5 of the story. In pairs, answer the questions.
1 Who was the fortune-teller?
2 Why did he pay Madame Yolanda £100?
3 What's the fifth card? What does Madame Yolanda think is going to happen?

5 GRAMMAR *be going to* (predictions)

a Look at the two sentences. Which one is a *plan*? Which one is a *prediction*?
1 She's going to be very lucky.
2 She's going to go on vacation next week.

b **G** p.142 Grammar Bank 10C

c Write four predictions, about the weather, sports, your town / country, and you. Use *I think… going to…*

I think it's going to snow tonight.

d Compare your predictions with a partner. Do you agree?

6 SPEAKING

Role-play fortune-telling.

A Look at the ten cards in **1**. Secretly, number the cards in a different order (1–10).
B Choose five numbers from 1–10.
A Predict **B**'s future using those cards.
B Ask for more information. Then change roles.

A *I'm going to tell you about your future. Your first card is a star. You're going to become famous. You're going to be on TV.*

B *Great! What TV show?*

Go online to watch the video and review the lesson

9 & 10 Review and Check

GRAMMAR

a Circle a, b, or c.
1 There's ____ milk in the refrigerator.
  a some b any c a
2 We don't need ____ bread.
  a no b any c a
3 How ____ fruit do you eat a day?
  a much b many c a lot
4 I drink ____ coffee.
  a much b a lot c a lot of
5 A How much salt do you eat? B ____.
  a A little b A few c Much
6 A Is there any sugar? B No, sorry, ____.
  a there isn't none
  b there isn't any
  c there isn't some
7 Tea is ____ coffee in this café.
  a cheaper that
  b more cheap than
  c cheaper than
8 This exercise is ____ than the last one.
  a more easy b easier c easyer
9 My English is ____ than my brother's.
  a gooder b better c more good
10 This is ____ size that we have.
  a the biggest
  b the most big
  c the bigger
11 It's ____ restaurant in the city.
  a the baddest b the worst
  c the worse
12 What's ____ park in your town?
  a the most beautiful b most beautiful
  c the more beautiful
13 ____ to buy my ticket this afternoon.
  a I go b I going c I'm going
14 ____ to get married?
  a Do they going b They are going
  c Are they going
15 I think ____ tomorrow.
  a it snows b it's snowing
  c it's going to snow

VOCABULARY

a Circle the word that is different.
1 breakfast dessert dinner lunch
2 mushrooms onions peas strawberries
3 milk water orange juice sugar
4 French fries tomatoes potatoes potato chips
5 cake chicken fruit salad ice cream

b Match the food to the containers.

chocolates fruit juice honey rice tomatoes

1 a box of _____   4 a package of _____
2 a can of _____   5 a carton of _____
3 a jar of _____

c Circle the correct word or phrase.
1 It's *a hundred twenties / a hundred and twenty* miles from here.
2 The population is about three *million / millions*.
3 That new *department shop / department store* is great.
4 Let's have a coffee at one of those cafés in the *square / bridge*.
5 Where is the train *center / station*?

d Complete the phrases with these verbs.

become book fall get go have meet rent stay visit

1 _____ in a hotel   6 _____ flights
2 _____ by bus   7 _____ somebody new
3 _____ famous   8 _____ a museum
4 _____ married   9 _____ a great meal
5 _____ in love   10 _____ an apartment

PRONUNCIATION

a Practice the words and sounds.

Vowel sounds

egg   owl   boy   tourist

Consonant sounds

key   girl   leg   right   monkey   television

b p.166–7 Sound Bank Say more words for each sound.

c What sound do the pink letters have in these words?
1 bread   2 oil   3 town   4 sugar   5 wrote

d Underline the stressed syllable.
1 cho|co|late   3 su|per|mar|ket   5 dan|ger|ous
2 des|sert   4 in|ter|est|ing

CAN YOU understand this text?

a Read the article once. Match the hotels and photos. Which one would you like to stay in?

b Read the article again. Match the hotels (A–C) to the sentences.

At which hotel can you…?
1. ☐ get a great view of the ocean
2. ☐ sleep a long way from other people
3. ☐ get married
4. ☐ spend time with working animals
5. ☐ do hard physical exercise
6. ☐ have a massage or facial
7. ☐ take a tour of geographical features
8. ☐ have a business meeting

▶ CAN YOU understand these people?

🔊 **10.21** Watch or listen and answer the questions.

1 Graziella   2 Kara   3 James   4 Kevin   5 Mica

1. Graziella eats a lot of ____.
   a fruit   b chocolate   c salt
2. Kara is good at cooking food from ____ country.
   a her   b her parents'   c her husband's
3. James loves Paris because ____.
   a it has tall towers
   b it's beautiful at night
   c it has beautiful flowers
4. When Kevin goes to Thailand he's going to visit ____ different places.
   a two   b three   c four
5. Mica thinks that the biggest difference between New York and the UK is ____.
   a the weather   b the people   c the food

CAN YOU say this in English?

Do the tasks with a partner. Check (✓) the box if you can do these things.

Can you…?
1. ☐ say what you usually have for breakfast
2. ☐ compare your country with the US in three ways
3. ☐ say what the best and worst things are about the town or city where you live
4. ☐ ask somebody what he / she is going to do…
   - tonight   • tomorrow   • next weekend

TRAVEL

The world's most unusual hotels

A For people who love nature, **Verana** in Puerto Vallarta in Mexico is an amazing spa hotel with beautiful views on all sides. It has ten guesthouses, and four new buildings with balconies above the trees, from where you can see the beautiful Bay of Banderas. The spa has an infinity pool and offers a variety of different spa treatments, as well as yoga classes. You can go whale-watching, go fishing for tuna, and explore the area on foot. This is the perfect place for your wedding, your honeymoon, or both. But remember, you can only get there by boat!

B Would you like to sleep in a mine? Then book the underground suite in **Sala Silvermine** in Sweden, and enjoy the world's deepest bedroom, 508 feet below the surface. Although the corridors are cold and dark, your rooms are warm (64°F), and the light comes from candles in beautiful silver candlesticks. You can also explore the caves and magical lakes with a guide. There are no other guests, so it's not for nervous people. Cell phones don't work, but you have a radio for emergencies. In the morning, they bring breakfast down to you. Perfect for romantic couples who like a little bit of adventure.

C You don't need to travel to the Arctic Circle to spend time with Siberian huskies. At the **Husky Lodge** in the mountains of Switzerland, dog-lovers can sleep in cabins, heated with wood fires, next to the dogs' kennels. During the day, you can join in with their training runs. They pull sledges in the winter and bikes and carts in the summer. In the evening, there's an excellent restaurant. And if you have to work, there are three rooms for small conferences and seminars. If you can't afford the cabins, there's a campsite, too – though maybe only in summer!

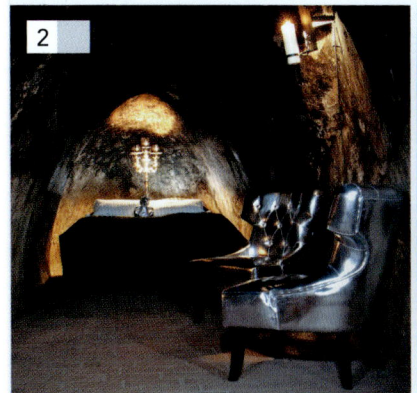

Go online to watch the video, review Files 9 and 10, and check your progress

11A Culture shock

G adverbs (manner and modifiers) **V** common adverbs **P** connected speech

> How do they drive? — They drive fast, but very well.

1 READING

a Think of a time when you went to another country or another city / region in your country for the first time. Was there anything that surprised you?

b Read some posts on a forum. Which topic *don't* they mention?

clothes   exercise   food   health   money   transportation

c Read the posts again. Match sentences 1–9 to the people who said them, **L** (Lena), **R** (Rahim), **N** (Natasha), **T** (Tara), or **J** (Julie).
1. ___ People can earn good salaries without working hard.
2. ___ Some people don't dress warmly in the winter.
3. ___ The president isn't paid very well.
4. ___ People don't always speak politely to older people.
5. ___ People have really big serving sizes when they eat out.
6. ___ Some hospitals are incredibly luxurious.
7. ___ You can travel safely on public transportation.
8. ___ Doctors speak very openly to their patients.
9. ___ You pay people well to do their job, and then you give them more money.

d Look again at sentences 1–9 about the US. Are they true in your country? If not, say why.

e Learn these words and phrases related to money. What do they mean? How do you pronounce them?

salary /ˈsæləri/   insurance /ɪnˈʃʊrəns/   tip /tɪp/
earn money /ərn ˈmʌni/   pay bills /peɪ bɪlz/
pay rent /peɪ rɛnt/

NEWS **COMMENT** **POLITICS** **TRAVEL** **SPORTS** **INFO**

THINGS I DIDN'T KNOW UNTIL I GOT HERE
What was a surprise for you when you came to live in the US?

LENA FROM UKRAINE

When I eat out with my husband or friends, we usually share because serving sizes are huge and we don't want all that food. But you can take home everything you don't eat, and I like that.

In the winter, you often see people on the street or the subway who are wearing just a T-shirt when it's really cold outside.

RAHIM FROM PAKISTAN

When people speak to their boss (and to their teachers), they call them by their first name. They do the same to old people, too, even when they don't know them well. It doesn't seem polite to me.

NATASHA FROM BELARUS

The American president's salary is about the same as a doctor's. He isn't the richest person in the country. That surprised me!

Some hospitals are like smart hotels – but a lot of people can't go there because they don't have medical insurance. Also, doctors don't always explain everything to their patients in my country. Here, they tell you everything.

TARA FROM INDIA

I couldn't believe the tipping system, for example, in places like a hair salon. You cut my hair and I pay you – a lot! Why do I need to give you a tip too?

Public transportation can be dangerous in India. But I was on the subway here in New York, going home late at night, when a group of people got on. They were very loud and we were frightened. But at the next stop, two police officers got on. The people stopped shouting when they saw the police. I felt really safe.

JULIE FROM CANADA

My husband is from Ecuador, and when he first arrived, he was really surprised by his salary. As a chef, he could earn enough money to pay bills, buy food, pay rent, have a good social life, and buy luxuries like our Xbox. In Quito, he worked 15 hours a day, and more on the weekend, and he earned half the money.

2 GRAMMAR adverbs

a Look at the highlighted phrases with adverbs in sentences 1–9 in **1c**. Choose **a** or **b** to complete the rules.

1 Regular adverbs
   An adverb is **a** adjective + -ly.
   　　　　　　 b adjective + -lly.

2 Use of adverbs
   Adverbs describe **a** nouns.
   　　　　　　　　 b verbs, adjectives, or other adverbs.

3 Position of adverbs
   Adverbs go **a** **before** a verb or verb phrase.
   　　　　　 b **after** a verb or verb phrase.
   Adverbs go **a** **before** another adverb or adjective.
   　　　　　 b **after** another adverb or adjective.

b **G** p.144 Grammar Bank 11A

c 🔊 11.3 Listen and say what's happening. Use an adverb.

1 *They're speaking quietly.*

3 LISTENING & PRONUNCIATION
connected speech

> Jack Horton lives in San José in Costa Rica, where he teaches computer science at a high school.

a 🔊 11.4 Listen to Jack talking about what surprised him when he arrived in Costa Rica. In general, is he positive, negative, or neutral about living there?

b 🔊 11.5 You're going to hear seven three- and four-word phrases that Jack says, linking the words. Listen and write the phrases.

1 *how incredibly friendly*

c Listen to the whole interview again. Then with a partner, complete the sentences.

The people (the ticos)
1 They are much _____ than people in his home country.
2 *Pura vida* really means "things _____ _____."
3 They are often _____ for appointments because they use "tico time."

The weather
4 The temperature is about _____ _____ all year round.
5 In September and October, it _____ really _____ for two hours a day.

The country
6 The scenery is even _____ _____ than he expected.
7 He was _____ _____ the first time a volcano erupted.

The food
8 The only things you can buy cheaply are _____, _____, and _____.
9 He really likes the _____.

San José
10 He thinks it's probably _____.
11 The roads are _____.

d Would you like to go to Costa Rica for a vacation? Would you like to live there?

4 VOCABULARY & SPEAKING
common adverbs

Answer the questions in small groups. If the answer is yes, give more details. If no, say how they do these things. How about you?

Do you think people in your country…?

drive dangerously
speak foreign languages fluently
treat tourists well
talk loudly
work hard
take life seriously
treat people in stores and restaurants politely
dress well
wait patiently in lines
behave calmly in a crisis

> *In Spain, I think that some young men drive dangerously. They drive very fast and they don't obey traffic rules. But I never drive dangerously. I drive very slowly and carefully.*

5 WRITING

Write three forum posts for people visiting your country, about habits that might surprise them. Use at least one adverb of manner or a modifier in each post.

We have our meals really late. We often have lunch at 2:30 and dinner at 10:00.

Go online to review the lesson

11B Experiences or things?

G verb + infinitive **V** verbs that take the infinitive **P** weak *to*, sentence stress

> Would you like to learn a new language?
>
> Yes, I want to learn Chinese.

1 READING & SPEAKING

a Read the dictionary definition of a *bucket list*. Do you have a similar phrase in your language?

> **bucket list** NAmE /ˈbʌkət lɪst/ 🔊; BrE /ˈbʌkɪt lɪst/
> 🔊 *noun* a list of things that you want to do before you die
> *Traveling to India is number one on my **bucket list**.*

b Read the **About me** section of Stef's blog. What does she say about…?

1 the Canary Islands and Argentina
 She worked there when she was a student.
2 Australia and New Zealand
3 an IT company
4 Istanbul, Indonesia, Chile, Prague
5 having experiences
6 three months ago

c Read the **My dreams** section. Check (✓) the five things you would most like to do. Compare with a partner and say why.

d Cover **My dreams**. Remember the missing verbs.

1 _____ a list
2 _____ on vacation
3 _____ a horse
4 _____ a language
5 _____ for a walk
6 _____ a dream come true
7 _____ a recipe
8 _____ in a taxi

e What do you think of Stef's lifestyle? Do you agree that experiences are more important than things?

HOME BLOG **ABOUT ME** MY DREAMS

About me

Hi! I'm Stef, a traveler from Germany with a passion for travel, food, and photography.

During my studies, I worked in the Canary Islands and in Argentina and I studied for two semesters in the UK. After I finished, I decided that I didn't want to work for the rest of my life. I was 21 and couldn't imagine sitting in an office for the next 40 years or more. So, I decided to go to Australia on
05 a working vacation visa. First, I worked for six months in Germany because I needed to save some money. I went to Sydney at the end of 2011. I spent Christmas on St. Kilda Beach in Melbourne, I worked in a restaurant, and then I traveled all over Australia and New Zealand.

After coming back, I got a job as a project assistant in an IT
10 company – an office job. I was happy to have a routine again, but I spent all my vacations traveling – to Thailand, Istanbul, Portugal, Indonesia, Chile, Belize, and Morocco.

Some months passed, but finally I realized what I wanted to do with my life, at least for now. Having experiences is
15 very important to me – more important than working in an office all week to pay for an apartment that I hardly ever spend time in, and to buy things I don't really need. Three months ago, I left my job. I decided to work in different
20 jobs, sometimes here, sometimes abroad, sometimes as a volunteer, sometimes for money. I have a lot of dreams and I want to make them come true.

HOME BLOG ABOUT ME **MY DREAMS**

My dreams

At the beginning of every year, I make a "bucket list" of 100 things I would like to do. These are some of them. You can probably do them in your country – you don't need to travel.

- Put a secret in a balloon and let it fly away.
- Go on vacation with my best friend.
- Take a photo every day for a year.
- Learn to windsurf.
05 • Ride a horse on the beach.
- Learn to play the guitar.
- Learn a new language.
- Read one book every week.
- Run through a field of flowers.
10 • Learn to dive and take underwater photos.
- Go for a walk in the summer rain.
- Go to a festival or an outdoor concert.
- Explore my hometown.
- Do karaoke.
15 • Make my best friend's dream come true.
- Do something that scares me.
- Make all the recipes in a cookbook.
- Get in a taxi and shout "follow that car."

2 GRAMMAR verb + infinitive

a Match the phrases to make sentences from Stef's blog. Which word is missing?

I decided ____	save some money.
I needed ____	play the guitar.
Learn ____	go to Australia.

b 🄶 p.144 Grammar Bank 11B

3 PRONUNCIATION weak *to*, sentence stress

a 🔊 11.7 Listen and write six sentences. Then listen and repeat them. How do you pronounce *to*?

b 🔊 11.8 Listen and repeat the conversation. <u>Copy</u> the <u>rhy</u>thm. Practice it with a partner.

> A Would you **like** to **go** to **Aus**tralia?
> B **No**, I **would**n't.
> A **Why not**?
> B **Because** I **don't like snakes** or **insects**.

c Work with a partner. Choose five more things from Stef's bucket list (not the five your partner checked) in **1c**. Ask your partner questions using *Would you like to…?*

> Would you like to learn to windsurf?
>
> Yes, I would. / No, I wouldn't.

4 VOCABULARY verbs that take the infinitive

a Look at ten verbs that take the infinitive. Which one is irregular?

decide   forget   hope   learn   need   plan   promise   remember   try   ~~want~~

b Complete the sentences with a verb from **a** in the past tense.
1 He *wanted* to know how much the salary was.
2 It was my mom's birthday yesterday – luckily I _____ to buy her a present!
3 They looked at some destinations on the internet, and finally they _____ to go to Phuket.
4 Oh no! I _____ to lock the door!
5 I _____ hard to open the bottle, but I couldn't.
6 She _____ to swim when she was eight years old.
7 We _____ to have good weather, but unfortunately it rained.
8 My neighbor _____ to water my plants while I was on vacation.
9 We _____ to have dinner outside, but sadly it was too cold.
10 I went to the bank because I _____ to talk to the manager.

5 SPEAKING

Work in pairs. Take turns.
A Tell your partner about the things below.
B Respond to what **A** says. Ask questions.
A Answer, then ask *What about you?*

a country you **want to go** to
something you **would like to learn** to do
something you **need to do** tomorrow
a vacation you **are planning to take** soon
a famous person you **hope to meet** one day
a movie you **want to see** soon
a dangerous sport you **would like to try**
something you **need to buy** soon
a singer or group you **hope to see** one day
a change you **are planning to make** to your lifestyle

> I really want to go New Zealand.
>
> Really? Why New Zealand?
>
> Because I have a cousin there. What about you?
>
> I want to go to Cuba…

6 WRITING

a Write your own bucket list of five things you would like to do this year.

b Compare your list with a partner. Did you choose any of the same things? Is there anything on his / her list that you'd like to add to yours?

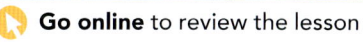

Go online to review the lesson

11C How smart is your phone?

> What do you use your phone for the most?
> I take photos and I play games.

G definite article: *the* or no *the* **V** phones and the internet **P** *the*

1 VOCABULARY phones and the internet

a Look at the phone screen below. How many of the apps and functions do you have on your phone?

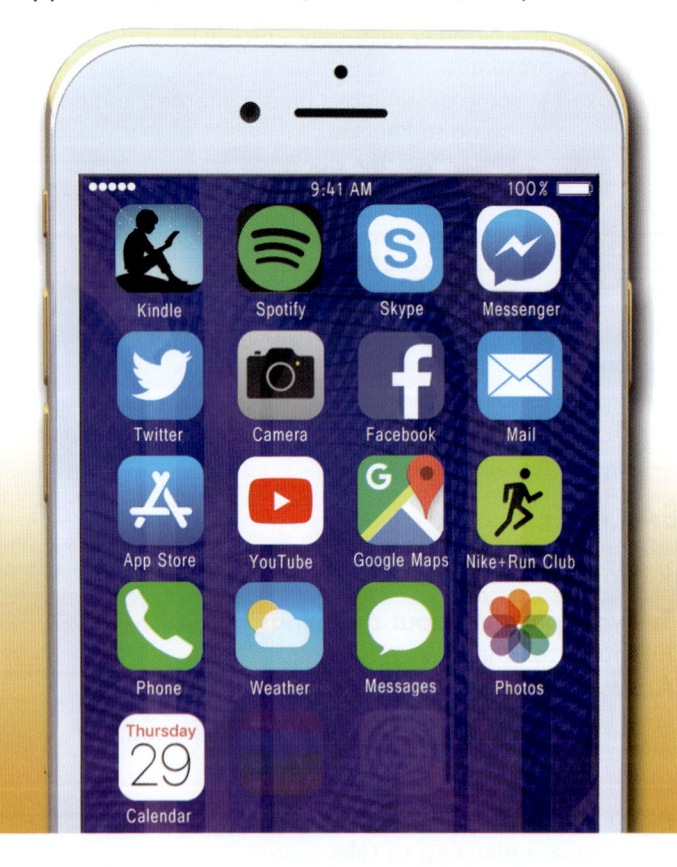

Kindle · Spotify · Skype · Messenger
Twitter · Camera · Facebook · Mail
App Store · YouTube · Google Maps · Nike+Run Club
Phone · Weather · Messages · Photos
Calendar (Thursday 29)

b Match icons in **a** to activities 1–13. Which can you use when you aren't online?

1. share a photo (on a social media website)
2. download an app
3. Skype a friend
4. send a text message
5. upload a video
6. message a friend
7. post a tweet
8. send an email
9. take a photo
10. get directions
11. read a book
12. get in shape
13. listen to a song

c 🔊 11.9 Listen and repeat activities 1–13.

d 🔊 11.10 Match the words and pictures. Listen and check.

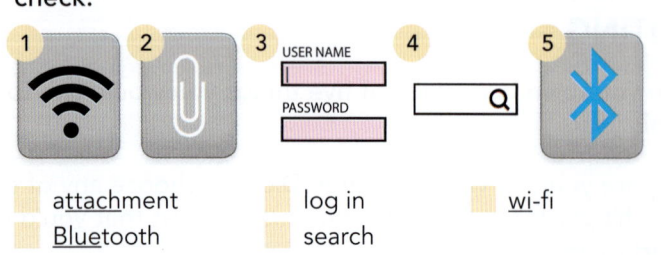

1. (wi-fi symbol)
2. (paperclip)
3. USER NAME / PASSWORD
4. (search box)
5. (Bluetooth symbol)

- attachment
- log in
- wi-fi
- Bluetooth
- search

2 LISTENING & SPEAKING

a 🔊 11.11 Listen to three people (A–C) talking about their phones. What's the first thing they say they use their phones for?

b Listen again. Which speaker (A–C)…?

1. ☐ doesn't want the newest phone
2. ☐ often checks train times on his / her phone
3. ☐ doesn't have an iPhone
4. ☐ prefers normal books to e-books
5. ☐ likes playing games on his / her phone
6. ☐ gets a new phone when the contract lets him / her
7. ☐ uses an app to track his / her money
8. ☐ has an app that he / she only uses at night
9. ☐ uses an app to help with his / her diet

c Answer the questions with a partner.

1. What phone do you have? How often do you change phones?
2. What three things do you do the most on it?
3. Is there anything on the list in **1b** that you never do on your phone? Why not?
4. Do you have any apps apart from the ones in **1a** that you use a lot? What are they?
5. Do you have any unusual apps on your phone? What are they?

3 READING

a Look at photos 1–6. What can you see?

b Read the article and check. What did people use each thing for?

c Talk to a partner. Do you do any of these things? How often? Why (not)?

- go to the bank
- go to travel agents
- buy CDs
- look something up in an encyclopedia
- use phone booths
- buy stamps
- look at paper maps
- write by hand
- read printed books

> I never go to the bank. I do everything with a banking app.

Life before the internet

This morning in the office somebody mentioned "carbon paper." "What's that?" our intern Francesca asked. She genuinely had no idea. For all of you who are too young to remember, we used carbon paper to make one or two copies of a document as it was typed. That's where the term "cc" or "carbon copy" came from. After that conversation, we started to remember life before the internet. Can you remember any of these?

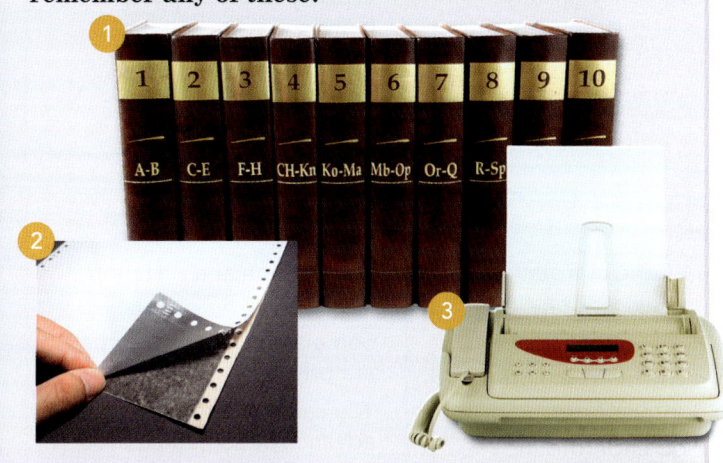

FAX MACHINES Sending an email is so easy these days, but some years ago, when you needed to send something to somebody urgently and the mail was too slow, you sent a fax. When they were introduced in the 1970s, people thought they were a technological miracle. "You can print something and send it over the phone in seconds! Magic!"

THE YELLOW PAGES If you needed to make an appointment with your hair stylist or call for Chinese take-out, what did you do? You looked up the phone number or address in a big fat yellow book – the Yellow Pages. Amazingly, it still exists online.

ENCYCLOPEDIAS When you needed information for your homework, or to win an argument, you looked it up in an enormous encyclopedia – sometimes ten or twelve books of information in alphabetical order. Some people had them at home, or they went to a library.

WALKMANS This is how we listened to music. A Walkman was a lot heavier than an MP3 player! And if you didn't have the cassette or CD of a song, you couldn't listen to it.

A THOMAS GUIDE If you had a meeting or job interview, or you wanted to go to a new restaurant in a part of town you didn't know, what did you always take with you? Your Thomas Guide maps. And your reading glasses to read the street names, because they were so small!

4 GRAMMAR definite article

a Look at the three sentences. Do you agree? Say why (not).
- Men use the internet more than women.
- The best place for children to learn how to use new technology is at school.
- It's bad manners to use your phone when you're having lunch or dinner.

b Look at the sentences in **a** again. Complete the rules with "Use *the*" or "Don't use *the*."
1 _____ before superlatives.
2 _____ when you talk about people or things in general.
3 _____ before meals and some general places, e.g., *lunch*, *work*, *college*.
4 _____ when there is only one of something (*sun*, *world*, etc.).

c **G** p.144 Grammar Bank 11C

5 PRONUNCIATION & SPEAKING *the*

a 🔶 11.13 Listen to the phrases below. How is *the* pronounced in the two groups? Why?

1 the alphabet   2 the president
  the end   the sun
  the internet   the world

b Practice saying the phrases.

c Work in pairs. **A** choose a circle, think of three things, places, etc. and tell **B**. **B** respond and ask for more information. Then change roles. Be careful to only use *the* when it's necessary!

I think women like shopping, but men don't.
I'm not sure. I'm a man and I like shopping!

Articles challenge

- 3 things men usually like doing (but women don't)
- 3 ways that the internet makes your life easier
- 3 things women usually like doing (but men don't)
- 3 things you did last night
- 3 kinds of food you love and 3 you hate
- 3 good ways you can travel around your town / city
- 3 places that you think are the most beautiful in your country
- 3 things you do before you go to work / school

Go online to review the lesson

Practical English Going home

EPISODE 6

getting to the airport   V public transportation

1 ▶ JENNY'S LAST MORNING

a 🔊 11.14 Watch or listen to Rob and Jenny. Mark the sentences **T** (true) or **F** (false).
1 Rob arrives late.
2 He has a coffee with Jenny.
3 Jenny has bad news for him.
4 Rob thinks *A writer in New York* is a good name for a column.
5 Rob needs time to think.

b Watch or listen again. Say why the **F** sentences are false.

2 VOCABULARY public transportation

a Match the words and pictures.

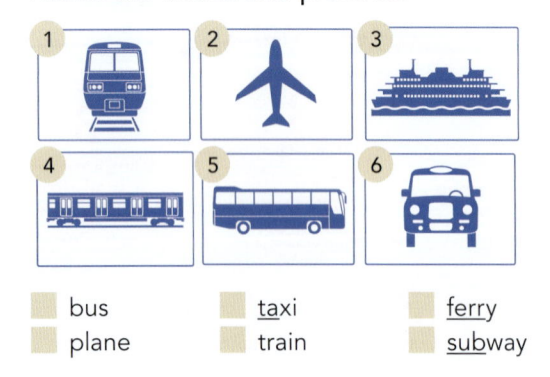

☐ bus   ☐ taxi   ☐ ferry
☐ plane   ☐ train   ☐ subway

b 🔊 11.15 Listen and check. Then cover the words and look at the pictures. Say the words.

c Complete the headings with a word from **a**.

1 _____
You get one at a ~ stand or by waving your hand.
They are also called cabs.
People usually give the driver a tip (= some extra money, about 15–20%).
In New York City, they are yellow.

2 _____
You get one at an airport.
First, you have to check in.
Then you go through security to the departure lounge.
Finally, you go to your gate.

3 _____
You get one at a station.
You usually need to get a ticket or a card first.
Then you need to find the right platform.
Most go underground in big cities.

4 _____
You get one at a ~ station or a ~ stop.
Some are public and some are private.
You can buy a ticket in advance or sometimes you can pay the driver.
In New York City, they are blue and white.

d Cover the facts and look at the headings. Try to remember two facts about each type of public transportation.

3 ▶ GETTING TO THE AIRPORT

a 🔊 11.16 Watch or listen to Jenny's three conversations. How does she get to the airport?

92

b   Watch or listen again. Complete the **You hear** phrases.

You say	You hear
Could you call me a taxi, please?	Yes, of course. ¹_____ to?
To Paddington Station.	And when would you like it ²_____?
Now, please.	
How much is it?	That's £³_____, please.
Make it £15. And could I have a receipt?	Thank you very much, ⁴_____.
Could I have a ticket to Heathrow Airport, please?	Single or ⁵_____?
Single, please.	Standard or ⁶_____ class?
Standard, please.	That's £18.
Can I pay by credit card?	Yes, of ⁷_____.

c   🔊 11.17 Watch or listen and repeat the **You say** phrases. Copy the rhythm.

d   Practice the conversation with a partner.

e   In pairs, role-play the conversation. Then change roles.

   A (book open) You are the receptionist, the taxi driver, and the ticket clerk. The taxi costs $12.60. The ticket costs $32.50.
   B (book closed) You want to get a taxi to Penn Station, and then a train to JFK Airport. Begin with *Could you call me a taxi, please?*

4 ▶ SAYING GOODBYE

a   🔊 11.18 Watch or listen and complete what happens.
   1 Jenny is worried because…
   2 Rob goes to the airport because…
   3 Rob tells Jenny that he wants to…
   4 Eddie isn't going to meet Jenny in New York because…
   5 Rob is happy because Eddie is…
   6 Jenny needs to go because…

b   Look at the **Social English** phrases. Who says them: **J**enny or **R**ob?

   💬 Social English
   1 ☐ I can't believe it!
   2 ☐ Thank you so much.
   3 ☐ I'm so happy.
   4 ☐ Have a good journey.
   5 ☐ See you in New York!

c   🔊 11.19 Watch or listen and check. Then watch or listen and repeat the phrases.

d   Complete conversations A–E with **Social English** phrases 1–5. Practice with a partner.

A	☐	Yes, see you there! It's going to be great!
B	Excuse me, is this your bag? It was under the chair.	Oh, yes it is. ☐ I'm usually so careful.
C	Is everything OK?	Yes, everything's great! ☐
D	☐ There are no taxis at the airport!	Oh no! How are we going to get to the hotel?
E	Bye! ☐ Call me when you get there.	Don't worry! Bye.

🔍 **American and British English**
one-way ticket = American English
single ticket = British English
round-trip ticket = American English
return ticket = British English
coach = American English
standard = British English

CAN YOU…?

☐ ask for a taxi
☐ buy a ticket for public transportation
☐ use common phrases, e.g., *Thank you so much, See you in (New York)*, etc.

Go online to watch the video, review the lesson, and check your progress

12A I've seen it ten times!

G present perfect **V** irregular past participles **P** sentence stress

> Have you seen Game of Thrones?
>
> No, but I've read the books.

1 GRAMMAR present perfect

a Look at the photos from two movies and a TV show. Can you match them to the books?

b 🔊 12.1 Listen to three conversations. Complete them with the phrases below.

I've read the book   I haven't seen it
~~Have you seen it~~   No, I haven't   Yes, I have

1 **Stella** The first *Jurassic Park* is on TV tonight. <u>Have you seen it</u>?
   Paul _____. And _____. The movie's better than the book, I think.
   Stella Let's watch it then. I know it's an old movie, but I haven't seen it.

2 **Matt** Have you read the *Game of Thrones* books?
   Tom _____. They're really long! Life's too short for 700-page books!
   Matt Have you watched the TV show?
   Tom Yes, I've watched the first three seasons, and I've downloaded the fourth.

3 **Ann** Have you seen the movie *It*? The recent one.
   Mike Is it the movie of the Stephen King book?
   Ann Yes.
   Mike I've heard of it, but _____. I've read the book – it's great.

c Listen to and read the conversations again. Complete the chart for *read*, and answer the questions with a partner.

Present perfect: *read*	
+	I've read the book.
–	_____ the book.
?	_____ the book?
✓	
✗	

1 What is the full form of *I've read*?
2 How do you think *have* and *haven't* change in the third person singular?
3 *Seen*, *read*, and *heard* are **irregular past participles**. What are the base forms?
4 *Watched* and *downloaded* are **regular past participles**. What are the base forms?
5 When Tom says *I've watched the first three seasons*, do we know when he watched them?

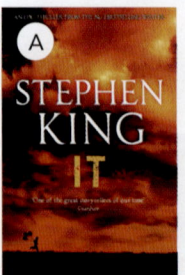

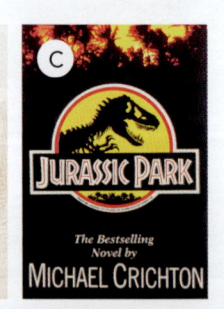

d **G** p.146 Grammar Bank 12A

e Complete 1–10 with a past participle from the list of regular verbs.

act   ask   believe   book   download   kill   ~~open~~
play   travel   work

I've never…
1. *opened* a bank account.
2. _____ a flight online.
3. _____ in a play or movie.
4. _____ a team sport.
5. _____ an insect.
6. _____ as a waiter.
7. _____ in horoscopes.
8. _____ somebody to marry me.
9. _____ to another continent.
10. _____ a movie or music without paying.

f With a partner, say which sentences are true for you.

2 PRONUNCIATION sentence stress

a ◯ 12.3 Listen and repeat the conversation. Copy the rhythm.

> A Have you **seen** The **Martian**?
> B **No**, I **haven't**.
> A Have you **read** the **book**?
> B **Yes**, I **have**. I've **read** it **twice**.

b Write down three more movies or TV shows from books. Have conversations with a partner as in **a**.

3 VOCABULARY irregular past participles

a Look at the past participles. Which verbs are they from? Write the base form and the simple past.

	base form	simple past	past participle
1	buy	bought	bought
2			fallen
3			given
4			heard
5			left
6			read
7			seen
8			told

b ◯ 12.4 Listen and check. How do you say *read* (base form) and *read* (simple past and past participle)?

c ◯ 12.5 Cover **a**. Listen and say the simple past and past participle.

>)) buy (bought, bought

d Complete the **Verb** column with a past participle from **a**.

                                                    Verb

1. Have you ever ☐ a Japanese novel? _____
2. Ben's ☐ in love with Sally. _____
3. Have you ☐ Mike about the party? _____
4. We've ☐ the news – congratulations! _____
5. She's never ☐ *X-Men*. _____
6. Tim's ☐ some tickets for the game. _____
7. Oh no! I've ☐ my bag on the train. _____
8. I've ☐ my old computer to my brother. _____

e Cover the **Verb** column. Say the sentences.

4 LISTENING & SPEAKING

a Complete the phrases with the past participle of the verb in parentheses.

Movies, books, and TV
Have you ever…?
1. _____ asleep at the movies (fall)
2. _____ the soundtrack of a movie (buy)
3. _____ the movie theater before the end of a movie (leave)
4. _____ a movie more than three times (see)
5. _____ during a movie (cry)
6. _____ a movie in English with subtitles (see)
7. _____ somebody to be quiet during a movie (tell)
8. _____ a book more than once (read)
9. _____ watching a TV show after the first or second season (stop)
10. _____ to an audiobook (listen)
11. _____ a book to a friend as a present (give)
12. _____ three or more episodes of a TV show in one evening (watch)

b ◯ 12.6 Listen to six people, A–F. Which question (1–12) in **a** does each person answer?
A ☐ B ☐ C ☐ D ☐ E ☐ F ☐

c Listen again. Make notes about their answers.

d Choose six of the questions in **a**. Ask a different person each question. If they answer *Yes, I have.*, ask *What movie / book / TV show was it?* Write their name and answer.

e Tell the class your two most interesting answers.

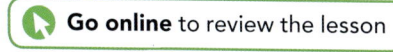

⟳ Go online to review the lesson

12B He's been everywhere!

G present perfect or simple past? V learning irregular verbs P irregular past participles

How about that Indian restaurant?

I've been there.

He's so annoying!

Have you been to the new Thai restaurant?

Yes, I have. I went there last week.

1 LISTENING

a Look at the list of ten popular types of foreign restaurant in the US. Answer the questions.

| Chinese | French | Greek | Indian | Italian |
| Japanese | Mexican | Spanish | Thai | Turkish |

1 Which do you think are the top three?
2 Which of these kinds of food have you eaten?
3 What are the most popular types of foreign restaurant where you live?

b ◉ 12.7 Listen to four people trying to decide where to go for dinner. Do they agree which restaurant to go to?

c Listen again. Check (✓) the restaurants Joe has been to, and write when. Write ? if he doesn't say when.

	Has he been there?	When?
Curry Up		
The Great Wall		
Thai-Chi		
Mexican Wave		
The Acropolis		

d Do you know any annoying people like Joe?

2 GRAMMAR present perfect or simple past?

a Look at part of the conversation in **1**. Answer the questions.

Alison	Have you been to Mexican Wave?
Joe	Yes, I have.
Alison	When did you go there?
Joe	Last month. I went for dinner with people from work.

1 What tense is Alison's first question?
2 What tense is Alison's second question?
3 Which of the two questions is about a specific time in the past?

b ◉ p.146 Grammar Bank 12B

c Write down the names of two restaurants you've been to recently, two movies you've seen recently, and two places you've visited recently.

d In pairs, ask and answer questions.

Have you been to...?

Yes, I have.

When did you go there? Did you like it?

3 VOCABULARY learning irregular verbs

a 🔊 **12.10** Write the base forms for the irregular verbs. Then listen and check.

base form	simple past
1 _____	got
2 _____	had
3 _____	lost
4 _____	met
5 _____	won

b 🔊 **12.11** Now look at some verbs where the past participle is different from the simple past. Write the base form and the simple past. Then listen and check.

base form	simple past	past participle
1 _____	_____	been
2 _____	_____	done
3 _____	_____	eaten
4 _____	_____	spoken
5 _____	_____	sung

c **p.165 Irregular verbs** Underline the verbs that have the same form for the simple past and the past participle.

4 PRONUNCIATION irregular past participles

a Put the irregular past participles in the correct column.

bought   done   eaten   fallen   given
got   left   lost   met   read   seen
spoken   sung   won

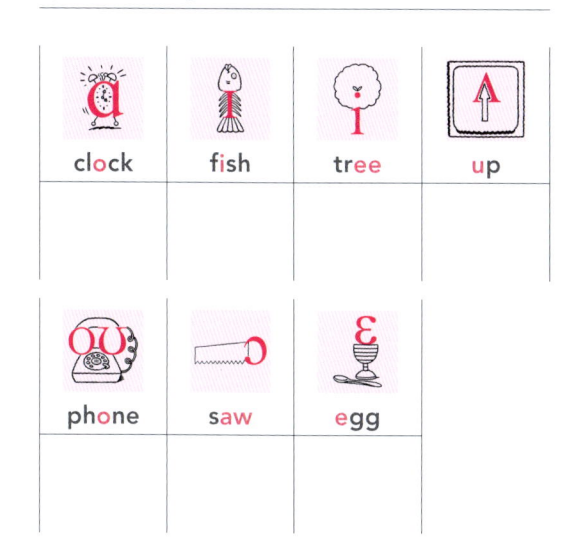

clock	fish	tree	up

phone	saw	egg	

b 🔊 **12.12** Listen and check. Practice saying them.

5 SPEAKING

a Look at question 1 below. What words are missing in the present perfect question? What form do you need of the verb in **bold**? What words are missing in the simple past question?

Recently…

		Present perfect	Simple past
1		/ **be** to the movies recently?	What / see? / like it?
2		/ **play** any sports recently?	What / play? Who / play it with?
3		/ **eat** out with friends recently?	Where / go? What / have?
4		/ **get** up really late recently?	Why? / miss anything important?
5		/ **buy** anything online recently?	What / buy? Where / buy it from?

In your life…

		Present perfect	Simple past
1		/ ever **sing** something in public?	What / sing? How / feel?
2		/ ever **lose** your phone?	Where / lose it? / find it?
3		/ ever **win** a trophy or medal?	What / win it for?
4		/ ever **speak** to a famous person?	Who / speak to? What / say?
5		/ ever **have** very long (or short) hair?	When / have it? / like it?

b Work in pairs. **A** ask **B** the questions. If **B** answers *Yes, I have.*, ask the simple past questions. Then change roles.

Have you been to the movies recently?   *Yes, I have.*
What did you see?

Go online to review the lesson

12C The *American English File* interview

G review: question formation

1 READING

a Look at the photos of Sir Ian McKellen. Do you know the names of any movies he has been in? Have you seen any of them?

b Sir Ian McKellen was interviewed especially for *American English File*. Read the interview and complete sections A–F with a heading from the list.

Your abilities   Your lifestyle
Your work experiences   Your places
Your home   ~~Your tastes~~

c Look at sentences 1–10 about Sir Ian McKellen. Some are true and some are false. In which section of the interview do you expect to find the information?

1 He became an actor when he was a student.
2 He lives outside London.
3 He gets up early every day.
4 He's never been to India.
5 He spends a long time on the internet every day.
6 He read *The Lord of the Rings* when he was young.
7 His desk isn't very neat.
8 He doesn't like animals.
9 He relaxes by playing games.
10 He's not interested in learning new things.

d Read the interview again and mark the sentences **T** (true) or **F** (false). Say why the **F** ones are false.

e Talk to a partner. What three things from the interview with Sir Ian McKellen did you find the most interesting?

2 GRAMMAR & SPEAKING review: question formation

a In pairs, look at the groups of questions (1–6). Complete them with *'s*, *are*, *can*, *do*, *did*, or *have*.

1 Your lifestyle
What *do* you usually do in the morning?
How _____ you relax?
What _____ you do last weekend?

2 Your home
What _____ your favorite room in your home?
_____ you neat or messy?
_____ you do a lot of housework last week?

as Gandalf

An interview with
Sir Ian McKellen

A Your tastes

What kind of music do you like? I hardly ever listen to music at home – I prefer going to concerts. I enjoy classical music and pop, but my favorite kind of music is traditional American jazz.

What book are you reading right now? I'm reading *The Hammersteins*, a biography of the American theater family written by Oscar Andrew Hammerstein.

Who's your favorite historical character? Perhaps William Shakespeare.

3 Your abilities
What languages _____ you speak?
_____ you sing or play a musical instrument?
Why _____ you learning English?

4 Your places
What _____ your favorite place to spend the weekend?
Where _____ you go for your last vacation?
Where _____ you going to go for your next vacation?

5 Your tastes
What _____ your favorite time of year?
What book _____ you reading right now?
What kind of TV shows _____ you like watching?

6 Your experiences
What movies _____ you seen recently?
What _____ the most beautiful place you've ever been to?
_____ you ever been to the US or Britain?

b 🔊 12.13 Listen and check.

B

What time do you usually get up in the morning? If I am working, I get up one hour before I have to leave the house. If I am not working, and I went to bed late the night before, I get up at about 10:00 in the morning.

How much time do you spend a day on the internet? I can very easily spend three or four hours on the internet, answering emails, reading the news, etc. I think of the internet as a wonderful encyclopedia of information.

How do you relax? I enjoy a late-night Sudoku, but especially being with friends.

C

What's your favorite room in the house? Perhaps the living room where I cook and eat, and from where I can see the River Thames in London.

What do you always have on your desk? I always have too many letters, papers, and books, which are waiting for me to read.

Do you have any pets? I love dogs, but I can't have one because I'm often away from home.

D

What languages do you speak? I only speak English, but I can remember a little of the French I learned at school.

Can you play a musical instrument? No.

Is there something you would like to learn to do? Yes – many things, e.g., to sing well, to play the piano, and to speak foreign languages.

E

What's your favorite place in London? I love the River Thames and the views from its many bridges.

Where are you going to go for your next vacation? I am going to go to India for the first time in February.

What's the most beautiful city you've ever visited? I can't choose between Edinburgh, Prague, and Venice.

F

What was your first job? The first money I earned as a professional actor was when I was a student at Cambridge University in 1959. I played small parts in audio recordings of Shakespeare's plays.

When did you first read *The Lord of the Rings*? I read it first when I was preparing to play Gandalf in the movie trilogy.

What was the best and worst thing about filming *The Lord of the Rings*? The best thing about filming was discovering the countryside and people of New Zealand. But the worst thing was living away from home for a year or more.

as Magneto

---

c Work with a partner.

A interview **B** with group 1. Ask more questions where appropriate, and show interest in **B**'s answers.

B answer the questions, giving as much information as you can. Then **B** interview **A** with group 2, etc.

> **A** *What do you usually do in the morning?*
> **B** *I get up at about 7:00. I have breakfast and then I go to class at school.*
> **A** *What time do your classes start?*
> **B** *At 8:00.*

3 ▶ VIDEO LISTENING

a Watch the documentary *Judi Dench – a life in acting*. Check (✓) the six movies you hear. Have you seen any of them?

Macbeth   A Room with a View   Tea with Mussolini
Henry V   GoldenEye   Mrs. Brown   Skyfall
Shakespeare in Love

Judi Dench and Ian McKellen in *Macbeth*

b Watch again. Put the events in the correct order.

- [ ] She appeared in *A Room with a View*.
- [ ] She played Queen Elizabeth I.
- [ ] She worked with the Royal Shakespeare Company.
- [1] She was born in York.
- [ ] She appeared in her first James Bond movie.
- [ ] She acted in the York Mystery Plays.
- [ ] She played Queen Victoria in the movie *Mrs. Brown*.
- [ ] She was in a production of *Macbeth* with Ian McKellen.
- [ ] She won an Oscar.

c Are there any famous actors from your country who are the same generation as Judi Dench and Ian McKellen? Do you like them?

> **Go online** to watch the video and review the lesson

11 & 12 Review and Check

GRAMMAR

Circle a, b, or c.

1. You speak ____.
   a very slow   b very slowly   c very slower
2. She plays tennis ____.
   a very well   b very good   c very goodly
3. My husband works ____.
   a incredible hard   b incredibly hard
   c incredibly hardly
4. I'd like ____ a Ferrari.
   a drive   b to drive   c driving
5. What do we need ____ next?
   a to do   b do   c doing
6. She wants to pass her exams, but she doesn't like ____.
   a study   b studing   c studying
7. ____ usually drive faster than women.
   a The men   b Men   c The man
8. It's ____ best place to eat in the city.
   a the   b a   c –
9. Do you go to ____ bed late on the weekends?
   a the   b a   c –
10. My grandfather never uses ____ internet.
    a the   b a   c –
11. I've read the book, but I ____ the movie.
    a haven't see   b haven't saw
    c haven't seen
12. A Have you ____ anyone famous?
    B Yes, I have. A famous movie actor.
    a ever met   b ever meet   c met ever
13. ____ he been to New York?
    a Has   b Did   c Have
14. We ____ to Los Angeles last year.
    a have gone   b have been   c went
15. She ____ in a restaurant before.
    a has never work   b have never worked
    c has never worked

VOCABULARY

a Write the opposite adjective or adverb.
1. quickly   _____
2. safe   _____
3. well   _____
4. noisy   _____
5. hot   _____
6. weakly   _____

b Complete the sentences with these verbs.

| need   learn   promise   want |

1. I'd like to _____ to dance the tango.
2. You don't _____ to wash it. You've only worn it once.
3. I can't _____ to be on time. It depends on the traffic.
4. Do you _____ to go to a restaurant or a food truck for lunch?

c Complete the sentences with these internet words.

| attachment   download   online   website   wi-fi |

1. I always shop _____ these days.
2. I can _____ the song for you tonight.
3. You can find all the information on the hotel's _____.
4. Don't open an _____ if you don't know who it's from.
5. I can't Skype you – our _____ isn't working right now.

d Complete the sentences with *for*, *in*, *up*, or *with*.
1. Log _____ with your username and password.
2. I looked _____ Coldplay on Wikipedia – the band started in 1996.
3. You can search _____ most information on the internet.
4. Have you ever seen a movie _____ subtitles?

e Write the past participle of these verbs.

1. see   saw   _____
2. go   went   _____
3. know   knew   _____
4. give   gave   _____
5. fall   fell   _____
6. take   took   _____

PRONUNCIATION

a **P p.166–7 Sound Bank** Review vowel and consonant sounds.

b What sound do the pink letters have in these words? Match them to the sound pictures.

bought   spoken   want   wi-fi   women

1. saw   2. clock   3. fish   4. bike   5. phone

c Underline the stressed syllable.
1. po|lite|ly   3. de|cide   5. web|site
2. dan|ger|ous|ly   4. at|tach|ment

CAN YOU understand this text?

a Read the reviews of Pizza West once. Which review is most positive and which is most negative?

PIZZA WEST

A ALAN
I go here often because it's very close to my apartment. The pizza is OK, and it's not too expensive. The atmosphere is great, perfect for a Friday or Saturday night. It's very popular, but if you don't mind waiting, you can usually get a table. Or book online!

B STEVE AND JANE
Very expensive. In most pizza places, we usually pay about $15 for a pizza; here it's $22 for more or less the same thing! The food is fine, but we definitely aren't going to eat there again.

C SARAH
We've been here a lot and we always enjoy it. The menu is very good, and they have great appetizers as well as pizzas. We went yesterday for an early dinner with our three-year-old daughter and they really made us feel at home – and they served a delicious birthday cake for her. Great food, friendly waiters, fantastic atmosphere.

D BRIDGET
We booked a table, but when we got there, they asked us to sit with a lot of other people at a big table. We didn't want to because there were only two of us. Then they asked us to wait until a different table was free, so we waited for 45 minutes! But I recommend it because the food is excellent!

E GEORGE
The pizza here isn't the best I've tasted, but it's OK (and the salads are delicious). The service is a little bit slow and the place is very busy – it can be really noisy. However, the atmosphere is great and it's obviously popular. Not the place for a romantic dinner – it's more of a fun, exciting place.

b Read the reviews again. Match them to the sentences. Who (A–E)...?

1 ____ says the waiters are nice
2 ____ says the food is too expensive
3 ____ says they have had better pizzas
4 ____ lives near the restaurant
5 ____ didn't like the table when they arrived
6 ____ went for a special family meal
7 ____ thinks the prices are good
8 ____ doesn't recommend it for couples who want a quiet dinner

CAN YOU understand these people?

▶ 12.14 Watch or listen and answer the questions.

1 Cara   2 Madeleine   3 Chris   4 Susan   5 Martin

1 When Cara came to the US she was surprised by ____.
   a the number of people
   b the weather and the food
   c the parks and the attractions
2 Madeleine thinks that she drives ____ other people from her area of the US.
   a better than   b worse than   c the same as
3 Chris would like to ____ soon.
   a go to Australia   c visit her parents
   b go to Austria
4 Susan has seen the movie ____ more than three times.
   a *Titanic*   c *Gone with the Wind*
   b *Casablanca*
5 Martin bought his phone ____ years ago.
   a two   b three   c four

CAN YOU say this in English?

Do the tasks with a partner. Check (✓) the box if you can do these things.

Can you...?
1 ☐ say how people in your country drive and dress
2 ☐ say three things you would like to do in the future
3 ☐ say which of the following you prefer and why
   • classical music or pop music
   • summer vacations or winter vacations
   • Chinese food or Japanese food
4 ☐ say what things you use the internet for, and how often
5 ☐ answer the questions below
   • What city have you been to recently?
   • When did you go there? What did you do there?
   • What's the best / worst thing about your town?

Go online to watch the video, review Files 11 and 12, and check your progress

Communication

1B WHERE ARE THEY FROM?
Student A

a Look at the chart. Take turns to ask and answer the questions about each person. Ask about person 1. Then answer **B** about person 2.

Where's Masako from?

Where in (country)?

	1	2	3
Name	Masako	Ali	Nadir
From		Turkey Ankara	

	4	5	6
Name	Maria	Sofia	Oliver
From	Mexico Acapulco		Germany Berlin

b Repeat for the other people.

1C WHAT'S HIS / HER REAL NAME?
Student A

a Look at list **1**. Read the names of your four people. Two are their real names and two aren't. Cross out (✗) the names you think are **not** their real names.

1
- Daniel Craig, actor _____
- Jay Z, singer _____
- Cate Blanchett, actress _____
- Helen Mirren, actress _____

2
- Leonardo DiCaprio, actor (real name)
- Pink, singer (real name Alecia Moore)
- Bruno Mars, singer (real name Peter Gene Hernandez)
- Dakota Johnson, actress (real name)

b Talk to **B**. Check your answers to **a**. Write the real name next to the photo.

Is _____ his / her real name?

What's his / her real name? How do you spell it?

c Now look at list **2** and answer **B**'s questions.

2A IN, ON, UNDER Student A

a Where are these things? Ask **B**. Draw them in the correct place in picture 1.

charger   glasses   keys   laptop   scissors   umbrella   wallet

Where's the charger?   *It's in the…*

b Look at picture 2. Answer **B**'s questions.

c Now compare your pictures. Are all the things in the correct place?

2B THE SAME OR DIFFERENT? Student A

a Describe picture 1 to **B**. Is your picture the same or different? Write **S** or **D** on the picture. Then listen to **B** describe picture 2, etc. Find eight differences.

A *Number 1. It's an old house.*
B *In my picture, it's a new house. They're different.*

b Compare your pictures and check.

2C WHAT'S THE MATTER? Student A

a Have this conversation in pairs. You are **A**.

A What's the matter?
B I'm sad.
A Cheer up.
B OK.

b Have four more conversations. Ask *What's the matter?* **B** answers. Then choose a phrase below.

Don't worry. It's OK.   Take a vacation.
Open the window.   Have a drink.

c Change roles. **B** asks *What's the matter?* Answer with 1 below. **B** responds. Then respond, e.g., *Thanks, OK, Good idea*, etc.

1 *I'm bored.*
2 *I'm cold.*
3 *I'm tired.*
4 *I'm hungry.*

d Have all eight conversations again. Try to do them from memory.

103

PE2 WHAT'S THE TIME?
Student A

Ask and answer questions with **B** and complete the times on the clocks. Then compare your clocks.

Clock 1: What's the time?/What time is it?

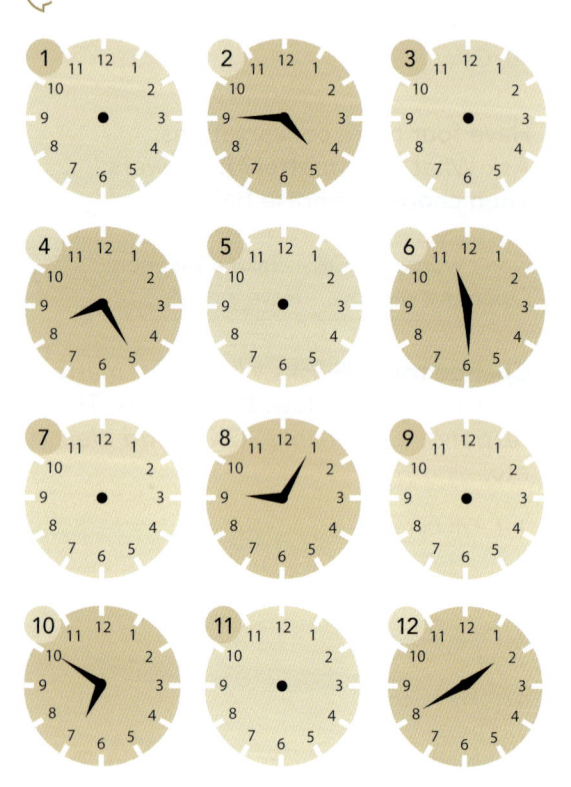

4C SHORT LIFE, LONG LIFE?
Students A+B

Interview your partner. **A** ask the questions in the questionnaire. **B** answer and give more information if you can. Then change roles.

How often do you…?
1 **have breakfast**
 a hardly ever / never
 b sometimes / usually
 c always
2 **eat fresh fruit and vegetables**
 a hardly ever / never
 b once a day
 c three times a day
3 **eat fast food**
 a often
 b sometimes, not often
 c hardly ever / never
4 **exercise**
 a hardly ever / never
 b once or twice a week
 c three or four times a week
5 **feel tired or stressed**
 a always / often
 b sometimes
 c hardly ever / never
6 **drink soda**
 a every day
 b sometimes
 c hardly ever / never
7 **see your friends**
 a sometimes
 b often
 c very often

How many…?
8 **hours do you usually sleep a day**
 a 0 to 4
 b 5 to 6
 c 7 to 9
9 **cups of coffee do you drink a day**
 a more than five
 b usually only one or two
 c I don't drink coffee.
10 **Which of these is true for you?**
 a I'm not very positive about life.
 b I'm usually positive about life.
 c I'm always positive about life.

Now calculate your partner's score.
a = 5   b = 7   c = 10
Total score = number of years you live

4C IKARIA Student A

a Read the article about Ikaria and answer the questions.
 1 Where is Ikaria?
 2 What do the people eat and drink?
 3 What exercise do they do?
 4 What do they do after lunch?
 5 Is Ikaria a safe place? How do you know?
 6 Do they have a good social life? What examples does the article give?
 7 What do people call the island?

b Listen to **B** describe life in Nicoya.

c Tell **B** about life in Ikaria. Use your answers to questions 1–7. What do the two places have in common?

Ikaria, Greece

Ikaria is a small Greek island near the coast of Turkey. How do the people there live? They eat a lot of beans, potatoes, and green vegetables, and they sometimes eat fish, but they hardly ever eat red meat or sugar. They drink a lot of herbal tea. They do a lot of exercise, but they never go to a gym. They work in their gardens, and they walk everywhere – not many people in Ikaria have a car. They also take a siesta every afternoon.

Ikaria is a very safe place. In the village of Raches, the police station is closed. The people say they don't need police. People also have a very good social life. The island is famous for its tradition of *panagiria*, or festivals. Between May and October, the island has between two and four festivals every week, where people eat, drink, and dance all night. They call Ikaria "the island where people forget to die."

Glossary
beans   **herbal tea**

siesta a rest or sleep taken in the early afternoon, especially in hot countries

5B SPOT THE DIFFERENCES Student A

You and **B** have the same picture but with eight differences.

a   Tell **B** what is happening in apartments 1–4 and in the yard on the left. What is happening in **B**'s picture? Listen and (circle) the differences.

b   Listen to **B** describe what is happening in apartments 5–8 and in the yard on the right. What is happening in your picture? Is it the same or different? Tell **B**. (Circle) the differences.

c   When you finish, compare the two pictures.

5C WHAT DO YOU DO? WHAT ARE YOU DOING NOW? Student A

a   Ask **B** your questions.

What do you do?
What are you doing now?
Are you wearing a watch today?
Do you usually wear a watch?
What kind of books do you usually read?
What are you reading right now?

b   Answer **B**'s questions.

6A READING IN ENGLISH Students A+B

Interview your partner.

What kind of things do you read in your own language?

a   books
b   newspapers
c   magazines
d   websites
e   work documents
f   movie subtitles or song lyrics
g   other (what?)

When and **where** do you usually read?

a   at work / school
b   when you are on a bus or train
c   on vacation
d   before you go to bed

Do you ever need to read in English? What?

> **Reading in English**
> Reading Graded Readers, e.g., the *Oxford Bookworms* series, helps you to learn and remember vocabulary and grammar. Buy a Starter (A1) or Stage 1 (A2/B1) level book with audio.

105

8A POLICE INTERVIEW Student A

Work in pairs with another **A**. You are police officers. There was a robbery last night. **B** and **B** are your suspects. They are friends. They say that they went out for dinner and went to the movies last night. You want to know if this is true.

a **A**s look at the police interview form and prepare to ask the **B**s the questions. Think of questions to get more details about the evening, e.g., *What did you eat and drink? What movie was it?*

Police interview form

Name: _____ Date: _____

	What time?	Where?	More details
/ meet?			
/ have dinner?			
/ go to the movies?			
What / do after the movies?			
What time / get home?			

b Interview one of the **B**s. Write down his / her answers in the form. (Your partner interviews the other **B**.)

c Compare with your partner. Did the two **B**s tell exactly the same story? If not, arrest them!

8B IS THERE…? ARE THERE…? Student A

a Make questions with *Is there a…?* or *Are there any…?* to ask **B**.

> *Is there a bathtub in your bathroom?*

1 bathtub in your bathroom
2 books in your living room
3 stores near your house
4 desk in your bedroom
5 dishwasher in your kitchen
6 supermarkets on your street

b Answer **B**'s questions with *Yes, there is / are.* or *No, there isn't / aren't*.

8C A HAUNTED ROOM Student A

a Some people say there are haunted hotel rooms all around the world. Look at the photo of a haunted hotel room in the UK for one minute. Try to remember what's in the room.

b Ask **B** the questions.

/ a single or a double bed? (*There was a double bed.*)
How many tables / ? (*There were three.*)
/ a rug on the floor? (*Yes, there was.*)
/ any armchairs? Where were they? (*Yes, there were. They were across from the bed, next to the windows.*)
/ any books in the room? (*No, there weren't.*)
What / over the bed? (*There was a light.*)

c Close your book. Answer **B**'s questions.

9B SUGAR AND SALT Students A+B

How much sugar?

According to the American Heart Association, a woman should have **no more than 24 g** (grams) of sugar a day (= 6 teaspoons) and a man **no more than 36 g** (= 9 teaspoons).

- a can of soda has approximately 35 g of sugar
- an apple has approximately 23 g of sugar
- a small (40 g) bar of dark chocolate has approximately 10 g of sugar
- an egg doesn't have any sugar

How much salt?

According to UK Government studies, an adult should eat **no more than 6 g** of salt a day.

- a large bag of potato chips has approximately 3 g of salt
- a slice of white bread has approximately 0.5 g of salt
- a bottle of mineral water has approximately 0.0023 g of salt
- a bottle of olive oil doesn't have any salt

9C QUIZ NIGHT Student A

a Complete your sentences 1–8 with the comparative form of the **bold** adjectives.

> 1 **small** Brazil is _____ than the US.
> (*True. Brazil is 3,300,000 million square miles and the US is 3,790,000 million square miles.*)
> 2 **cold** Alaska is _____ than Greenland.
> (*False. The lowest recorded temperature in Alaska was –80 degrees Fahrenheit, but in Greenland it was recorded at –87 Fahrenheit.*)
> 3 **old** Oxford University is _____ than Cambridge University.
> (*True. Oxford University was founded in about 1170 and Cambridge 40 years later, in 1209.*)
> 4 **short** The English alphabet is _____ than the Arabic alphabet.
> (*True. There are 26 letters in the English alphabet and 28 in the Arabic alphabet.*)
> 5 **expensive** Taxis in Tokyo are _____ than taxis in New York.
> (*True. A 2-mile trip in Tokyo costs approximately $16, but in New York it costs $12.*)
> 6 **dry** The Sahara Desert is _____ than the Atacama Desert.
> (*False. In the Sahara Desert, the average rainfall is 1 inch, and in the Atacama Desert, it's 0.0004 inches.*)
> 7 **far** New Zealand is _____ south than Australia.
> (*True. It's about 1,250 miles southeast of Australia.*)
> 8 **hot** The Earth is _____ than the moon.
> (*False. The temperature of the moon during the day can be 250 degrees Fahrenheit, but the maximum temperature of the Earth is about 140 degrees Fahrenheit.*)

b Play *Quiz Night*. You are the host.

Read sentence 1 to **B**. **B** says "true" or "false."

Tell **B** if he / she is right and give the extra information in parentheses. If **B** is right, he / she wins $100.

Then read sentence 2 for $200, sentence 3 for $400, sentence 4 for $800, etc.

If **B** gets a question wrong, he / she loses all the money but continues to play. The prize starts again from $100.

c Play *Quiz Night* again. You are the contestant. Listen to **B**'s sentences and answer. Who won more money?

10A I'M A TOURIST. HELP! Student A

a Imagine you are an English-speaking tourist in your town (or the nearest big town). **B** lives in the town. Ask **B** six questions about the town using superlative adjectives. Get as much information as you can.

What's the most beautiful square?
I think it's the Jemaa el-Fnaa.

Where is it?
It's in the center, near the Koutoubia Mosque. It has…

1 What's _____ square? (beautiful)
2 What's _____ way to get around? (easy)
3 What's _____ museum? (interesting)
4 What's _____ time of year to visit? (good)
5 What's _____ place to eat typical food? (nice)
6 What's _____ shopping area? (famous)

b Then change roles. **B** is an English-speaking tourist in your town. Listen and answer his / her questions about the town. Explain everything very clearly and give as much information as you can!

10B WHAT ARE YOU GOING TO DO?
Student A

a Ask **B** the questions below. Use *going to*.

Tonight
What / do after class?
/ study English? Why (not)?

Tomorrow
What time / get up tomorrow?
Where / have lunch?

Next weekend
/ go away next weekend? Where to?
What / do on Saturday night?

What are you going to do after class?

b Answer **B**'s questions.

1B WHERE ARE THEY FROM?
Student B

a Look at the chart. Take turns to ask and answer the questions about each person. Answer **A** about person 1. Then ask about person 2.

Where's Ali from?

Where in (country)?

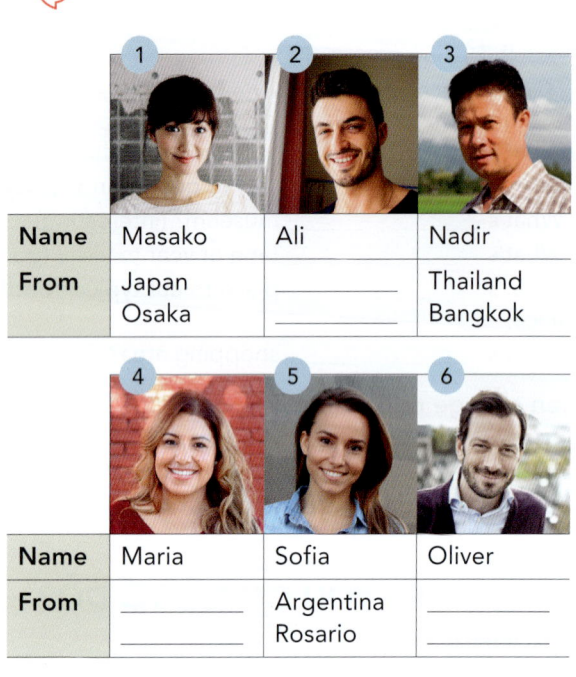

	1	2	3
Name	Masako	Ali	Nadir
From	Japan Osaka	_____	Thailand Bangkok

	4	5	6
Name	Maria	Sofia	Oliver
From	_____	Argentina Rosario	_____

b Repeat for the other people.

1C WHAT'S HIS / HER REAL NAME?
Student B

a Look at list **2**. Read the names of your four people. Two are their real names and two aren't. Cross (✗) the names you think are **not** their real names.

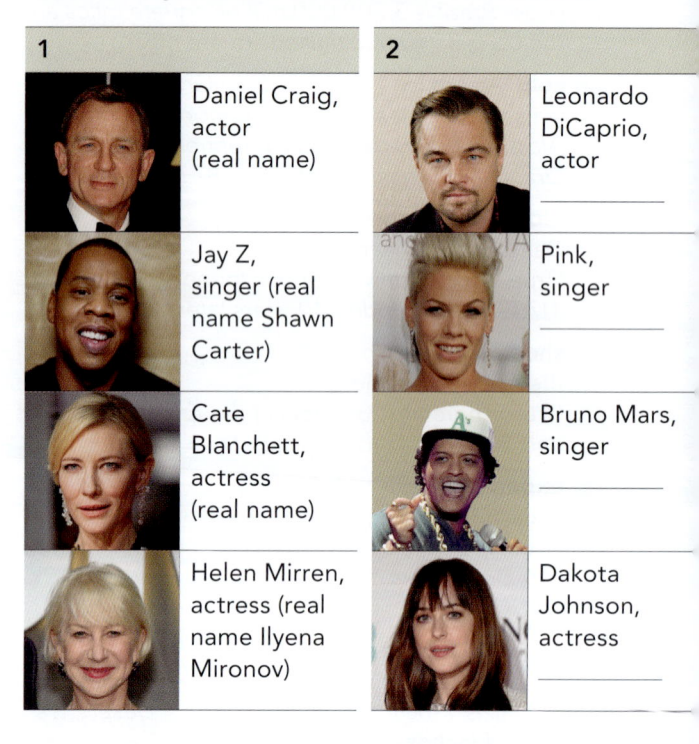

1		2	
	Daniel Craig, actor (real name)		Leonardo DiCaprio, actor _____
	Jay Z, singer (real name Shawn Carter)		Pink, singer _____
	Cate Blanchett, actress (real name)		Bruno Mars, singer _____
	Helen Mirren, actress (real name Ilyena Mironov)		Dakota Johnson, actress _____

b Now look at list **1** and answer **A**'s questions.

c Talk to **A**. Check your answers to **a**. Write the real name next to the photo.

Is _____ his / her real name?

What's his / her real name? How do you spell it?

2A IN, ON, UNDER Student B

a Look at picture 1. Answer **A**'s questions.

Where's the charger? *It's in the…*

b Where are these things? Ask **A**. Draw them in the correct place in picture 2.

file   headphones   magazine   phone
photo   tissues   watch

c Now compare your pictures. Are all the things in the correct place?

2B THE SAME OR DIFFERENT? Student B

a Listen to **A** describe picture 1. Is your picture the same or different? Write **S** or **D** on the picture. Then describe picture 2 to **A**, etc. Find eight differences.

   B *Number 2. They're expensive watches.*
   A *In my picture, they're expensive watches, too. They're the same.*

b Compare your pictures and check.

2C WHAT'S THE MATTER?
Student B

a Have this conversation in pairs. You are **B**.

   A What's the matter?
   B I'm sad.
   A Cheer up.
   B OK.

b Have four more conversations. **A** asks *What's the matter?* Answer with 1 below. **A** responds. Then respond, e.g., *Thanks, OK, Good idea*, etc.

   1 I'm hot.
   2 I'm thirsty.
   3 I'm worried.
   4 I'm stressed.

c Have four more conversations. Ask *What's the matter?* **A** answers. Then choose a phrase below.

   Close the window.   Have a sandwich.   Read a book.   Sit down.

d Have all eight conversations again. Try to do them from memory.

PE2 WHAT'S THE TIME?
Student B

Ask and answer questions with **A** and complete the times on the clocks. Then compare your clocks.

   Clock 2: What's the time?/What time is it?

4C NICOYA Student B

a   Read the article about Nicoya and answer the questions.

   1 Where is Nicoya?
   2 What do people there do?
   3 What do they eat and drink?
   4 What exercise do they do?
   5 When do they get up and go to bed?
   6 How long do they sleep?
   7 What is a *plan de vida*? How does it make a difference in their lives?

b   Tell **A** about life in Nicoya. Use your answers to questions 1–7.

c   Listen to **A** describe life in Ikaria. What do the two places have in common?

Nicoya, Costa Rica

Nicoya is in northwest Costa Rica, near the border with Nicaragua. Most of the people who live there are farmers. In Nicoya people eat small meals. They usually have beans, rice, sweet potatoes, and sometimes a little meat, an egg, or some cheese. They also have some unusual fruits, for example, the *marañón*, a fruit similar to an orange, with a lot of vitamin C. They drink a lot of water – the local water is unusually rich in calcium and magnesium.

They are very active during the day – they work outside, and they walk everywhere, or ride horses. They don't watch television and they don't use the internet, so they go to bed when it's dark and get up when it's light. They sleep well, usually eight hours a night.

All people in Nicoya have something called a *plan de vida*. It means "a reason to get up every morning." This may be work or family, and it's what makes even people who are over 100 still feel necessary.

Glossary
beans

5B SPOT THE DIFFERENCES Student B

You and **A** have the same picture but with eight differences.

a   Listen to **A** describe what is happening in apartments 1–4 and in the yard on the left. What is happening in your picture? Is it the same or different? Tell **A**. Circle the differences.

b   Tell **A** what is happening in apartments 5–8 and in the yard on the right. What is happening in **A**'s picture? Listen and circle the differences.

c   When you finish, compare the two pictures.

5C WHAT DO YOU DO? WHAT ARE YOU DOING NOW? Student B

a Answer **A**'s questions.

b Ask **A** your questions.

Do your parents work? What do they do?
Think of someone in your family. What do you think they are doing now?
What kind of TV shows do you like?
What TV shows are you watching right now?
Is it raining now?
Does it rain a lot at this time of year?

8A POLICE INTERVIEW Student B

Work in pairs with another **B**. You are friends. Last night you met, had dinner, and went to the movies. There was a robbery last night. **A** and **A** are police officers. You are their suspects, and they want to interview you separately. If you both tell exactly the same story, you are innocent!

a **B**s prepare your story. Answer these questions. Think of more details, e.g., *What did you eat and drink? What movie was it?*

What time / Where did you meet?
What time / Where did you have dinner?
What time / Where did you go to the movies?
What did you do after the movies?
What time did you get home?

b Answer **A**'s questions. (Your partner answers the other **A**.)

c Did you and your friend tell the same story?

8B IS THERE...? ARE THERE...? Student B

a Answer **A**'s questions with *Yes, there is / are.* or *No, there isn't / aren't.*

b Make questions with *Is there a...?* or *Are there any...?* to ask **A**.

Is there a TV in your kitchen?

1 TV in your kitchen
2 pictures in your classroom
3 park near your house
4 mirror in your living room
5 plants in your hall
6 shelves in your bedroom

8C A HAUNTED ROOM Student B

a Some people say there are haunted hotel rooms all around the world. Look at the photo of a haunted hotel room in the UK for one minute. Try to remember what's in the room.

b Close your book. Answer **A**'s questions.

c Ask **A** the questions.

/ any plants or flowers in the room? (*No, there weren't.*)
/ a table between the armchairs? (*Yes, there was.*)
How many windows / ? (*There were two.*)
What / at the end of the bed? (*There was a TV.*)
/ a sofa? (*No, there wasn't.*)
/ a phone? Where was it? (*Yes, there was. It was on the table next to the bed.*)

9C QUIZ NIGHT Student B

a Complete your sentences 1–8 with the comparative form of the **bold** adjectives.

> 1 **old** The Great Wall of China is _____ than the pyramids in Egypt.
> (*False. The pyramids are about 4,500 years old, but the Great Wall of China was only finished 600 years ago.*)
>
> 2 **small** Monaco is _____ than San Marino.
> (*True. Monaco is .77 square miles, but San Marino is 23 square miles.*)
>
> 3 **high** The mountains on Earth are _____ than the mountains on Mars.
> (*False. Olympus Mons on Mars is about 15 miles high, but Everest is only about 5.6 miles high.*)
>
> 4 **big** China is _____ than Canada.
> (*False. Canada is 3,900,000 square miles and China is about 3,700,000 square miles.*)
>
> 5 **popular** In the UK, coffee is _____ than tea. (*False. On average, the British drink 165,000,000 cups of tea a day and 70,000,000 cups of coffee.*)
>
> 6 **large** A gigabyte is _____ than a megabyte.
> (*True. A megabyte is 1,024 kilobytes and a gigabyte is 1,024 megabytes.*)
>
> 7 **warm** The Mediterranean Sea is _____ than the Red Sea.
> (*False. The average temperature of the Mediterranean Sea is 66 degrees Fahrenheit, but the average temperature of the Red Sea is 82 degrees Fahrenheit.*)
>
> 8 **busy** Heathrow Airport in London is _____ than Atlanta Airport in the US.
> (*False. 100 million people a year travel through Atlanta, but only 70 million go through Heathrow.*)

b Play *Quiz Night*. You are the contestant.

A reads you his / her sentence 1. Say if it's true or false.

A tells you if you are right and gives you extra information. If you are right, you win $100.

A then reads you his / her sentence 2 for $200, sentence 3 for $400, sentence 4 for $800, etc.

If you get a question wrong, you lose all the money but continue to play. The prize starts again from $100.

c Play *Quiz Night* again. You are the host. Use your sentences 1–8. Who won more money?

10A I'M A TOURIST. HELP! Student B

a **A** is an English-speaking tourist in your town. Listen and answer his / her questions about the town. Explain everything very clearly and give as much information as you can!

b Then change roles. Imagine you are an English-speaking tourist in your town (or the nearest big town). **A** lives in the town. Ask **A** six questions about the town using superlative adjectives. Get as much information as you can.

What's the oldest building?
  I think it's the cathedral.
How old is it?
  I'm not sure. About 500 years, maybe?

1 What's _____ building? (old)
2 What's _____ place to go for a day trip? (nice)
3 What's _____ place to go to with children? (good)
4 What's _____ souvenir? (typical)
5 What's _____ area to go at night? (popular)
6 Where do you have _____ view? (beautiful)

10B WHAT ARE YOU GOING TO DO? Student B

a Answer **A**'s questions.

b Ask **A** the questions below. Use *going to*.

Tonight
What / do after dinner?
What time / go to bed?

Tomorrow
/ go to work (or school) tomorrow?
What / do in the evening?

Next weekend
/ go out on Friday night? What / do?
What / do on Sunday?

What are you going to do after dinner?

Writing

1 COMPLETING A FORM

> 🔍 **Capital letters**
> In English, these words start with a CAPITAL letter.
> - names and last names   **M**elissa **R**ogers
> - continents, countries, nationalities, and languages   **A**sia, **C**hina, **C**hinese
> - towns and cities   **N**ew **Y**ork
> - days of the week   **M**onday
> - the first word in a sentence   **H**er father is from Vancouver.
> - the pronoun I   She's Russian and **I**'m Mexican.

a   Read the information box.

b   Complete the online form with your information.

VISIT AND SHORT STAY
Visa application form for a visitor or student

About you
First name   Last name (Family name)

Mr. / Mrs. / Ms.   Date of birth
                                        M M   D D   Y Y Y Y

Gender   male   female
Marital status
    married   single   divorced   separated
Nationality
Place of birth: country   town / city

Contact information   Home address and zip code

Email address
Phone number:
home (landline)   cell
Passport / Identity card number

c   Write this paragraph again with CAPITAL letters where necessary.

> my name's omar. i'm from lima in peru, and i speak spanish, french, and a little english. my teacher is american. her name's kate. my english classes are on tuesdays and thursdays.

d   Write a similar paragraph about you. Check that the capital letters are correct.

⤴ p.11

2 A PERSONAL PROFILE

a   Read Jill's profile. Do you have similar interests?

netlinks

Jill Mauer

MY PROFILE

Hometown
I'm from Chicago, but I live in Los Angeles.

Occupation
I'm a web designer. I work for an international company.

Languages
I speak English and a little Spanish.

INTERESTS

Music   I like pop and rap music. I don't like opera or jazz.

Movies   I like action movies. I love the old James Bond movies, e.g., *From Russia with Love*.

TV   I don't watch a lot of TV, but I like comedy shows.

Sport   I don't watch basketball or other sports. I go to the gym after work.

> 🔍 **and, but, or**
> **and**   I speak English **and** a little Spanish.
>   I like pop **and** rap music.
> **but**   I'm from Chicago, **but** I live in Los Angeles.
>   I don't watch TV very much, **but** I like comedy shows.
> **or**   I don't like opera **or** jazz.
>   I don't watch basketball **or** other sports.
> **e.g.** e.g. = for example. We often use it when we write informally.
>   I like pop music, **e.g.**, Ariana Grande.

b   Read the information box. Then write a profile of yourself. Use the same headings (Hometown, Music, etc.). Attach a photo if you can. Use *and*, *but*, and *or* to join your ideas together.

c   Check your profile. Make sure you use *and*, *but*, and *or* correctly.

⤴ p.27

Go online for more Writing practice   113

3 AN ARTICLE

a Read Cristina's article. Find her answers to questions 1–4.

1. What's your favorite day of the week? Why?
2. What do you usually do in the morning?
3. Where do you have lunch? Who with? What do you usually do after lunch?
4. What do you usually do in the evening?

> **after and then**
> Use *after* + another word, e.g., **after** lunch, **after** work, **after** that, etc.
>
> Use *then* to say what happens next, e.g., I get up and **then** I have breakfast.

b Look at the highlighted words to check that you understand them, and read the information box. Then use them to complete the sentences below.

1. Jack usually gets up at 7:30. _____ he takes a shower.
2. _____ lunch, I often sleep for half an hour.
3. She always takes a bath _____ she goes to bed.
4. _____ the week, I work _____ 9:00 _____ 5:00.
5. I get home at about 7:30, take the dog for a walk, and after _____, I have dinner.
6. We usually watch TV _____ it's time to go to bed.

c Plan an article called *My favorite day*. Plan four paragraphs. Make notes to answer questions 1–4 in **a**. What other information could you include to make the article interesting?

d Now write your article. Choose the ideas you want to use. Don't forget to use some of the highlighted words to link together your ideas.

e Check your article. Make sure you use the highlighted words correctly.

f Show your article to another student. Can you find one thing in your partner's article that is the same for you?

← p.33

My favorite day

March 24 #favorite#weekend#family#food

My favorite day of the week is Saturday because it's the first day of the weekend!

I get up very early during the week, so on Saturday it's nice to get up late, and I always stay in bed until about 10:30. Then I usually go shopping with a friend. In Mexico, stores are sometimes closed on Sundays, so Saturday is the only day for shopping. We don't always buy something, but we have fun just looking.

I often have lunch with my mother and my brother. It's great because my mom is a really good cook – she always makes things we like, and my brother and I have time to talk about our week. After lunch, I sometimes study from about 4:00 to 6:00, especially if I have exams.

In the evening, I usually go out with my friends. We often go to the movies, and after that, we have a pizza or tacos. I never go to bed before 1:00, or sometimes later.

4 POSTING ON SOCIAL MEDIA

a Nick is on vacation in Los Angeles. He posts news and photos from his vacation. Read his posts and match them to the photos.

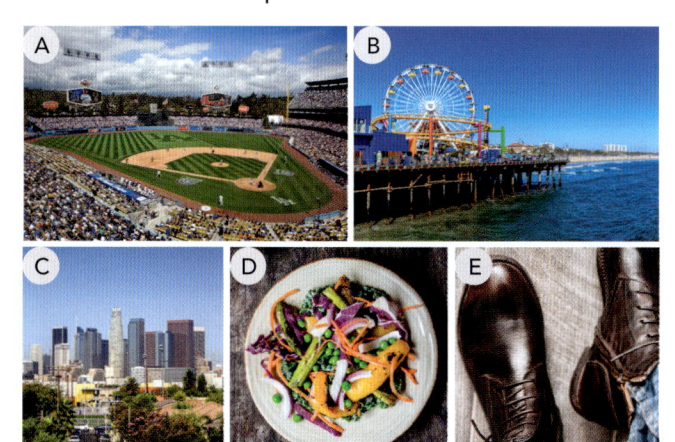

A   B   C   D   E

1
Thur June 8
Do you like my new boots? They're from The Grove, and I'm wearing them for the first time. I love the fashion in California! 11:10 am

2
Thur June 8
I'm sitting at a café in Venice Beach and watching the amazing street artists. It's cold for June, but it's sunny! Venice Beach is full of tourists (like me!). 2:15 pm

3
Fri June 9
Beautiful weather today – the sun's shining! I'm on a bus tour of the Hollywood Hills – great views of downtown LA. 10:30 am

4
Fri June 9
I'm having a typical Californian lunch at an outdoor café – a salad and a smoothie. It's OK, but I prefer a hamburger and French fries! 1:20 pm

5
Fri June 9
I'm at Dodger Stadium with tickets for the Dodgers – Giants game! I usually root for the Cubs, but I'm rooting for the Dodgers today! 7:15 pm

b Imagine you are on vacation in your country or abroad. Plan four posts or messages of about 30 words. Think about the following:

Where are you? What are you doing?
Who are you with? What's the weather like?

c Write your posts. Make sure they are about 30 words.

d Check your posts. Make sure you use the simple present and present continuous correctly.

➜ p.43

5 AN INFORMAL EMAIL

a Read the email. Who do you think Stefan is?

From: Carmen <carmensanchez@hotmail.com>
To: Stefan <stefan7541200@moebius.ch>
Subject: Hi from Buenos Aires

Hi Stefan,

My name's Carmen. I'm 19, and I'm from Mendoza, in Argentina. I'm a receptionist at a hotel. I'm studing English becuse I need it for my job.

I live with my parents and my brother and sister. My father is an arkitect and my mother works in a clothing store. My brother and sister are at school.

I don't have very much free time because I work six days a week. I usualy go shoping on my day off. In the evening, I like seeing freinds or listening to music. I really like hip hop. What kind of music do you like?

Please write soon.

Best wishes,
Carmen

b Cover the email. What personal information can you remember about Carmen? What does she say about her family and her free time? Look at the email again and check.

c Look at the six underlined spelling mistakes. Can you spell the words correctly?

d Plan a similar email. Make notes about the following information.

Paragraph 1: Your name, age, and where you are from. Say what you do, and why you are studying English.
Paragraph 2: Who you live with. Say something about them.
Paragraph 3: What you like doing in your free time.

> **Informal emails**
> **Beginning:** *Hi* + name
> **Middle:** Use contractions, e.g., *I'm from Mendoza.*
> **End:** *Best wishes* or *Love* (for a good friend)

e Write your email. Use your notes and the language in the information box.

f Check your email for spelling mistakes.

> To practice your English, you can write to a friend in another country. You can find "pen pal" websites on the internet.

➜ p.51

Go online for more Writing practice   115

6 DESCRIBING YOUR HOME

a Read the website and the description of an apartment for rent. Imagine you want to go on vacation to Hermosa Beach, California for a week. Would you like to stay there?

b Number the information in the order it comes in the description.

- ___ Details about some of the rooms
- ___ How far it is from downtown Los Angeles
- ___ What floor the apartment is on
- ___ What rooms there are
- ___ What places or services there are nearby
- ___ What you can see from the apartment
- ___ Where it is

c What adjectives does the writer use to describe…?

1 the street 2 the kitchen 3 the view
4 the community swimming pool

> 🔍 **so**
>
> There's a sofa bed in the study, **so** you can use it as an extra bedroom.
>
> We can use *so* to express a result or consequence, e.g.,
> I was very tired, **so** I went to bed early.
> My office is near my house, **so** I walk to work.

d Read the information box. Then plan a description of your house or apartment for the website. Make notes on the topics in **b**.

e Write your description.

f Check your description. Make sure you use *there is / there are* correctly. Show it to another student. Can you find one thing in your partner's description that is the same as yours?

⬅ p.65

| | Search | Bookings | Contact | BECOME A HOST |

List your home

Home type	Bedrooms	Bathrooms	City	Rent
Apartment	2	1	Hermosa Beach	$125 per night

Summary

My apartment is on a quiet street in Hermosa Beach, California. It's on the second floor. There are two bedrooms, two bathrooms, a living room, a study, and a light, pretty kitchen. The kitchen is small, but it has a stove, a refrigerator, and a dishwasher. There's a sofa bed in the study, so you can use it as an extra bedroom. The bedrooms have a great view of the Pacific Ocean — you can see the sun set over the ocean in the evening. There isn't a yard, but the apartment building has a beautiful community swimming pool. The apartment is a five-minute walk from stores, restaurants, and a bus stop. It's also about a 30-minute car ride from downtown Los Angeles.

7 A FORMAL EMAIL

a Read the advertisement and Hannah's email, and complete it with the words in the list.

about   are   confirm   Dear   double   from
hope   Sincerely   would

b You booked a room last night at The Bay House. Plan a similar email. Think about these things.

Are you traveling with someone or alone?
What kind of room(s) did you book?
How many nights did you book for? Which dates?
How are you planning to get there?
When are you planning to arrive?
Do you want to have dinner there? When?

> 🔍 **Formal emails** (e.g., to a hotel, a language school, etc.)
>
> **Beginning:**
> *Dear Mr. / Mrs. / Ms.* _____ (+ last name),
> *Dear Sir or Madam* (if you don't know the person's name),
>
> Use a comma (,) not a colon (:), e.g.,
> *Dear Mr. Brown,* **NOT** ~~Dear Mr. Brown:~~
>
> **Middle:**
> Don't use contractions, e.g.,
> *I would like to make a reservation* **NOT** ~~I'd like to...~~
>
> **End:**
> *Sincerely,*
> (your first name + last name)

c Read the information box. Then write your email. Check that there aren't any contractions.

⬅ p.81

🔍 Search   🏠 Bookings   💬 Contact

The Bay House
Bed and Breakfast in Bath, Maine

| Overview | Photos | Reviews |

Gary and Rebecca Brewster and their family welcome you to their 100-year-old home in a small town in Maine. Five double bedrooms, three singles, and a family suite. TV, wi-fi. Breakfast 7:30–9:30. Dinner optional. We can pick you up from the Portland airport.

Places to stay in Bath

---

[1]_____ Mr. and Mrs. Brewster,

I booked a [2]_____ room and a single room on your website this morning for three nights, [3]_____ June 24th to June 27th.

We [4]_____ planning to arrive by car at [5]_____ 5:00 in the afternoon on the 24th. Is there a place where we can park near your house?

My husband and I and our son [6]_____ also like to have dinner at The Bay House on the evening of the 24th. My son is vegetarian – I [7]_____ that is not a problem. Could you please [8]_____ that this will be possible?

[9]_____,

Hannah Cho

Listening

🔊 **1.15**

1 A A turkey and cheese sandwich, please.
   B That's $9.15.
2 A So, Anna, your classes are on Tuesday and Thursday mornings.
   B What? Sorry?
3 The JetBlue flight to Burbank is now boarding at gate number 5.
4 A Where to?
   B 16 Manchester Road, please.
5 A Here's your key. Room 12.
   B Thank you.
6 A Here we are.
   B Oh, no! It's closed.
   A Look, it says "Closed on Monday"!

🔊 **1.23**

1 A Hi. Where are you from?
   B We're from Fortaleza, in Brazil.
   A OK. Good luck to the Brazilian team!
   B Thank you!
2 A Hello. I'm Mike from *USA News*. Where are you from?
   B I'm from Australia.
   A Are you from Sydney?
   B No, I'm not. I'm from Cairns.
   A Where's Cairns? Is it near Sydney?
   B No, it isn't. It's north. Am I on TV?
   A Yes, you are.
   B Wow!
3 A Hi. Are you American?
   B No, we aren't. We're from Japan.
   A Oh, sorry!

🔊 **1.30**

1 Announcer The 6:12 train to Poughkeepsie, making stops at Harlem, Beacon, New Hamburg, and Poughkeepsie is departing from track 30.
   A That's our train. Track 30. Come on.
   B OK. Let's go.
2 A Excuse me! How far is it to Austin?
   B It's about 40 miles.
   A Thanks a lot.
3 A Just one more set. Come on!
   B 15–love.
   A Great serve!
4 A Will all passengers on Delta flight 1182 to Portland please go to gate 16 immediately.
   B Gate 16. Is that our flight?
   C No, it's to Portland, Maine, not Portland, Oregon.
5 A How much for this?
   B Two slices of pizza, a salad, and a soda. That's $17.
6 A What's your address?
   B It's 80 Park Street.
   A Sorry?
   B 80, eight–oh. Park Street.
7 A OK, be quiet, please. Open your books to page 90.
   B What page?
   A Page 90.

🔊 **1.41**

Mark Hello? Hello? Can you hear me?
Micaela Hi, yes, fine. I can hear you.
Mark Good! I'm Mark, from English House Language School.
Micaela Hi, Mark.
Mark OK, can I check your information first?
Micaela Yes, of course.
Mark What's your first name?
Micaela Micaela.
Mark How do you spell it?
Micaela M-I-C-A-E-L-A.
Mark M-I-C-A-E-L-A – is that right?
Micaela Yes, that's right.
Mark And what's your last name?
Micaela Vazquez.
Mark Vazquez. Is that V-A-S…?
Micaela No, it's V-A-Z-Q-U-E-Z.
Mark V-A-Z-Q-U-E-Z. OK. And how old are you?
Micaela I'm 20.
Mark Where are you from?
Micaela I'm from Argentina.
Mark Where in Argentina?
Micaela From Buenos Aires.
Mark What's your address?
Micaela It's Florida one six five.
Mark Florida's the street? Number one six five?
Micaela Yes.
Mark What's your zip code?
Micaela Sorry?
Mark You know, the zip code?
Micaela Ah yes. It's C- one zero zero five A-A-C.
Mark C- one zero zero five A-A-C. Great. What's your email address?
Micaela It's m dot vazquez at mail dot com.
Mark And what's your phone number?
Micaela My cell phone or my home phone, my landline?
Mark Both – cell and landline.
Micaela My cell is one one, one five, eight nine three four, five five six eight.
Mark One one, one five, eight nine three four, five six eight. Great. And your landline?
Micaela Five four, one one, six zero two three, five four four two.
Mark Five four, one one, six zero two three, five four four two.
Micaela That's right.
Mark OK, that's great. So, what do you do, Micaela?
Micaela I'm in college. I'm a nursing student…

🔊 **1.45**

Snoop Dogg isn't his real name. His real name is Calvin Cordozar Broadus. He's American.
Shakira is her real name. Her full name is Shakira Isabel Mebarak Ripoll. She's from Colombia.

🔊 **2.5**

1 On my desk, I have my computer. I have some pens and pieces of paper. I have a lamp, and a photo of my family. Oh, and a phone. It's very neat.
2 In my study, I have a desk, a table, and two chairs. I have a lot of books and a big dictionary on the desk – it isn't very neat! And I have a map of the world on the wall.
3 I have a lot of things in my bag. I have my phone. I have the charger for my phone. I have my sunglasses, tissues. And I have my house keys and my change purse.

🔊 **2.15**

Lisa The Highland Hotel's 20 miles from here. Let's go there.
John 20 miles? No problem.
Lisa John! Slow down!
John Oh no!…Here she comes.
Police Officer Good evening. Turn off the engine, please. Thank you.
John What's the problem, officer?
Police Officer The problem? Well, 70 miles an hour is the problem. That's very, very fast. The speed limit on this road is 50 miles an hour. Can I see your driver's license?
John 70? Oh. Uh, I'm very sorry, officer.
Police Officer Ah, what a beautiful baby! What's his name?
Lisa Henry. He's *very* tired, officer. And it's 20 miles to our hotel.
Police Officer Well…OK…go to your hotel. But please slow down.
John Yes – thank you, officer.
Police Officer Goodbye, sir, ma'am. Goodbye, Henry!

🔊 **3.14**

Part 1
Host And now your favorite radio show, *His Job, Her Job*.
Host Good evening and welcome again to the jobs quiz *His Job, Her Job*. And our team tonight is David, a teacher…
David Hello.
Host Kate, who's unemployed…
Kate Hi.
Host …and Lorna, who's a writer.
Lorna Good evening.
Host And our first couple tonight is…
Alex Alex.
Host And?
Sue Sue.
Host Welcome to the show, Alex and Sue. OK team, you have one minute to ask Alex questions about his job and then one minute to ask Sue about her job, starting now. Let's have your first question for Alex.
David Hi, Alex. Do you work in an office?
Alex No, I don't.
Lorna Do you work in the evening?
Alex It depends. Yes, sometimes.
Kate Do you make things?
Alex No, I don't.
Lorna Do you wear a uniform or special clothes?
Alex Uh, yes – I wear special clothes.
Kate Do you drive for your job?
Alex No, I don't.
Lorna Do you work on a team?
Alex Yes, I do. With ten other people.
Kate Do you have any special qualifications?
Alex Qualifications? No, I don't.
David Do you speak foreign languages?
Alex No, only English.
Host You only have time for one more question, team…
David Uh, do you travel?
Alex Yes, I do. On weekends. Well, not every weekend…
Host Your time's up.

🔊 **3.15**

Part 2
Host Now team, you have a minute to ask Sue about her job.
Kate Hello, Sue. Do you work outside?

Sue It depends. Outside and inside.
Lorna Do you work on the weekend?
Sue Yes, I do.
David Do you work with the public?
Sue No, I don't.
Kate Do you get vacation time?
Sue No, I don't. I never get vacation time.
Kate Do you work at night?
Sue Sometimes. It depends.
Lorna Do you earn a lot of money?
Sue No, nothing! I don't have a salary.
David Do you like your job?
Sue Yes, I do! I love it.
Host That's time. OK, team…

🔊 3.17

Becca He's beautiful. Is he a fox terrier? Sorry, he or she?
Dave She. Yes, she's a fox terrier. Her name's Dolly. And your dog?
Becca He's a Labrador.
Dave What's his name?
Becca Barry. Barry come here!
Dave Dolly. Here. Stop it.
Becca I think Barry likes her.
Dave Yes! Sorry, I'm Dave. What's your name?
Becca Becca. Hi.
Dave Nice to meet you, Becca! How old is Barry?
Becca Uh…He's, uh, two. And Dolly?
Dave Uh…The same. Hey, Dolly! Come back!

🔊 3.20

Becca Hi, Dave.
Dave Hi, Becca. Hi, Barry! So nice to see you both again!
Becca What a cute restaurant. I really like it. And look at all the dogs.
Dave I know, right! It has good food, too…for people and for dogs!
Becca Mmm. Sit Barry. Good boy. Uh, where's Dolly?
Dave She isn't here. Uh, Becca, I need to tell you something. Dolly isn't my dog. She's my friend's dog. I sometimes help and take her for a walk.
Becca You don't have a dog?
Dave No. Uh…I don't like dogs very much. And my apartment's so small. I'm so sorry. I know you love dogs.
Becca Phew! Don't worry! Barry isn't my dog either! He's my sister's dog. I like dogs, but… in fact…I have two cats. How do you feel about cats?
Dave I love cats – in fact, I prefer cats to dogs! Let's sit down and order lunch.
Becca Great! So, what's good here?
Dave The spaghetti carbonara is fantastic—and so is the homemade chocolate ice cream!
Becca Yum! All for me this time!

🔊 4.6

Anna Who's that?
Grace That's my boyfriend, Mark.
Anna He's good-looking. How old is he?
Grace 26.
Anna What does he do?
Grace He's a medical student. He finishes this year – I hope!
Anna Where does he study?
Grace At Indiana University School of Medicine.
Anna Does he like it?
Grace Yes, he loves it. And this is my sister Celia and her kids.
Anna Ah. She looks like you.
Grace Yes, she does.
Anna How old is she?
Grace She's 35.

Anna How old are the kids?
Grace Carlos, the little one, is two, and Daniel, the older one's, uh, six, I think. They live in Chile, so I don't see them very often.
Anna Is that another sister?
Grace No, she's my sister-in-law, Miriam. She's married to my brother Tim.
Anna What does Tim do?
Grace He's a lawyer, and Miriam's a teacher.
Anna How old are their children?
Grace Alex is four, and Helen's 13 months now.
Anna They're so cute!…So how about you and Mark? When's the wedding?
Grace Wedding! No, thanks! I'm too young!

🔊 4.11

Interviewer What time do you get up in the morning?
Darius I get up at about seven-thirty.
Interviewer How do you feel when you get up?
Darius I know seven-thirty isn't that early, but it's early for me, and I usually feel tired and in a little bit of a bad mood.
Interviewer Do you have breakfast?
Darius Absolutely. I have cereal and milk, and some bread with honey or jam. I love honey!
Interviewer Do you walk to school?
Darius No, it's very far away. I go to school by Tube. I usually get to school about eight twenty. I like to be early.
Interviewer What time does your first class start?
Darius It starts at nine. I have four or sometimes five classes before lunch.
Interviewer Where do you have lunch?
Darius I usually have lunch at school at about one o'clock. I know people usually say that school food is terrible, but actually at my school the food is really good.
Interviewer And after lunch?
Darius We start classes again at 1:45. I usually have two or three classes in the afternoon.
Interviewer What time does school finish?
Darius At 4:15. But I don't go home then. I stay at school to do extra things – I study in the library or play music.
Interviewer What kind of music?
Darius Well, I sing in the school choir on Tuesdays, and on Thursdays, I play percussion in the orchestra. I love music – it's my main hobby.
Interviewer So what time do you usually get home?
Darius At about six o'clock.
Interviewer What's the first thing you do?
Darius I take a shower, and then I have dinner. And then, of course, homework.
Interviewer How much homework do you have?
Darius Two or three hours. It's my last year at school and I have my A levels this summer. I need to do really well to get into a good university.
Interviewer Do you watch TV in the evening?
Darius No, never. I don't have time. When I finish my homework, I practice the piano and then I go to bed.
Interviewer What time do you go to bed?
Darius At about ten-thirty. I'm usually so tired I go to sleep right away. All I really do these days is study, eat, and sleep.
Interviewer So no social media or anything like that?
Darius Well…I do spend a little bit of time on Facebook. But not much, I promise!

🔊 5.2

Amy 12:30. In a long line outside the Conference Center in Portland.

Guard Remember, you need ID. You can't come in if you don't have ID.
Amy Here's my passport.
Guard Thanks "Amy Jones." Yup, that's you! OK, come in. Next, please!
Amy 12:45. In the waiting area with 350 other singers!
Organizer 1 OK Amy, sit here and wait until we call your name.
Amy Thanks.
Organizer 1 Are you here for the audition, too?
Friend No, I'm not. I'm Amy's friend. Can I wait with her?
Organizer 1 Yeah, sure.
Friend Thanks.
Amy Let's sit here. I'm so nervous…
Organizer 1 Mike Smith, Pat Jones, Tony Cash, come with me. This way.
Amy Good luck!
Amy 4:00. Three hours later! My turn at last!
Organizer 2 Amy Jones, Naomi Williams, Justin Elliot? Can you come with me, please? It's your turn now.
Amy Oh my goodness! It's my turn.
Friend Good luck, Amy! You can do it!
Amy Excuse me. Can my friend come with me?
Organizer 2 No, she can't. She can wait there. And you can't take your bag into the audition. Leave it with your friend.
Amy OK.
Amy 4:15. In the audition, with three judges. Really nervous!
Judge Amy…Jones? What's your song?
Amy One Day.
Judge We can't hear you. Is the microphone on?
Amy Sorry…Sorry. Can you hear me now?
Judge Yes, that's fine.
Amy My song's One Day.
Judge Can you start, please?
Amy Oh no! I can't remember the first line.
Judge Take your time.
Amy I'm OK now!

🔊 5.11

Woman Oh, hi Paul. Jack, it's Paul, from next door. Come in! We're having a party. It's my birthday.
Paul Oh! Uh, Happy Birthday!
Woman Thanks. Would you like a drink?
Paul Actually, I want to talk to you about the noise.
Woman Sorry?
Paul The NOISE. It's very noisy.
Woman Yes. We're having a great time! Do you want a soda? Or a glass of iced tea?
Paul Oh, well, yes, OK. A soda, please.
Woman Here you are. Come and meet our friends. Hey, everyone, say hello to Paul. He's our neighbor.
All Hello, Paul.
Paul Hello.
Woman Do you want to dance, Paul?

🔊 5.15

A Good afternoon. How can I help you?
B Hello. I have a reservation for two nights.
A Your name?
B Carter.
A Carter. Here we are. Can you sign here, please?…Here's your key card. You're in room 212, on the second floor.

🔊 5.16

1 **A** Can I help you?
  B Yes, I'd like a latte, please.
  A Regular or large?
  B Large, please.
  A To have here or to go?

B To have here.
   A That's $3.40, please.
   B Here you are. $3.40.
2 A Where are my car keys? I can't find them anywhere.
   B I don't know. In your jacket pocket?
   A No, they aren't there.
   B How about on the hall table?
   A No.
   B Are you sure you don't have them?
   A Absolutely sure.
   B Look in the living room.
3 A Oh no, it's 20 minutes late.
   B Is there a waiting room somewhere? It's really cold here on the platform.
   A No, I don't think so.
   B What time is it now?
   A 6:15. We can take the 6:20, but it's a slow train.
   B No, let's wait then.
4 OK, come on everyone, out here. Stand together under the tree. OK! Are you ready? Carole, I can't see you. Can you stand next to Jim? OK, ready? Say cheese!
5 A …So, Mr. Bartlett, do you have any questions you'd like to ask?
   B Uh, yes. On the website, it says the hours are from 10 to 6. What about the weekends?
   A The hours are 10 to 6 on the weekends too, but you get paid overtime on Sundays. Saturday counts as a normal day. But if you work on a Saturday, you have a weekday free. The contract clearly says five days a week, with possibilities of overtime.
   B Oh right.

🔊 5.19

The best (or worst) thing about the weather in Chicago is that it's always changing. It can be very hot or very cold. In the summer, it's mostly sunny and sometimes cloudy, with temperatures of about 84 degrees. And of course, sometimes it rains.
In the winter, the temperature is usually between 29 and 14 degrees. It can be below freezing (32 degrees) for weeks at a time. Brrr! It snows about 38 inches a year.
In the spring and the fall, the weather is very changeable. You can have all four seasons in one week. It can be cold and snowing on Monday, cool and foggy on Tuesday, and warm and sunny on Wednesday. I always tell tourists to bring a winter coat, gloves, sunglasses, sandals, and an umbrella when they visit Chicago in the spring and the fall—that way they are prepared for any kind of weather!
But one thing that isn't always true about Chicago is the wind. Even though Chicago's nickname is "The Windy City," it's not always windy there. In fact, Boston has more windy days a year than Chicago. Some people think Chicago's nickname is from politicians who talk too much!

🔊 6.5

Part 3 Walid walks for five days through the mountains. The sun shines, and at night it's very cold. Then one evening, he finds the palace. The prince welcomes him and gives him food and drink, and a comfortable bed. But Walid can't sleep. He's thinking about the 1,000 gold coins.
The next morning, he says to the prince, "I want to say thank you to you. Please have this silver ring. It's my mother's."
The prince is very happy. "This is a beautiful ring," he says. "Thank you. Let me give you something in return."
He gives Walid a box. "Don't open this until you get home," he says. "Be careful with it. It's very, very valuable."

Walid runs through the mountains, and after three days, he arrives home.
"Where's my silver ring?" shouts his mother.
"Don't worry about your ring!" says Walid. "Look at this!"
Hassan and their mother watch as he opens the box. Inside he finds…

🔊 6.14

1 A Hi, Kim. Do you want come to the theater with me this Saturday?
   B Saturday? I can't – it's my brother's 21st birthday! We're having a big party at my parents' house.
   A Oh, that sounds great! Have a wonderful time – and say "Happy Birthday" from me!
2 A Are you in the office next week?
   B No, I'm on vacation.
   A Where are you going?
   B Australia!
   A Lucky you! When do you get back?
   B On the 30th.
   A Wow! That's a long vacation.
   B Yeah, three weeks! I can't wait.
3 A You drink a lot of coffee!
   B Yes, this is my fifth this morning.
   A It's not good for you, you know.
   B I know, but I can't wake up without it.
4 A Where's the restaurant?
   B It's not far. It's on the corner of Park Avenue and 53rd.
   A Great. See you there at 7:30.
5 A Good morning. I'm here to see Maria Diaz. My name's Brian Sanders.
   B Just a moment, sir, I'll call her…Hi, Maria. There's a Mr. Sanders here to see you…OK, sir. Could you sign in here? Great. You can go right up. She's on the sixth floor. The elevators are over there.
   A Thank you.

🔊 7.1

This painting is a self-portrait by the Dutch painter Vincent van Gogh.
Van Gogh was born in the Netherlands on March 30th, 1853. His parents weren't poor – his father was a church minister, and his mother was an artist. Van Gogh's first job was in his uncle's company, selling paintings, but later he was a teacher, and finally a painter. We only really know what he looked like because of his many self-portraits. Only three photographs of him exist, and they are all from when he was young. This portrait is from his time in Arles in the South of France, in 1888, when he was 35. He was very poor, but he was happy because of the beautiful light and colors there. This portrait was a present for his friend, the painter Paul Gauguin. Gauguin and van Gogh were together in Arles for a month. Van Gogh was not strong mentally, and the relationship between them was difficult. After a big fight, van Gogh cut off his ear, and was in a mental hospital for some time. He died on July 29th, 1890. He was only 37 years old. His paintings weren't popular during his lifetime, and he was never rich or famous. But today, people think that Vincent van Gogh is one of the greatest painters in the world, and his paintings, like *Sunflowers* and *The Starry Night*, sell for millions of dollars.

🔊 7.6

Edward Gamson lives in Washington, D.C. A few years ago, he and his friend Lowell decided to go on vacation to Granada in Spain. Edward wanted to visit the Alhambra, a famous palace. They researched flights online and booked tickets for the two of them. Their tickets were expensive, but Edward decided to spend extra money on first-class seats. On the day of their flight, they arrived at Dulles Airport and parked their car in the long-term parking lot. Edward and Lowell checked in for the first part of their trip. They traveled safely to London, changed planes at Heathrow Airport, and settled into their second flight. Twenty minutes into the flight, Lowell looked at Edward with surprise.

🔊 7.7

Lowell Edward, I think we're going west and not south to Granada.
Edward Hmm. Let's ask the flight attendant. Excuse me, why aren't we going south to Spain?
Flight Attendant Spain? We're not going to Spain. We're going to Grenada, the island in the Caribbean.
Edward The Caribbean? But I booked tickets to to Granada, Spain.
Flight Attendant Let me check your ticket. Oh, I see. I'm really sorry, but your ticket isn't for Granada, Spain. It's for Grenada, in the West Indies.
Edward No, it can't be.
Flight Attendant I'm very sorry, but it is. Look, it clearly says Grenada – it's spelled correctly.
Lowell I don't believe it. Edward, did you check the airport when you booked?
Edward Well, no, I didn't. I was in vacation mode and I didn't think about it.
Lowell Ugh! What are we going to do?
Flight Attendant When we land, you need to book new tickets to fly from Grenada in the Caribbean to Granada in Spain.

🔊 7.17

Friend What was your best ever New Year's Eve? One you always remember?
Denisa Oh, definitely 2014, when I was in Rio.
Friend Who were you with?
Denisa I was with my boyfriend Marcelo, who's Brazilian.
Friend Why was it so special?
Denisa Well, Brazil has special traditions for New Year's Eve, and they were all new for me. For example, it's a Brazilian tradition to wear white clothes for New Year's Eve because white is a symbol of peace, so I wore a beautiful white dress that Marcelo's mother bought me. I have a photo somewhere on my phone. Yes, here, look!
Friend How pretty. So what did you do?
Denisa Uh, let me think. Well, first we had a typical New Year's Eve dinner with Marcelo's family. And then, I guess it was about ten, we got a bus to Copacabana.
Friend What was the atmosphere like there?
Denisa Oh, it was amazing! The streets were already full of people. We went to a show at a place near the beach. It was great, and we danced the samba.
Friend Wow. Were you there at midnight?
Denisa No, no. When we saw it was almost midnight, we went to the beach, and the typical countdown started, you know – ten, nine, eight…Happy New Year! Everywhere we heard the sound of people celebrating, and we watched the wonderful fireworks.
Friend It sounds great. What did people do when the fireworks finished?
Denisa Most people went to other parties, or they went home.
Friend And what about you?
Denisa We decided to go to a different beach, a beach called Praia do Arpoador, and we took our first swim of the new year. It was magical.

🔊 8.4

Then the detective questioned Barbara Travers.
Detective What did you do after dinner yesterday evening?
Barbara After dinner? I played cards with Gordon, and then I went to bed.

Detective What time was that?
Barbara It was about eleven thirty. I remember, I looked at my watch.
Detective Did you hear anything in your father's room?
Barbara No. I didn't hear anything.
Detective Miss Travers, did you have any problems with your father?
Barbara No, I didn't have any problems with him at all. Daddy was a wonderful man and... a wonderful father. I'm sorry, Detective.
Detective Don't worry, Miss Travers. No more questions.

🔊 8.5
Next, the detective questioned Gordon Summers.
Detective What did you do after dinner, Gordon?
Gordon I played cards with Barbara. Then she went to bed.
Detective Did you go to bed then?
Gordon No. I stayed in the living room, and I had a cup of tea. Then I went to bed.
Detective What time was that?
Gordon I don't remember exactly. I didn't look at the time.
Detective Did you hear anything during the night?
Gordon No, I didn't. I was very tired. I slept very well.
Detective You and Mr. Travers were business partners, weren't you?
Gordon Yes, that's right.
Detective And it's a very good business, I understand.
Gordon Yes, Detective, it is.
Detective And now it's your business.
Gordon Listen, Detective, I did not kill Jeremy. He was my partner, and he was my friend.

🔊 8.6
Finally, the detective questioned Claudia Pasquale.
Detective What did you do yesterday evening, after dinner?
Claudia I went to my room and I took a bath and I went to bed.
Detective What time was that?
Claudia About 11 o'clock.
Detective Did you hear anything?
Claudia Yes. I heard somebody go into Jeremy's room. It was about 12 o'clock.
Detective Who was it?
Claudia It was Amanda, his wife.
Detective Are you sure? Did you see her?
Claudia Well, no, I didn't see her. But I'm sure it was Amanda.
Detective You were Mr. Travers's secretary, Claudia.
Claudia Yes, I was.
Detective Were you just his secretary?
Claudia What do you mean?
Detective Were you in love with Mr. Travers?
Claudia No, I wasn't.
Detective The truth please, Claudia.
Claudia Fine, Detective. Yes, I was in love with him, and he said he was in love with me. He said he wanted to leave his wife – Amanda – and marry me. I was stupid. I believed him. But he didn't leave her. He used me, Detective! I was very angry with him.
Detective Did you kill him?
Claudia No, Detective. I *loved* Jeremy.

🔊 8.12
Barbara Let's go upstairs. Follow me…Be careful. The ceiling is very low here.
Leo It's a very old house.
Barbara Yes, the house is 300 years old. My family lived here for nearly 80 years. There are six bedrooms. This was my father's bedroom.
Kim Is there heat in the house?
Barbara Yes, there is. Why do you ask? Are you cold?
Kim Yes, it's very cold in here.
Leo That's because we're from California.
Barbara Let's go and see the other bedrooms.
Leo Yes, of course.
Leo Well, what do you think, Kim? I love it! Don't you?
Kim I'm not sure. There's something about the house I don't like.
Leo Kim, it's perfect for the kids. Think of the yard. And it's a real, authentic country house. What do you say?
Kim I guess so. If you're sure.
Leo I am sure! Miss…uh, Barbara. We want it. We want to rent the house.
Barbara Excellent.
Leo When can we move in?
Barbara As soon as you like.

🔊 8.14
Leo Hello.
Waiter Good evening, sir, madam. What can I get you?
Kim How about a coffee? I'm still cold.
Waiter Yes, madam. And you, sir?
Leo You know, I'm cold, too. I'll also have a coffee, thanks.
Waiter Here you are!
Leo Well, here's to our new house!
Kim Yes!
Waiter You're new around here, aren't you?
Leo Yes, that's right.
Kim We just rented the big house on Darwin Road.
Waiter Which house? The Travers family house?
Leo Yes.
Waiter Oh.
Leo Is something wrong?
Waiter Who showed you the house?
Kim Barbara. The old lady who lived there before.
Waiter Ah, Barbara. Old Mr. Travers's daughter. Some people thought that she was the one who did it.
Kim The one who did what? What happened?
Waiter Didn't she tell you?
Kim Tell us what?
Waiter About the murder.
Leo & Kim Murder?
Waiter Yes, Mr. Travers was murdered in that house in 1965…in his bed.
Kim Oh, how horrible!
Waiter The man who killed Mr. Travers was Barbara's lover. The family never lived there again. They tried to sell the house, but nobody wanted to buy it. Not after a murder. That's why that house is always rented. Barbara never married, of course.
Leo Kim?
Kim Yes?
Leo Are you thinking what I'm thinking?
Kim Yes – I don't want to live in a house where somebody was murdered. Come on. Let's go.
Waiter Hey, hey, your coffee! You didn't drink your coffee…Ah, well.

🔊 8.19
1 We stayed at The Roosevelt Hollywood for two nights. It's a really nice place – a very elegant, very LA hotel. The service, atmosphere, and room were excellent, and we really enjoyed our stay. But we had a really strange experience. On the first night, we woke up at 3:30 in the morning. There was a strange noise outside our door, like someone softly playing a trumpet. To tell you the truth, we were a little bit frightened. Why would someone play the trumpet in the middle of the night? Then we thought that it was probably another guest in the hall, and maybe they were listening to music on their cell phone or something, and we went back to sleep. But on the second night, the same exact thing happened. So we just thought, strange, maybe it's because it's an old hotel and the walls are thin. But when we got home, we told the story to a friend, and he told us that The Roosevelt Hollywood is haunted. We looked on the internet, and we read that people say that room 924 has a ghost! And our room was 922, the next room! We sent an email to The Roosevelt Hollywood and told them about it, and they sent us some really interesting information about the ghost stories. We'd really like to stay in this fantastic hotel again, but maybe not in room 924!

2 I stayed at The Roosevelt Hollywood in May of last year with my husband. It's a beautiful hotel, with a great location. It's right on Hollywood Boulevard. We were in a room on the eighth floor. We knew that people said there were ghosts, and we knew about room 924, but we weren't worried at all. We had a nice meal at a nearby restaurant and then we went to bed. But in the middle of the night – about 3:00 in the morning – we suddenly woke up and we could hear loud noises from the room above us. They were really loud noises – like people were dropping their heavy suitcases on the floor. Anyway, after two or three minutes, the noises stopped and we went back to sleep. There weren't any more strange noises, and we slept for the rest of the night. The next morning, we went to reception and said, "We slept very poorly last night – the people in the room above us made so much noise." The man at reception asked for our room number and said, "Let me check." He looked on the computer and he said, "The room above you is empty." So I said, "Are you sure?" And he said, "Yes. The room above yours is room 924. There wasn't anybody in that room last night." We checked out of the hotel the same morning. Never again!

🔊 9.3
Woman We need food for the weekend – can you go to the store on your way home this evening?
Man OK, I guess so. What do we need?
Woman Let's see. We need some coffee, we don't have *any*.
Man OK…coffee…
Woman And some milk. And some juice.
Man Orange juice?
Woman Yeah. And maybe apple juice, too.
Man OK. What else?
Woman Get a pineapple if they have them.
Man One pineapple…
Woman And some oranges – four or five oranges – and some bananas. And I want to make a vegetable curry, so get some onions, some potatoes, some tomatoes…
Man Hold on, wait a minute…! Potatoes…
Woman Yes, two or three big ones. Oh, and forget the tomatoes – we have some in the refrigerator. And a bottle of soda.
Man Coke? Pepsi?
Woman Any kind is fine. Oh, and some lettuce, I want to make a salad.
Man Some lettuce…Do we need any tomatoes?
Woman No, I said no tomatoes!
Man Sorry, yes, you did. Is that everything?
Woman Yes, I think so. And don't forget anything!

9.4

1 This is for my foodie friends. In case you thought lettuce was only for salads, here I'm cooking it in some butter with an onion. Then I add some mushrooms, chicken, fresh tomatoes, and some other things – not sure yet. Lettuce is also great in soups, or you can grill it and serve it with blue cheese.

2 We didn't feel like cooking last night, and besides, we didn't have any food in the house, so we decided to order some take-out salads from our wonderful local pizzeria. They were all very good, but my favorite was a chicken salad with carrots, tomatoes, peppers, lettuce, and some pieces of fried bread.

3 Brunch Sunday afternoon at a restaurant in the East Village, called Timna. We had lots of different sharing plates. I loved everything, especially this dish called *shakshuka*, which is North African, and it's basically eggs in a tomato sauce, but the mixture of herbs and spices makes it taste great. And the bread we had to dip in the sauce was wonderful, too. Go there. Soon.

4 OK guys, this is it! Our Thanksgiving dinner – which we had at 6:30 last night. All the usual things: turkey with cranberry sauce, mashed potatoes, sweet potatoes, lots of vegetables, and more…and more…Mom said, "why not go to a restaurant this year, maybe have seafood," but I said, "no – I want it homemade and traditional" – so she did it. Thanks, Mom. I now need to spend a few hours on the sofa before I even think about going to bed. So how was yours?

9.7

1 **A** Hi. I'd like a bottle of oil.
   B Olive oil?
   A Yes, please.
2 **A** Can I help you?
   B Yes, I'm looking for a package of rice.
   A Ordinary rice, basmati, brown rice?
   B Uh, basmati, please.
3 **A** Excuse me. I need a can of tomatoes, but I can't find them anywhere.
   B They're over there, next to the pasta.
   A Thanks.
4 **A** Hi. I want a box of chocolates – a nice one. It's for my girlfriend's birthday.
   B How much do you want to spend?
   A Oh, not very much, I mean, nothing too expensive…
5 **A** A carton of juice, please.
   B Apple juice? Orange juice?
   A Uh, orange juice.
   B That's $2.59, please.

9.13

Host Question 1. What is the population of the Canada? Is it approximately a, 27 million, b, 37 million, or c, 57 million?
Contestant I think it's b, 37 million.
Host B is the right answer! Question 2. How far is it from New York City to Los Angeles? Is it a, about 1,500 miles, b, about 2,500 miles, or c, about 3,100 miles?
Contestant About 3,100 miles.
Host Are you sure?
Contestant Yes. I'm sure.
Host C is the right answer! Question 3. How many politicians are there in the British Parliament? Is it a, 450, b, 650, or c, 750?
Contestant I think it's c, 750.
Host Final answer? I'm sorry, the right answer is b. There are 650 politicians in the British Parliament.

9.16

Host Good evening. Welcome to *Quiz Night*. Our first contestant is Eddie from Washington, D.C. Hi, Eddie. Are you nervous?
Eddie No, not really. I think I'm, uh, ready.
Host Well, let's hope so. The rules are the same as always. I'm going to read you some sentences, and you have ten seconds to say if the sentence is true or false. If you get the first answer right, you win $100. Then for each correct answer, you double your money, so if you get the second answer right, you win $200, and for the third correct answer, you win $400. For eight correct answers, you win $12,800. But if you get an answer wrong, you lose all the money. Remember, you can also call a friend, so if you're not sure about one of the answers, you can call your friend to help you. Is that OK, Eddie?
Eddie Yeah, OK.

9.17

Host OK, Eddie, first question for $100. A whale can make a louder noise than a lion. True or false?
Eddie A whale can make a louder noise than a lion. Uh, true.
Host Correct. Blue whales can make a sound of up to 188 decibels whereas a lion's roar is never more than 114 decibels. Ro-a-rrrr. Now, for $200, World War I was shorter than World War II. True or false?
Eddie Uh, I think it's true.
Host Correct. It's true. World War I lasted four years, from 1914 to 1918, but World War II lasted six years, from 1939 to 1945. Next, for $400, the American movie industry is bigger than the Indian movie industry.
Eddie I think it's false. You know, Bollywood and all that is huge. I think it's false.
Host Correct. The Indian movie industry is much bigger than the American one. It produces about 1,000 movies every year, which is double what Hollywood produces. In fact, the US isn't even the second country that makes the most movies, which is Nigeria. Next, for $800, in July, Seattle is hotter than Sydney. True or false?
Eddie In July, Seattle is hotter than Sydney. Uh, true.
Host Correct. The average temperature in July in Seattle is 75 degrees Farhenheit, and in Sydney it's 62 degrees Farhenheit. Of course, Australia's in the southern hemisphere, so it's winter there. Next, for $1,600, silver is heavier than gold. True or false?
Eddie Uh, true. No, uh, false.
Host Do you want to call a friend?
Eddie I think it's false. I remember from science class at school. Gold is heavier than silver.
Host Correct. Gold weighs about 10.16 ounces per cubic inch and silver weighs only 5.53 ounces. That means that gold is almost twice as heavy as silver. OK, for $3,200, the mountain K2 is more difficult to climb than Mount Everest.
Eddie Uh, true.
Host Correct. 30% of the people who try to climb K2 die, usually on the way down, whereas only 5% of the people who try to climb Everest die. OK, Eddie, now for $6,400, driving in Italy is more dangerous than driving in the US. True or false?
Eddie Uh, I think that's a trick question. We all think Italians drive really fast, but maybe they're good drivers. I think it's false.
Host Good job, Eddie! It may be hard to believe, but in fact, out of every 100,000 people, six people died because of car accidents in Italy, compared to approximately 12 in the US. And finally, the last question. Be very careful, Eddie. If you get it right, you win $12,800, but if you get it wrong, you win nothing. Are you ready?
Eddie Yes, ready.
Host OK, for $12,800, it's better to exercise in the morning than in the afternoon.
Eddie Uh…uh…
Host Quickly, Eddie, your time is almost up.
Eddie I think it's false, but I'm not sure. I want to call a friend.
Host OK, Eddie. So, who do you want to call?
Eddie Sandra.
Host Is she your girlfriend?
Eddie Yes, she is.
Host OK, then. Hello, is this Sandra?
Sandra Yes, it is.
Host I'm calling from *Quiz Night*. Eddie needs some help. You have 30 seconds, Eddie. Here she is.
Eddie Hi. Sandra?
Sandra Yes.
Eddie Listen. It's the last question. "It's better to exercise in the morning than in the afternoon." True or false? I think it's false.
Sandra Uh, I think it's true. I always see people running in the park in the morning…
Eddie Google it. Quickly. On your phone.
Sandra What do I put in?
Eddie That sentence and see what comes up! "It's better to exercise in the morning than in the afternoon." Come on!
Sandra OK, I'm typing it. Oh sorry, I just got a message.
Eddie Hurry up, Sandra!
Host Time's up, I'm afraid. OK, Eddie. So, true or false?
Eddie Uh. True.
Host Final answer?
Eddie Final answer. True.
Host I'm sorry, Eddie, it's false. It's better to exercise in the afternoon, between 4:00 and 5:00. Eddie, you had $6,400, but now you go home with…nothing.
Eddie Why did I call Sandra? Why didn't I call my friend Dave?

10.10

Interviewer Gunnar, can you give us a quick update on your trip?
Gunnar OK, so we left Istanbul 20 minutes late, at 1:30 in the morning – not a good start. But we arrived in Casablanca more or less on time. We visited the mosque at 4:30 in the morning. We couldn't go inside though – we just saw it from the outside! Then we went back to the airport and flew to Paris. When we arrived, we rushed outside and took some photos, and then went back in to a different terminal. It was really stressful, the most stressful part of the trip – but we got to the gate just in time for our flight to Punta Cana. When we got there, we went to a beach that was about 12 miles from the airport, and we relaxed there for a little bit, and then went back to the airport and got our flight to Caracas. And we arrived here at 10:00 at night, and we officially entered the country at 10:15. So – five continents in one day! We did it!

10.12

If you're thinking of taking a vacation or traveling somewhere nice, the planning can be complicated. The internet is full of reviews of hotels, restaurants, and attractions. There are so many different ways of traveling, and thousands of places to go. Where do you start? Why not follow these three simple steps to find the right vacation for you.
Step 1. Think about what you want to do on your vacation. The first thing people usually try to decide is *where* they want to go, but it's probably

better to start by thinking about *what* you want to do. Do you want to relax? Then think about *how* you relax. For example, do you like reading, or doing yoga, or do you like doing something more active? Do you want to go somewhere completely different? Do you want to visit an exciting new city, or see some scenery and animals that are different from where you live? Seeing something completely new is a great way to forget about your normal life. Do you want to go on an adventure? Perhaps you're dreaming about climbing Everest or living with an African tribe. You could use your vacation to make one of those dreams come true. Do you want to learn something new? Not everybody wants to sit in a classroom learning Spanish or be in a kitchen learning to cook when they're on vacation, but some people love it. And nowadays, you can take courses in many countries and experience a different culture at the same time.
So now, Step 2. Think about the people you're going to go with. Are they family or friends? Do they have children? What do they want to do? People have different needs and interests, and if you're all going to enjoy the vacation, you need to make sure you all want the same things. But if what you really want to do is to meet new people, maybe it would be better to travel alone.
And finally, Step 3. Think about good vacations you had in the past. Why were they good? Maybe it was the people you were with. Maybe it was something you learned, or an experience you had. What can you repeat from those vacations? Of course, there are always other things you need to consider, like how much money you can spend, and how much time you can be away. But first, follow these three steps, and then you're ready to start thinking about where you want to go!

🔊 10.15
Part 2
Jane Well, I have a problem with my boyfriend. We argue all the time. I'm not sure that he loves me. I want to know if we're going to stay together.
Jim Please choose five cards, but don't look at them…Ah, this is a good card. This means you're going to be very lucky.
Jane But am I going to stay with my boyfriend?
Jim Maybe…We need to look at the other cards first.

🔊 10.17
Part 4
Jim Now I can see everything clearly. You're going to leave your boyfriend and go away with the other man, with Jim…to another country. And very soon, you're going to get married.
Jane Married? To Jim! But am I going to be happy with him?
Jim You're going to be very happy together. I'm sure of it.
Jane Oh no, look at the time. I'm going to be late for work.

🔊 11.4
The first thing that I really noticed when I arrived here was how incredibly friendly the people are. The "ticos" – that's what they're called – are much friendlier than people from my home country. They always say *buenos días* to you, even if they don't know you. And if something's good, like a beautiful day or a good meal, they say *pura vida*, which I love. It literally means "pure life," but I think it really means "things are great," or something like that. One thing that can be difficult though, their sense of time is completely different from ours – they call it "tico time." If they have an appointment at, let's say, seven in the evening, they probably leave home at seven o'clock, so they're always late. Luckily, my school works on what they call "British time," so classes start punctually!
Another thing that surprised me was the weather. I thought Costa Rica was hot and sunny all the time. That's true in the dry season, and the temperature's about 77 degrees all year round, but in the rainy season, especially in September and October, it rains really heavily for maybe two hours a day. Really amazing rain, nothing like at home.
Everyone told me that the scenery was beautiful in Costa Rica, but it was even more beautiful than I expected. Incredible animals, birds, trees – and volcanoes. Some of them are active and smoke quietly, and then suddenly there's a big bang and they start erupting. I was very frightened the first time it happened.
What else? Uh, I thought that life here was going to be very cheap, but in fact, food is very expensive, especially imported food. The only thing that's cheap is fruit, vegetables, and coffee – wonderful, wonderful coffee. And the fruit and vegetables are very different from what we have at home. One day, I went to a market and I didn't recognize any of the fruit.
I like San José. I don't feel that it's dangerous, but it probably is. A colleague of mine was in a taxi the other day, and the taxi driver robbed him of his money! And the roads are terrible, especially in the rain! But in general, I love it here.

🔊 11.11
A I What kind of phone do you have?
   A I have an iPhone.
   I How old is it?
   A Uh, about two years old.
   I How often do you change phones?
   A Not very often, I would say. I like to, uh, I'm not particularly worried about having the latest phone. I just want one that works well. Uh, I usually keep my phone about four years – if I don't lose it, that is.
   I What do you use your phone for the most?
   A Probably the internet. And messaging. Things like Snapchat, Facebook Messenger.
   I So you don't use it much to actually talk to people?
   A No, I don't.
   I What other apps do you use a lot?
   A I use the weather one a lot. And I have a couple of games I like playing. And Skype. I use Skype from time to time to talk to my brother because he lives in Toronto.
   I Do you have any unusual apps that you sometimes use?
   A I have one to track the food that I eat, but I don't use it every day. And I have a photo-editing app.
B I What kind of phone do you have?
   B An Android smartphone. A Samsung, uh, Galaxy, I think.
   I Is it new?
   B About six months old.
   I How often do you change phones?
   B About every two to three years.
   I What do you use it for the most?
   B Receiving phone calls from other people, or looking up things on the internet.
   I What apps do you have that you use a lot?
   B An online banking app. I use that a lot. Email, of course. And the Kindle app, the e-reader.
   I Do you like reading on your phone?
   B No, I prefer reading real books, paper books, but I always have my phone with me so there are lots of times like, on the bus or if I'm waiting for somebody, I can read a book on my phone.
   I Do you have any unusual apps that you sometimes use?
   B Uh, I have an app so I can order a taxi from my local taxi company.
C I What kind of phone do you have?
   C An iPhone.
   I How often do you change your phone?
   C When my contract lets me upgrade it, which is, I don't know, every two or three years.
   I What do you use your phone for the most?
   C Uh, email, text messages, internet, and phone, I mean, talking. In that order.
   I What apps do you use a lot?
   C Apart from mail and Google, you mean?
   I Yes.
   C Uh, Twitter, uh, CNN news, and various transportation apps for buying train tickets or seeing what time they are.
   I Do you have any unusual apps that you sometimes use?
   C I have a "night sky" app. If it's a starry night, I sometimes use that. You point your phone at the sky and it tells you the names of the stars and planets and things.

🔊 12.6
A Yes, I have. I drive a lot for my job, several hours a day, and I like listening to books – it's much better than listening to the radio. I probably listen to a couple of books every week.
B Yes, I've seen *Blade Runner* at least ten times. It's a really great movie, I never get tired of it, I always notice something new.
C No, never. I've definitely fallen asleep watching TV, but never at the movies.
D Yes, I have. When I'm stressed, I sit on the couch with my blanket, turn on Netflix, and spend the evening watching my favorite TV show, *Parks and Recreation*. I can easily watch four or five episodes one after the other.
E No, I haven't. It usually takes me a long time to finish a book, so I never read them again.
F Yes, I bought the soundtrack of *Catching Fire*, you know, *The Hunger Games*, after I saw the movie. It has some amazing music: Coldplay, Imagine Dragons, Christina Aguilera.

🔊 12.7
Alison Let's go out for dinner next Saturday. We can celebrate the end of the semester.
Brett Good idea. Where?
Alison Let's try somewhere new, somewhere that we haven't been to before.
Brett Yeah, good idea.
Clare How about that Indian restaurant near the train station, Curry Up?
Joe Curry Up? I've been there. It wasn't very good.
Clare OK. Joe says it's not great. What about Chinese then? Somebody told me The Great Wall is very good.
Alison Yeah, I haven't been there, but people say it's great.
Joe The Great Wall? I've been there. I went there last week. It's good, but I don't really want to go again.
Brett Well, there's a new Thai place, Thai-Chi. It opened just recently.
Joe Thai-Chi? I've been there, too. I went on Wednesday.
Alison Well, I don't know. Have you been to Mexican Wave?
Joe Mexican Wave? Yes, I have.
Alison When did you go there?
Joe Last month. I went for dinner with people from work.
Alison The Acropolis? That Greek place?
Brett I'm sure Joe's been there!
Joe No, I haven't. I haven't been to The Acropolis. But it closed a few months ago.
Brett Oh, this is ridiculous.
Alison OK, Joe, here's the answer. You cook dinner for us!

GRAMMAR BANK

1A simple present verb *be* +, subject pronouns

+ = affirmative form 🔊 1.4

full form	contraction
I am a student.	**I'm** a student.
You are my partner.	**You're** my partner.
He is Matt.	**He's** Matt.
She is Sally.	**She's** Sally.
It is a salsa class.	**It's** a salsa class.
We are students.	**We're** students.
You are partners.	**You're** partners.
They are teachers.	**They're** teachers.

- In contractions ' = a missing letter, e.g., *'m* = *am*.
- We use contractions in conversation and in informal writing, e.g., an email to a friend.
- We always use a subject pronoun (*you, he*, etc.) with a verb. **It's** a school. **NOT** ~~Is a school~~.
They're teachers. **NOT** ~~Are teachers~~.
- We always use capital *I*. With other pronouns we only use a capital letter when it's the first word in a sentence. *He's Ben and I'm Sally.* **NOT** ~~i'm Sally~~.
- *you* = singular and plural.
- We use *he* for a man, *she* for a woman, and *it* for a thing.
- We use *they* for people and things.

1B simple present verb *be* – and ?

I'm **not** American. 🔊 1.24
She **isn't** from London.
They **aren't** Spanish.
"**Are** you Turkish?" "Yes, I **am**."
"**Is** she Russian?" "No, she **isn't**."
"**Are** we in class 2?" "No, we **aren't**."

– = negative form

full form	contraction	
I am not	I'm not	
You are not	You aren't	
He / She / It is not	He / She / It isn't	Canadian.
We are not	We aren't	Moroccan.
You are not	You aren't	American.
They are not	They aren't	

- We put *not* after the verb *be* to make negatives –.
I'm not Canadian.
- We can also contract *are not* and *is not* like this:
You're not Canadian. She's not Spanish.

? = question form		affirmative short answer		negative short answer
Am I		I am.		I'm not.
Are you		you are.		you aren't.
Is he / she / it	Brazilian? Turkish? Thai?	he / she / it is.		he / she / it isn't.
Are we		Yes, we are.	No,	we aren't.
Are you		you are.		you aren't.
Are they		they are.		they aren't.

- In questions we put *am, are, is* before *I, you, he*, etc.
***Are** you Brazilian?* **NOT** ~~You are Brazilian?~~
*Where **are** you from?* **NOT** ~~Where you are from?~~
- We don't use contractions in affirmative short answers.
"*Are you Turkish?*" "*Yes, I am.*" **NOT** ~~"Yes, I'm."~~

1C possessive adjectives

I'm Peruvian.	**My** family is from Cusco. 🔊 1.43
You're in Class 1.	This is **your** classroom.
He's the director.	**His** name is Michael.
She's your teacher.	**Her** name is Tina.
It's a language school.	**Its** name is English House.
We're an international school.	**Our** students are from South America and Asia.
They're French students.	**Their** names are Luc and Marie.

- We use possessive adjectives for people and things.
***My** family* is from Peru. ***My** car* is Japanese.
- *his* = of a man, *her* = of a woman, *its* = of a thing.
- *their* = of people or things.
- Possessive adjectives don't change with plural nouns.
***our** students* **NOT** ~~ours students~~

> 🔍 **it's or its?**
> Be careful with *it's* and *its*.
> *it's* = it is   ***It's** a school.*
>   ***It's** American.*
> *its* = possessive   ***Its** name is English House.*
>   ***Its** sign is red and yellow.*

1A

a Complete with *am*, *is*, or *are*.

I <u>am</u> Mike.
1. We _____ from Manaus.
2. He _____ early.
3. They _____ teachers.
4. Today _____ Wednesday.
5. I _____ sorry.
6. It _____ a hotel.
7. You _____ in room 402.
8. She _____ a student.
9. My name _____ Carla.
10. I _____ in a taxi.

b Write the sentences with contractions.

He is late. <u>He's late.</u>
1. It is Friday. _____
2. They are at school. _____
3. I am well. _____
4. You are in my class. _____

c Write the sentences with a subject pronoun (*I*, *They*, etc.) and a contraction.

Mike and Hannah are students. <u>They're</u> students.
1. **John is** in room 5. _____ in room 5.
2. **Sam and I are** friends. _____ friends.
3. **Julia is** a teacher. _____ a teacher.
4. **The school is** in Oakland. _____ in Oakland.
5. **Nico and Fernanda are** in my class _____ in my class.

← p.7

1B

a Write negative sentences.

She's Australian. <u>She isn't Australian.</u>
1. I'm American. _____
2. They're Brazilian. _____
3. It's in South America. _____
4. You're French. _____

b Make questions and short answers.

/ you American? <u>Are you American?</u> ✓ <u>Yes, I am.</u>
1. / I in room 10? _____ ✓ _____
2. / it Spanish? _____ ✗ _____
3. / they students? _____ ✗ _____
4. / he from Peru? _____ ✓ _____
5. / you Mike Bell? _____ ✗ _____

c Complete the conversation. Use contractions, e.g., 'm, 's, if possible.

A Hi. I<u>'m</u> Mark.
B Hello, Mark. My name ¹_____ Maria.
A ²_____ you Spanish, Maria?
B No. I ³_____ not. I ⁴_____ from Mexico.
A ⁵_____ you from Mexico City?
B No. I ⁶_____ from Tijuana.
A ⁷_____ Tijuana near Mexico City?
B No, it ⁸_____. It ⁹_____ north.
A ¹⁰_____ you in class 1?
B No. I ¹¹_____ in class 2.

← p.9

1C

a Complete the sentences with a possessive adjective.

<u>My</u> name's Gloria. I'm from Brazil.
1. The students are from Turkey. _____ names are Sabina and Ahmet.
2. She's in my class. _____ name is Rebecca.
3. We're in class 2. _____ teacher is Richard.
4. New York City is famous for _____ yellow taxis.
5. How do you spell _____ last name?
6. This is my teacher. _____ name is John.
7. I'm from London. _____ address is 31, Old Kent Road.
8. Sit down and open _____ books, please.
9. Laura is in my class. _____ desk is near the window.
10. We're from Dallas. _____ last name is Walters.

b Circle the correct word.

Mark and Eric are friends. (They) / Their are in class 2.
1. She's a new student. *She* / *Her* name's Ipek.
2. Is *they* / *their* teacher Canadian?
3. My name's Soraya. I'm in *you* / *your* class.
4. Is *she* / *her* Chinese?
5. Peter is a teacher. *He* / *His* is from the United States.
6. What's *he* / *his* name?
7. Where are *you* / *your* friends from?
8. We're French. *We* / *Our* names are Marc and Jacques.
9. I'm Karen. *I* / *My* last name is White.
10. *She* / *Her* is from Mexico City.

← p.11

Go online to review the grammar for each lesson

2 GRAMMAR BANK

2A singular and plural nouns

a / an, plurals

singular nouns	plural nouns	2.2
It's **a** book.	They're **books**.	
It's **a** watch.	They're **watches**.	
It's **a** dictionary.	They're **dictionaries**.	
It's **an** umbrella.	They're **umbrellas**.	
It's **an** ID card.	They're **ID cards**.	

- We use *a / an* with singular nouns.
- We use *an* with a noun beginning with a vowel (*a, e, i, o, u*).
- We use *a* with nouns beginning with *u* or *eu* when the sound = /yu/, e.g., *a university, a euro*.
- We don't use *a / an* with plural nouns.
  They're books. **NOT** ~~They're a books~~.

> 🔎 **the**
> *Look at **the** board.*
> *Answer **the** questions.*
> - We use *the* when we know which board, questions, etc.
>   *Look at the board.* **NOT** ~~Look at a board.~~
> - We use *the* with singular and plural nouns
>   (*the board, the questions*).

regular plurals

singular	plural	spelling
a book a key	books keys	add -s
a watch a box	watches boxes	add -es after *ch, sh, s, x*
a country a dictionary	countries dictionaries	consonant + y = ~~y~~ -ies

- We add *-s* (or *-es* or *-ies*) to make plural nouns.
  It's a pen. They're pens.
- With two-word nouns, we add *-s* (or *-es* or *-ies*) to the second noun.
  credit card, credit cards **NOT** ~~credits cards~~

irregular plurals

singular	plural
a man /mæn/	men /mɛn/
a woman /ˈwʊmən/	women /ˈwɪmən/
a child /tʃaɪld/	children /ˈtʃɪldrən/
a person /ˈpɜrsn/	people /ˈpipl/

2B adjectives

1. The **White** House is in Washington, D.C. 🔊 2.8
   It's a **beautiful** picture.
   It's an **old** book.
2. They're **blue** jeans.
   We're **new** students.
3. He's **strong**.
   We aren't **rich**.
   Is your car **new**?
4. It's a **very big** city.
   We're **really tired**.

1. Adjectives go before a noun.
   It's a beautiful picture. **NOT** ~~It's a picture beautiful.~~
   - If an adjective begins with a vowel in an adjective + noun phrase, we use *an*. **NOT** ~~It's a old house.~~
2. Adjectives don't change before a plural noun.
   They're blue jeans. **NOT** ~~They're blues jeans.~~
3. We also use adjectives after the verb *be*. The word order is:
   ⊕ or ⊖: subject, *be*, adjective, e.g., *My car's new. The computer isn't cheap.*
   ❓: *be*, subject, adjective, e.g., *Is your car new? Is the computer cheap?*
4. We often use *very* and *really* before adjectives.
   a *He's very (or really) tall.*
   b *He's tall.*
   c *He isn't very tall.*

2C imperatives, *let's*

1. **Open** the door. **Turn** right. 🔊 2.16
   Don't worry. Don't stop.
   Be quiet, please. Please **sit down**.
2. **Let's go** home. **Let's not stop**.

> 🔎 **Can you...?**
> Use *Can you* + verb (base form) as a polite alternative to an imperative.
> *Open the window.* → *Can you open the window, please?*

1. We use imperatives to tell somebody to do (or not do) something.
   - ⊕ imperatives = verb (base form).
     ⊖ imperatives = *don't* + verb (base form).
   - We add *please* to be polite.
     Open the door, please.
   - We often use *be* + adjective in imperatives, e.g., *Be quiet., Be careful.*, etc.
   - We don't use a pronoun with imperatives.
     Be quiet. **NOT** ~~You be quiet.~~
2. We use *Let's* + verb (base form) to make suggestions.
   We use *Let's not* + verb (base form) to make negative suggestions.

2A

a Complete with *a* or *an*. Write the plural.

singular		plural
_a_	photo	_photos_
1 _____	window	_____
2 _____	key	_____
3 _____	ID card	_____
4 _____	country	_____
5 _____	watch	_____
6 _____	exercise	_____
7 _____	person	_____
8 _____	email	_____
9 _____	box	_____
10 _____	woman	_____

b Write sentences with *It's* or *They're* (and *a* or *an* if necessary).

pen — _It's a pen._
buses — _They're buses._
1 children _____
2 change purse _____
3 men _____
4 umbrella _____
5 sunglasses _____
6 scissors _____
7 charger _____
8 dictionaries _____
9 coin _____
10 egg _____

← p.15

2B

a Circle the correct sentence.

He's a rich man. / He's a man rich.
1 It's a very big house. / It's a house very big.
2 Is Louis French? / Is French Louis?
3 It's a watch expensive. / It's an expensive watch.
4 Is it an easy exercise? / Is it an exercise easy?
5 Is Vietnamese your girlfriend? / Is your girlfriend Vietnamese?
6 These questions are very difficult. / These questions are very difficults.
7 Are they tickets cheaps? / Are they cheap tickets?
8 My new glasses are very good. / My news glasses are very goods.

b Put the words in the correct order.

Is Chinese he ? _Is he Chinese?_
1 a day very It's hot
2 your Australian Is teacher ?
3 car fast isn't That very
4 a idea bad It's
5 Are students you good ?
6 easy is English very
7 strong My is brother really
8 train slow is This a

← p.16

2C

a Complete with a verb from the list. Use a ⊞ or a ⊟ imperative.

be (x2) go have open read speak take watch worry

A It's hot. B _Open_ the window.
A I'm very sorry. B _Don't worry._ It's OK.
1 A I'm bored.
  B _____ a book.
2 A *Me puedes dar una fotocopia, por favor?*
  B This is an English class. Please _____ Spanish.
3 A I'm tired.
  B It's late. _____ to bed.
4 A Is this show good?
  B No, it isn't. _____ it.
5 A I'm hungry.
  B _____ a sandwich.
6 A It's a dangerous street.
  B Yes. _____ careful.
7 A It's raining.
  B _____ an umbrella.
8 A It's dark. I'm frightened.
  B _____ frightened. I'm here with you.

b Complete with *Let's* or *Let's not* and a verb from the list.

do go (x2) open stop
take turn off watch

It's hot. _Let's open_ the window.
1 Come on, it's late. _____.
2 It's 11:00 p.m. _____ the TV and go to bed.
3 This exercise is difficult. _____ it together.
4 _____ a taxi. They're very expensive. The bus is fine.
5 There's a rest area. _____ and have a coffee.
6 It's very cold. _____ to the movies. _____ a DVD at home.

← p.18

Go online to review the grammar for each lesson

3 GRAMMAR BANK

3A simple present + and −

I **speak** English.
Americans **like** fast food.
My mother **cooks** great food.
I **don't drink** tea.
We **don't live** in a large city.
He **doesn't play** the guitar.

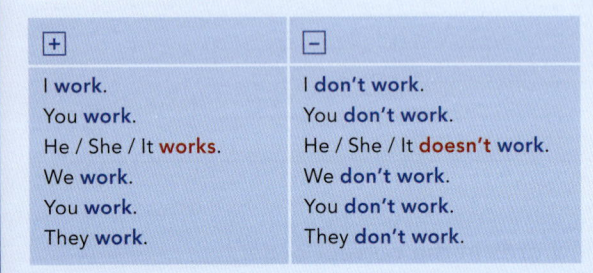

🔊 3.5

+	−
I work.	I don't work.
You work.	You don't work.
He / She / It works.	He / She / It doesn't work.
We work.	We don't work.
You work.	You don't work.
They work.	They don't work.

- We use the simple present for things that are generally true or are habits.
- **Contractions:** don't = do not, doesn't = does not.
- To make negatives, we use don't / doesn't + verb (base form).
  He doesn't **work**. **NOT** He doesn't works.

spelling rules for he / she / it	
I work / play / live.	He works / plays / lives.
I watch / finish / go / do.	She watches / finishes / goes / does.
I study.	She studies.

- The spelling rules for the he / she / it forms are the same as for regular plurals (see **Grammar Bank 2A** p.126).

🔍 Be careful with some he / she / it forms
I have   he has /hæz/   **NOT** he haves
I go   he goes /goʊz/
I do   he does /dʌz/

3B simple present ?

"**Do** you live in New York?"   "No, we **don't**."
"**Does** he work at night?"   "Yes, he **does**."

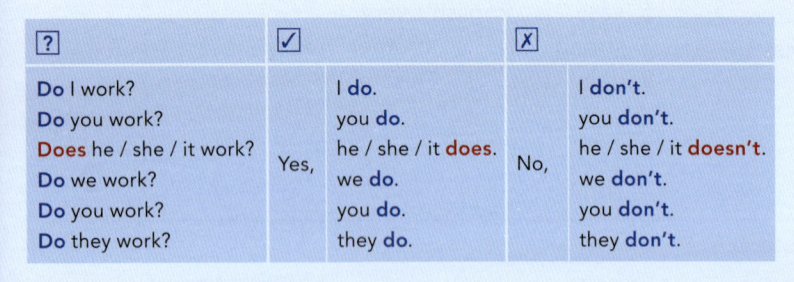

🔊 3.9

?	✓		✗
Do I work?		I do.	I don't.
Do you work?		you do.	you don't.
Does he / she / it work?	Yes,	he / she / it does.	No, he / she / it doesn't.
Do we work?		we do.	we don't.
Do you work?		you do.	you don't.
Do they work?		they do.	they don't.

- We use do (or does with he, she, it) + base form to make questions.
- The word order for simple present questions is auxiliary (do, does), subject (I, you, he, she, etc.), base form (work, live, etc.).

🔍 **do and does**
do = /du/, does = /dʌz/
do and does can be:
1 the auxiliary verb to make simple present questions.
   Do you speak English? **Does** she live here?
2 a normal verb.
   I **do** my homework in the evening.
   He **does** yoga every day.

3C word order in questions

Questions with be

Question word / phrase	be		🔊 3.22
	Is	she from Peru?	
	Are	your friends here?	
What	's	your dog's name?	
Where	's	your office?	
How many students	are	in the class?	
How	are	you?	
How old	is	she?	

- Remember the word order in questions with be. We put be before the subject.

Questions with other verbs

Question word / phrase	Auxiliary	Subject	Base form 🔊 3.23
	Do	you	live near here?
	Does	your mother	know?
What	do	you	do?
Where	does	he	live?
How many children	do	you	have?
What kind of music	does	she	like?
How	do	you	spell your last name?

- The word order for simple present questions with do and does is auxiliary, subject, base form, e.g., *Do you live here?* **OR** question word, auxiliary, subject, base form, e.g., *Where do you live?*
- We often use question phrases beginning with What, e.g., *What color…?, What time…?*, etc.

3A

a Change the sentences.

My mom drinks tea.   I *drink tea.*
1 I go to the movies.   She _____.
2 We live in a house.   He _____.
3 She has two children.   They _____.
4 My dad doesn't like cold weather.   I _____.
5 The stores close at 9:00.   The supermarket _____.
6 We don't study French.   My sister _____.
7 My husband does housework.   I _____.
8 I want a guitar.   My son _____.
9 I don't work on Saturdays.   My friend _____.
10 The show finishes at 5:00.   Our classes _____.

b Complete the sentences with a ⊕ or a ⊖ verb.

eat   have   listen   play   read   speak   ~~study~~   wear   work

⊕ They *study* economics.
1 ⊖ Pedro _____ in an office.
2 ⊕ Eva _____ books in English.
3 ⊕ You _____ Arabic very well.
4 ⊖ I _____ games on my phone.
5 ⊕ Paolo _____ glasses.
6 ⊕ We _____ to music in the car.
7 ⊖ They _____ fast food.
8 ⊕ Julia _____ three children.

← p.22

3B

a Complete the questions with *do* or *does*.

Do you work with a computer?
1 _____ you have a dog?
2 _____ you speak a foreign language?
3 _____ she play the guitar?
4 _____ he work or study?
5 _____ school children in your country wear uniforms?
6 _____ Jamie study Japanese?
7 _____ your husband cook?
8 _____ it rain a lot in your country?
9 _____ the students in this class speak good English?
10 _____ Angela like her job?

b Make questions using a pronoun and the bold verb.

A She **works** at night.   B *Does she work* on the weekend?
A I don't **play** the guitar.   B *Do you play the* piano?
1 A He **likes** sports.   B _____ tennis?
2 A She **speaks** foreign languages.   B _____ Chinese?
3 A I don't **eat** fast food.   B _____ sushi?
4 A They **cook** Italian food.   B _____ lasagna?
5 A Ali doesn't **live** in an apartment.   B _____ in a house?
6 A I **want** a new phone.   B _____ an iPhone?
7 A My dad **drives** a Ferrari.   B _____ fast?
8 A Sarah **drinks** a lot of tea.   B _____ it with milk?
9 A We **have** two children.   B _____ boys or girls?
10 A I don't **listen** to the radio.   B _____ to music on your phone?

← p.24

3C

a Order the words to make questions.

you   live   where   do   ?
Where do you live?
1 children   how   many   do   you   have   ?
2 interesting   is   job   your   ?
3 color   is   his   what   car   ?
4 brother   your   where   work   does   ?
5 you   with   work   computers   do   ?
6 read   of   what   do   kind   you   magazines   ?
7 do   what   does   weekend   he   on   the   ?
8 stressed   you   your   job   are   in   ?
9 your   where   does   sister   live   ?
10 do   how   English   you   say   that   in   ?

b Complete the questions in the conversation.

A Who *do you live* with?
B I live with my parents.
A ¹What _____ your father _____?
B He's retired. My mother's a doctor.
A Where ²_____?
B In Bristol. She works in a hospital there.
A ³_____ your mother _____ her job?
B Yes, she loves it. She doesn't want to retire!
A ⁴What _____ your father _____ during the day?
B He works in the yard, and he cooks in the evening.
A ⁵_____ a good cook?
B Yes, fantastic. He makes very good curries.
A ⁶_____ he also _____ housework?
B Yes, he does. I help, too.
A What ⁷_____?
B I make breakfast and I clean the bathrooms.

← p.27

Go online to review the grammar for each lesson

4 GRAMMAR BANK

4A possessive 's, Whose...?

1 He's Brad Pitt**'s** brother.   It's James**'s** laptop.   🔊 4.2
2 It's my parent**s'** car.
3 "**Whose** bag is this?"   "It's Maria's."
4 The end of the movie is fantastic.   I live near the city park.

1 We use a person + **'s** to talk about family and possessions.
  He's Brad Pitt**'s** brother. **NOT** ~~He's the brother of Brad Pitt.~~
2 With regular plural nouns we put the **'** after the **s**.
  It's my parent**s'** car. **NOT** ~~It's my parent's car.~~
• With irregular plural nouns, e.g., children, men, we use **'s**,
  e.g., the children**'s** room, men**'s** clothes.

3 We use **Whose...?** to ask about possessions.
  We can ask *Whose bag is this?* **OR** *Whose is this bag?*
  We can answer *It's Maria's bag.* **OR** *It's Maria's.*
4 We don't usually use a thing + **'s**, e.g., *the end of the class*
  NOT ~~the class's end~~, *the city park* **NOT** ~~the city's park~~.

> **'s**
> Be careful with **'s**. It can be two things:
> *Maria's mother* – 's = of Maria   *Maria's Spanish* – 's = is
>
> **Whose / Who's**
> *Who's* = Who is, e.g., "**Who's** that girl?" "She's my sister."
> *Whose* = of who, e.g., "**Whose** bag is this?" "It's Jack's."
> *Whose* and *Who's* are pronounced the same /huz/.

4B prepositions of time and place

Time

in	on	at	🔊 4.13
the morning	Monday (morning)	three o'clock	
the afternoon	January 1	noon / midnight	
the evening	the weekend	lunchtime	
the summer		night	
December			
2018			

• We use *in* for parts of the day, seasons, months, and years.
• We use *on* for days, dates, and *the weekend*.
• We use *at* for times of the day and *night*.

Place and movement

1 He has lunch **at** work.   🔊 4.14
  He works **in** an office.
2 He goes **to** work at 8:00.

1 We use *at* and *in* for place.
• We use *at* + *work, home, school*.
• We use *in* + other places, e.g., *a house, an office, a room*, etc.
• We can use *in* or *at* with some public places, e.g.,
  a restaurant, the movies, etc.
  On Saturdays, he usually has lunch in / at a restaurant.
2 We use *to* for movement or direction.
  She goes to the gym. **NOT** ~~She goes at the gym.~~
  We don't use *to* before *home*.
  go home **NOT** ~~go to home~~

4C position of adverbs, expressions of frequency

1 I **always** watch TV in the evening.   🔊 4.20
  Do you **usually** sleep eight hours a day?
  She **sometimes** plays sports.
  She doesn't **often** go to bed late.
2 They're **hardly ever** late.
  He isn't **often** stressed.
  Are you **usually** in this classroom?
3 I have English classes **twice a week**.
  She doesn't work **every day**.

1 We use adverbs and expressions of frequency to say how
  often you do something.
  "How often do you cook?"   "I cook every evening."
• Adverbs of frequency go <u>before</u> the main verb.
• In negative sentences, the adverb of frequency goes
  between *don't / doesn't* and the verb.
2 Adverbs of frequency go <u>after</u> *be* in ➕ and ➖ sentences.
  In ❓ with *be*, the adverb of frequency goes after the subject.
• We use a ➕ verb with *hardly ever* and *never*.
  He's never stressed. **NOT** ~~He isn't never stressed.~~
3 Expressions of frequency usually go at the end of a
  sentence or verb phrase.

4A

a Look at the pictures. Answer the questions with a short sentence.

Whose laptop is this? — *It's Ryan's laptop.*
1 Whose cars are these? _____
2 Whose wallet is this? _____
3 Whose magazines are these? _____
4 Whose watch is this? _____
5 Whose glasses are these? _____

b Circle the correct form.

Monica Cruz is *Penelope's sister* / *sister's Penelope*.
1 It's *my mother's birthday* / *my birthday's mother*.
2 That's *her parent's house* / *her parents' house*.
3 I'm tired when I go home at *the end of the day* / *the day's end*.
4 Those are *friends' my sister* / *my sister's friends*.
5 *The door of the classroom* / *The classroom's door* is open.
6 Those are *the students' desks* / *the desk's students*.

c Complete with *Whose* or *Who's*.

Whose car is this?
Who's the man with dark hair?
1 _____ book is this?
2 _____ phone is that?
3 _____ your favorite singer?
4 _____ Kevin's girlfriend?
5 _____ bag is this?
6 _____ their English teacher?

← p.30

4B

a Complete with *at*, *in*, or *on*.

on Saturday
1 _____ the evening
2 _____ September 22nd
3 _____ the summer
4 _____ 7:30
5 _____ night
6 _____ Wednesday afternoon
7 _____ the weekend
8 _____ January
9 _____ 2020

b Complete with *at*, *in*, or *to*.

We go *to* school by bus.
1 Sorry, John isn't here. He's _____ work.
2 It's a beautiful day. Let's go _____ the beach.
3 Sally's boyfriend works _____ a factory.
4 My brother studies math _____ New York University.
5 I go _____ the gym on Tuesdays and Thursdays.
6 I work _____ an office.
7 We live _____ a modern apartment.
8 It's Monday. The children are _____ school.
9 My father is a doctor. He works _____ a hospital.
10 Jack isn't _____ home. He's with a friend.

← p.33

4C

a Put the adverb of frequency in the correct place in the sentence.

They drive – they don't have a car. **never**
They never drive – they don't have a car.
1 I walk to work. **always**
2 Do you wear glasses? **usually**
3 I'm bored. **hardly ever**
4 She does the housework. **sometimes**
5 We go to the movies. **hardly ever**
6 Why are you late? **always**
7 My girlfriend is stressed. **never**
8 Does it rain in December? **often**

b Order the words to make sentences.

always she at six up gets
She always gets up at six.
1 for late never I am class
2 eat ever fast hardly we food
3 what work you usually time do finish ?
4 parents out night often my go don't at
5 always brother lunchtime is my hungry at
6 don't homework always our we do
7 you work usually to do drive ?
8 hardly teacher angry is our ever

← p.34

Go online to review the grammar for each lesson

GRAMMAR BANK

5

5A can / can't

1 I **can** sing, but I **can't** dance. 🔊 5.5
2 I **can** come on Tuesday, but I **can't** come on Wednesday.
3 **You can** park here. **You can't** park there.
4 **Can you** help me? **Can I** open the window?

+			−		
I / You / He / She / It / We / They	can	swim. come. help.	I / You / He / She / It / We / They	can't	swim. come. help.

?			+			−		
Can	I / you / he / she / it / we / they	swim? come? help?	Yes,	I / you / he / she / it / we / they	can.	No,	I / you / he / she / it / we / they	can't.

- **can** + base form has different meanings:
  1 *I can (sing)* = I know how to.
    I can't (dance) = I don't know how to.
  2 *I can (come)* = It's possible for me.
    I can't (come) = It's not possible for me.
  3 *You can (park here)* = It's OK. / It's permitted.
    You can't (park here) = It's not OK. / It's not permitted.
  4 *Can you (help me)?* = Please do it.
    Can I (open the window)? = Is it OK if I do it?

- *can* and *can't* are the same for all persons (*I, you, he,* etc.).
  NOT ~~He cans.~~
- **Contraction:** *can't* = *cannot*.
- We don't use *to* after *can*.
  I can swim. **NOT** ~~I can to swim.~~

5B present continuous

They're **having** a party next door. 🔊 5.12
Oh no! The baby's **crying**.
It's **raining**.
A What **are you doing**?
B **I'm waiting** for my brother.

+	−	
I'm You're He / She / It's We're They're	I'm not You aren't He / She / It isn't We aren't They aren't	having a party.

?		✓		✗	
Am I Are you Is he / she / it Are we Are they	having a party?	Yes,	I am. you are. he / she / it is. we are. they are.	No,	I'm not. you aren't. he / she / it isn't. we aren't. they aren't.

- We use the present continuous for things that are happening now.
- *At the moment* can mean *around now*.
  I'm reading a good book at the moment.
  (= not exactly now)
- We also use the present continuous with longer periods of time, e.g., *today, this week, this month*. The present continuous emphasizes that the action is <u>temporary</u>, not a habit.
  I'm working at home this week because my daughter isn't very well.

base form	verb + *-ing*	spelling
cook, read study, try	cooking, reading studying, trying	+ *-ing*
dance, live	dancing, living	~~e~~ *-ing*
shop, swim	shopping, swimming	one vowel + one consonant: double consonant + *-ing*

5C simple present or present continuous?

simple present	present continuous 🔊 5.20
It always **snows** here in the winter.	Look! It**'s snowing**.
What **do you** usually **do** at work?	What **are you doing** now?
My sister **works** in a bank.	Today, she**'s working** at home.

> **What do you do?** or **What are you doing?**
> A What **do you do**? (= What's your job?)
> B *I'm a teacher.*
> A What **are you doing**? (= now, at the moment)
> B *I'm waiting for a friend.*

- We use the **simple present** to say what we <u>usually</u> do, or things that are normally true.
- We often use the **simple present** with adverbs and expressions of frequency, e.g., *always, often, once a week,* etc.
- We use the **present continuous** to say what is happening now or around now.
- We often use the **present continuous** with *at the moment, today, this week.*

5A

a Complete the sentences with *can* or *can't* and the verbs.

I'm sorry. I *can't remember* your name. (remember)
1. My girlfriend _____ French, but not Spanish. (speak)
2. _____ you _____ me? This box is very heavy. (help)
3. I _____ you tonight. I have a lot of homework. (see)
4. _____ I _____ the window? It's cold in here. (close)
5. _____ you _____ your email address, please? (repeat)
6. It says "No parking." We _____ here. (park)
7. Andy doesn't want to go to the beach. He _____. (swim)
8. _____ I _____ your phone? I want to call my parents. (use)

b Rewrite the sentences using the correct form of *can* or *can't*.

I know how to play the piano.
I *can play the piano.*
1. It's possible for her to meet me after work.
   She _____.
2. Please open the door.
   _____ you _____?
3. My boyfriend doesn't know how to ski.
   My boyfriend _____.
4. Is it OK if I use your car?
   _____ I _____?
5. It's not permitted to take photos here.
   You _____.

← p.39

5B

a Write a question and an answer.

What's he doing? He's cooking.
1. _____.
2. _____.
3. _____.
4. _____.
5. _____.

b Put the verbs in parentheses in the present continuous.

A Hello, Tina. Where are you?
B I'm in Seattle. I*'m visiting* (visit) my parents.
  I ¹_____ (stay) with them for a week.
  ² What _____ you _____ (do)?
A I ³_____ (look for) a job. Right now
  I ⁴_____ (look) at job ads online.
B Good luck! ⁵_____ you still _____ (live) with your parents?
A Yes. But I'm not at home really. I'm usually at my friend's apartment.
B ⁶ What _____ she _____ (do) now?
  ⁷_____ she still _____ (study) drama?
A No, she ⁸_____ (work) at a café, but she ⁹_____ (not enjoy) it much.
  She ¹⁰_____ (look for) a job as an actress.
B Well, maybe we can all get together next week.
A Good idea. How about Friday?

← p.41

5C

a Circle the correct form.

A What *do you cook* / *(are you cooking)*? I'm really hungry.
B Spaghetti. We can eat in ten minutes.
1. A Hello. Is Martin home?
   B No, he isn't. *He plays* / *He's playing* soccer with his friends.
2. A *Do your parents live* / *Are your parents living* near here?
   B Yes. They *have* / *are having* an apartment in the same building as me.
3. A How often *do you go* / *are you going* to the hair stylist?
   B About once a month. When my hair *needs* / *is needing* a cut.
4. A Don't make so much noise! Your father *sleeps* / *is sleeping*!
   B Is he OK? He *doesn't usually sleep* / *isn't usually sleeping* in the afternoon.

b Put the verbs in the simple present or present continuous.

Look. It*'s raining*. (rain)
1. A Hi, Sarah! What _____ you _____ here? (do)
   B I _____ for a friend. (wait)
2. A Let's have lunch. _____ you _____ hamburgers? (like)
   B No, sorry. I'm a vegetarian. I _____ meat. (not eat)
3. A Listen! The neighbors _____ a party again. (have)
   B They _____ a party every weekend! (have)
4. A What _____ your boyfriend _____? (do)
   B He's a teacher. He _____ at the local school. (work)

← p.42

Go online to review the grammar for each lesson

133

6 GRAMMAR BANK

6A object pronouns

subject pronoun	object pronoun	🔊 6.2
I	me	Can you help **me**?
you	you	I love **you**.
he	him	She doesn't love **him**.
she	her	He calls **her** every day.
it	it	I don't like **it**.
we	us	Wait for **us**!
they	them	Please help **them**.

- Pronouns take the place of nouns.
- We use **subject** pronouns when the noun is the subject of a verb (i.e., the person who does the action).
  John is a doctor. He lives in Houston.
- We use **object** pronouns when the noun is the object of a verb (i.e., the person who receives the action).
  Anna knows John. She sees him every week.
- Object pronouns go <u>after</u> the verb.
  I love you. **NOT** ~~I you love.~~

> 🔍 **Object pronouns after prepositions**
> We also use object pronouns after prepositions (*with, to, from,* etc.).
> *I'm in love with **her**.*
> **NOT** ~~I'm in love with she.~~
> *Give this money to **him**.*
> **NOT** ~~Give this money to he.~~

6B like + (verb + -ing)

😄	I **love**	**shopping**.	🔊 6.15
🙂	I **like**	**going** to the movies.
😐	I **don't mind**	**getting** up early.
🙁	I **don't like**	**doing** housework.
😠	I **hate**	**driving** at night.

base form	verb + -ing	spelling
cook, read	cooking, reading	+ -ing
study, try	studying, trying	
dance, live	dancing, living	~~e~~ -ing
shop, swim	sho**pp**ing, swi**mm**ing	one vowel + one consonant: double consonant +-ing

- We use verb + -ing after *like, love, don't mind,* and *hate*.
- We can also use verb + -ing after *enjoy* and *prefer*.
  *I enjoy watch**ing** soccer on TV, but I prefer be**ing** there.*

6C be or do?

be

1. Hi. I**'m** Jim.   🔊 6.19
   She **isn't** very friendly.
   Are you Thai?
2. I can't talk. I**'m** driving.
   They **aren't** working today.
   Is it raining?

1. We use *be* as a main verb.
2. We also use *be* to form the present continuous. *Be* here is an auxiliary verb.
- Remember to invert *be* and the subject to make questions.
  *He's Spanish. **Is he** Spanish?*

do / does

1. I'm **doing** my homework.   🔊 6.20
   Do you **do** your homework regularly?
2. **Do** you speak English?
   Where **do** they live?
   They **don't** have children.
   Does your sister have a car?
   Where **does** your father work?
   Alan **doesn't** like jazz.

1. We use *do* as a main verb.
2. We also use *do / does* to make questions and *don't / doesn't* to make negatives in the simple present. *Do* here is an auxiliary verb.
- Remember the word order for simple present questions: auxiliary, subject, base form OR question word, auxiliary, subject, base form (see **Grammar Bank 3C** p.128).

6A

a Rewrite the sentences. Change the highlighted words to object pronouns.

I call *my mother* once a week.
I call her once a week.

1. I can't find *my wallet*.
   _____
2. She speaks to *her father* in Chinese.
   _____
3. He meets *his friends* after work.
   _____
4. Can you help *my friend and me*?
   _____
5. Ryan is angry with *his girlfriend*.
   _____
6. My son doesn't like *cats*.
   _____

b Complete the sentences with subject pronouns (*I*, *he*, etc.) or object pronouns (*me*, *him*, etc.).

John is American. *He* lives in California, with his parents. *He* argues with *them* a lot.

1. My mother has a big house in the country. _____ likes _____ a lot. We often visit _____ on Sundays – she invites _____ for lunch.
2. I am lucky to have great neighbors. _____ often help _____ with my children. They pick _____ up from school when _____ work late.
3. Mark loves Ruth, but she doesn't like _____. He calls _____ every day, but _____ doesn't want to speak to _____.
4. My brother has two big dogs. _____ takes _____ for a walk twice a day. I don't like _____ very much because _____ bark at _____.
5. We often take my grandfather some magazines, but _____ never reads _____. He watches TV all day and never turns _____ off.

⬅ p.46

6B

a Write the *-ing* form of the verbs in the chart.

~~come~~   cook   dance   eat   get   have
run   sleep   stop   study   swim   write

1 verb + -ing	work	work**ing**	
2 verb ending in *e*	live	liv**ing**	*coming*
3 double consonant	shop	shop**ping**	

b Write sentences about Matt with *love*, *like*, *not mind*, *not like*, or *hate*, and a verb.

He loves playing tennis.

1. _____
2. _____
3. _____
4. _____
5. _____
6. _____
7. _____
8. _____
9. _____

😃	tennis, to the movies
🙂	the dog for a walk, music
😐	housework, in an office
🙁	soccer on TV, novels
😠	lunch with his parents, a tie

⬅ p.49

6C

a Put the phrases in the correct column.

~~doing your homework~~   have a car   hungry
know those people   like classical music
listening to me   live downtown   stressed
tired   speak Russian   waiting for a friend

Are you...?	Do you...?
doing your homework	

b Complete the conversations with the correct form of *be* or *do*. Use contractions where possible.

A *Do* you speak German?
B Yes, but I *don't* practice it very often.

1. A Where _____ Gemma going?
   B She _____ going to the gym.
2. A _____ you play tennis?
   B Yes, but I _____ play very well.
3. A _____ Matt like shopping?   B He _____ mind it.
4. A Why _____ you crying?   B Because I _____ sad.
5. A _____ your boyfriend cook?
   B Yes. He _____ making dinner right now.
6. A _____ you busy?
   B Yes. We _____ doing our homework.
7. A How old _____ your father?
   B He's 66, but he _____ want to retire.
8. A _____ you watching TV?
   B No. I _____ playing a video game.

⬅ p.50

▶ **Go online** to review the grammar for each lesson

7 GRAMMAR BANK

7A simple past of be: was / were

Vincent van Gogh **was** an artist. 🔊 7.2
Was he Dutch or French?
She **wasn't** in class yesterday.
The Beatles **were** famous in the 1960s.
Where **were** you last night? You **weren't** at home.

- We use *was / were* to talk about the past.
- We often use *was / were* with past time expressions, e.g., *yesterday, last night, in 2014*, etc.
- We use *was / were* with *born*.
  I **was born** in Canada.

+			−		
I / He / She / It	**was** there.		I / He / She / It	**wasn't** there.	
You / We / They	**were** there.		You / We / They	**weren't** there.	

?			✓	✗
Was	I / he / she / it	famous?	Yes, I **was**.	No, I **wasn't**.
Were	you / we / they		Yes, you **were**.	No, you **weren't**.

7B simple past: regular verbs

1 I **booked** the flights yesterday. 🔊 7.9
  We **arrived** at the airport at 10:00 this morning.
2 When I was young, I **watched** TV every night.
  I **worked** as a waiter every weekend when I was in college.

- We use the simple past for:
  1 finished actions that happened once in the past.
  2 finished actions that happened more than once in the past.

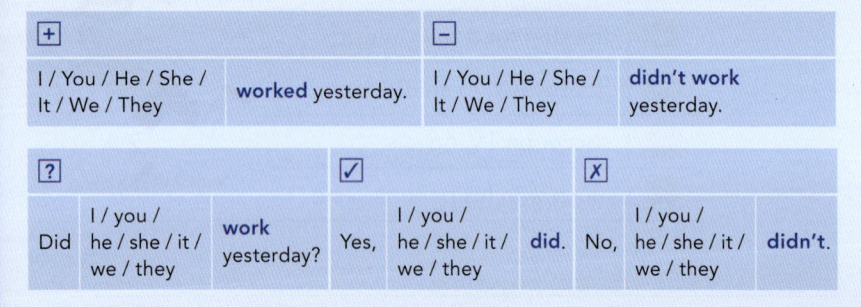

+		−	
I / You / He / She / It / We / They	**worked** yesterday.	I / You / He / She / It / We / They	**didn't work** yesterday.

?			✓			✗		
Did	I / you / he / she / it / we / they	**work** yesterday?	Yes,	I / you / he / she / it / we / they	**did**.	No,	I / you / he / she / it / we / they	**didn't**.

- **Contraction:** *didn't = did not*.
- Regular verbs in the past ⊞ end in *-ed*, e.g., *worked, lived, played*.
- The simple past is the same for all persons (*I, you, she*, etc.).
- We use *did / didn't* + base form for simple past ? and −. *Did* is the past of *do*.

base form	past	spelling
watch	watch**ed**	add *-ed*
play	play**ed**	
arrive	arriv**ed**	add *-d*
study	stud**ied**	consonant + *y*: ~~y~~ *-ied*
stop	stop**ped**	one vowel + one consonant: double consonant + *-ed*

7C simple past: irregular verbs

I **went** to Iceland in December. I **didn't go** to New York. 🔊 7.15
Did you **go** to a party? Who **did** you **go** with?

base form	past +	past −
buy	bought	didn't buy
come	came	didn't come
feel	felt	didn't feel
find	found	didn't find
get	got	didn't get
go	went	didn't go
have	had	didn't have
know	knew	didn't know
put on	put on	didn't put on
say	said	didn't say
take	took	didn't take
think	thought	didn't think
wear	wore	didn't wear

- Some verbs are irregular in the past ⊞ and change their form, e.g., *go → went, have → had*.
- We only use the irregular past form in ⊞ sentences.
  I **bought** a bag last night.
- We use the base form after *did / didn't*.
  Did you **go** out last night? **NOT** ~~Did you went…?~~
- Remember the word order in questions: auxiliary, subject, base form, e.g., *Did you go out last night?* or question word, auxiliary, subject, base form, e.g., *Where did you go?*
  Look at the list of irregular verbs on p.165.

> 🔍 **can / could**
> The simple past of *can* is *could*. We add *not* to make negatives and reverse the subject and verb to make questions.
> ⊞ We **could** see the whole city from the plane.
> − I **couldn't** see him. **NOT** ~~I didn't can see him.~~
> ? **Could** you wear jeans when you were at school?

7A

a Rewrite the sentences in the simple past.

simple present	yesterday
My father's at work.	My father was at work.
1 She's at home today.	_____ at home.
2 Where are you now?	Where _____?
3 I'm in Tokyo.	_____ in Tokyo.
4 Is it hot today?	_____ hot?
5 It isn't open now.	_____ open.
6 They aren't in the office.	_____ in the office.
7 We're in Lima now.	_____ in Lima.
8 They're tired.	_____ tired.
9 We aren't late.	_____ late.
10 I'm not at school.	_____ at school.

b Complete the conversation with *was*, *wasn't*, *were*, or *weren't*.

A *Were* you and Charlie at the concert last night?
B Yes, we ¹_____.
A ²_____ it good?
B No, it ³_____. The singer ⁴_____ terrible.
A ⁵_____ the tickets expensive?
B Yes, they ⁶_____.

C Where ⁷_____ your mother born?
D She ⁸_____ born in Argentina in 1955.
C ⁹_____ her parents Argentinian?
D No, they ¹⁰_____. Her father ¹¹_____ German and her mother ¹²_____ from Italy.

← p.54

7B

a Rewrite the sentences in the simple past.

simple present	simple past
We watch TV.	We watched TV yesterday evening.
1 I study English.	_____ at school.
2 Do you listen to the news?	_____ yesterday?
3 He doesn't cook.	_____ last night.
4 Does she play sports?	_____ in college?
5 They work late.	_____ last week.
6 She travels a lot.	_____ in 2018.
7 Jack works in New York.	_____ five years ago.
8 I call my parents every day.	_____ yesterday.
9 We don't live in France.	_____ ten years ago.
10 Anna asks a lot of questions.	_____ at the meeting.

b Complete the sentences with a verb in the simple past.

book   not call   cry   dance   ~~finish~~
not listen   play

We *finished* work late yesterday.
1 I _____ my mother on her birthday.
2 The movie was very sad. _____ you _____?
3 My brother _____ video games all day yesterday.
4 I _____ to the news this morning.
5 _____ Sarah _____ with Martin at the party?
6 We _____ our hotel rooms online.

← p.57

7C

a Correct the information using the word in parentheses.

She put on a coat. (jacket)
She didn't put on a coat. She put on a jacket.
1 She wore a red dress. (blue)
_____
2 I came home early. (late)
_____
3 We went by train. (bus)
_____
4 He said hello. (goodbye)
_____
5 You had a sandwich. (salad)
_____
6 He knew her last name. (first name)
_____

b Complete the text with the verbs in parentheses in the simple past. All the verbs are irregular.

Last New Year's Eve, I *went* (go) to San Francisco with some friends. We ¹_____ (have) dinner at a Chinese restaurant, and at 10:00 p.m. we ²_____ (take) a taxi to Union Square. We ³_____ (be) there for an hour, and then we ⁴_____ (go) to the water. We ⁵_____ (can) see the fireworks very well, and we ⁶_____ (have) a great time. We ⁷_____ (get) home at 4:00 a.m. We ⁸_____ (feel) tired, but we ⁹_____ (be) very happy!

c Complete the questions in the simple past.

A *Did you go out* last night?
B No, I stayed at home.
1 A What _____ yesterday?
   B I wore jeans.
2 A Where _____ her shoes?
   B She bought them in Paris.
3 A What time _____?
   B We got home late.

← p.58

> Go online to review the grammar for each lesson

8 GRAMMAR BANK

8A simple past: regular and irregular

1 was / were and could 🔊 8.9

+ Gordon **was** Jeremy's business partner. They **were** at his country house.
  They **could** hear a strange noise.
− She **wasn't** at home last night. You **weren't** very nice to her.
  I **couldn't** sleep.
? **Were** you sick yesterday? When **was** he born?
  Could you see anybody in the library?

2 regular verbs

+ I really **liked** the present. She **wanted** to be a doctor.
− She **didn't enjoy** the concert. They **didn't arrive** until very late.
? **Did** you **watch** the game last night? When **did** you **finish** the book?

3 irregular verbs

+ I **went** to Paris last summer. She **slept** on the sofa.
− He **didn't come** home last night. They **didn't hear** the music.
? **Did** you **speak** to your sister yesterday? Where **did** you **have** lunch?

1 The past of *be* is *was / were*, and the past of *can* is *could*. We add *not* to make negatives and reverse the subject and verb to make questions.

2 Regular verbs add *-ed* or *-d* in the simple past +, e.g., *want–wanted, like–liked*.

3 Irregular verbs change their form in the simple past +, e.g., *go–went, see–saw*.

- Regular and irregular verbs (except *can*) use:
  – *didn't* + base form to make negatives, e.g., *I didn't like it. She didn't see him.*
  – *did* + subject + base form to make questions, e.g., *Did you want to come? Where did she go?*

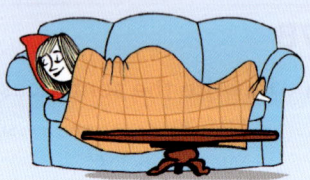

I went to Paris last summer.   She slept on the sofa.

8B there is / there are, some / any + plural nouns

singular	plural	🔊 8.15
+ There's a garage.	There are some pictures on the wall.	
− There isn't a swimming pool.	There aren't any plants in the room.	
? Is there a bathroom downstairs?	Are there any neighbors with children?	
✓ Yes, there is.	Yes, there are.	
✗ No, there isn't.	No, there aren't.	

there is / there are

- We use *there is / there are* to say that something exists or doesn't exist, e.g., *There's a bathroom upstairs. There isn't a bathroom downstairs.*
- We use *there is* + a singular noun and *there are* + plural nouns.
- *There is* is often contracted to *There's. There are* is not usually contracted.
- When we talk about a list of things, we use *there is* if the first word in the list is singular or *there are* if the first word in the list is plural.
  In my bedroom, **there's a** bed, two chairs, and a desk.
  In the living room, **there are** two armchairs and a sofa.

a / an, some, and any

- We often use *there is / isn't* with *a / an*, and *there are / aren't* with *some* and *any*.
- We use *some* and *any* with plural nouns. *Some* = not an exact number, e.g., *There are some eggs in the refrigerator.*
- We use *some* in + sentences and *any* in − and ?.

> *There is / There are* or *It is / They are*?
> Be careful. *There is* and *It is* are different.
> **There's** a key on the table. **It's** the key to the kitchen.
> **There** are three bedrooms in the apartment. **They're** all very small.

8C there was / there were

singular	plural	🔊 8.21
+ There was a big mirror.	There were four lamps.	
− There wasn't a TV.	There weren't any ghosts.	
? Was there a bathroom?	Were there any windows?	
✓ Yes, there was.	Yes, there were.	
✗ No, there wasn't.	No, there weren't.	

- *there was / there were* is the past of *there is / there are*. We use *there was / there were* to say that something existed or didn't exist, e.g., *There were two computers in the office, but there wasn't a printer.*

8A

a Complete the conversation using the simple past of the verbs in parentheses.

A Where _were_ (be) you last night at 8:00?
B I ¹_____ (be) at home, Detective. With my wife. We ²_____ (be) at home all evening.
A ³What _____ you _____ (do)?
B We ⁴_____ (watch) TV and then we ⁵_____ (have) a light dinner. We ⁶_____ (not be) hungry. After that, we ⁷_____ (go) to bed.
A ⁸What time _____ you _____ (go) to bed?
B About 10 o'clock.
A ⁹_____ you _____ (hear) a noise during the night?
B No, I ¹⁰_____ (not hear) anything.

b Complete the sentences with the simple past of a verb from the list.

arrive   not can   hear   read   see   sit
sleep   speak   not want

They _spoke_ quietly for a few minutes.
1 I _____ very badly last night.
2 She _____ a strange noise.
3 We _____ find our keys.
4 I _____ three books last week.
5 They _____ at the airport at 11:30.
6 He _____ her with an old friend.
7 We _____ next to each other in class.
8 You _____ to come.   ⬅ p.63

8B

a Complete with ➕ or ❓ of *There's* or *There are*.

There's a dishwasher in the kitchen.
Are there any people in the room?
1 _____ any books on the shelf?
2 _____ a bathroom downstairs?
3 _____ some stairs over there.
4 _____ a rug on the floor.
5 _____ some pictures on the wall.
6 _____ a shower in the bathroom?
7 _____ some chairs in the yard?
8 _____ a lamp in the bedroom?
9 _____ a motorcycle in the garage.
10 _____ any glasses in the cupboard?

b Write ➕ or ➖ sentences or ❓ with *there is / are* + *a / an*, *some*, or *any*.

➕ trees / the yard
There are some trees in the yard.
1 ➕ table / the kitchen.
2 ❓ fireplace / the living room?
3 ➖ plants / my apartment.
4 ❓ people / the yard?
5 ➕ pictures / my bedroom.
6 ➖ TV / the kitchen.
7 ➕ computer / the study.
8 ➖ cupboards / the dining room.
9 ❓ bathtub / the bathroom?
10 ➖ light / the garage.

⬅ p.65

8C

a Complete with the correct form of *there was* or *there were*.

A How many guests _were_ _there_ in the hotel?
B ¹_____ _____ four including me. ²_____ _____ a Brazilian tourist and ³_____ _____ two business people.
A ⁴_____ _____ a restaurant?
B No, ⁵_____ _____, but ⁶_____ _____ a coffee shop.
A ⁷_____ _____ a TV in your room?
B Yes, ⁸_____ _____, but ⁹_____ _____ any chairs.
A How many beds ¹⁰_____ _____?
B One. A double bed.

b Complete the sentences with *there was / were / wasn't / weren't* + *a*, *some*, or *any*.

There were some ghosts in the haunted hotel I stayed in.
1 My sister didn't take a shower because _____ spider in the bathtub.
2 We couldn't watch the news because _____ TV in our room.
3 I couldn't sleep on the plane because _____ noisy children behind me.
4 They couldn't play tennis because _____ tennis balls.
5 She didn't have a coffee because _____ cups.
6 He took a lot of photos because _____ beautiful view of the town.
7 They couldn't park near the restaurant because _____ parking lot.   ⬅ p.67

🔵 **Go online** to review the grammar for each lesson

9 GRAMMAR BANK

9A countable / uncountable nouns, a / an, some / any

Countable
an apple 
three apples

Uncountable
rice
meat 

- English nouns can be **countable** or **uncountable**.
  countable = things you can count, e.g., *apples*. Countable nouns can be singular (**an** apple) or plural (apple**s**).
  uncountable = things you can't count, e.g., *rice, meat*
  NOT *two rices, three meats.*
  Uncountable nouns are usually singular.
- Some nouns can be countable and uncountable, e.g., *ice cream*.

an ice cream (countable)    some ice cream (uncountable)

a / an, some / any

	countable	uncountable 🔊 9.2
➕ We need	**an** apple. **some** apples.	**some** butter.
➖ We don't need	**a** tomato. **any** tomato**es**.	**any** rice.
❓ Do we need	**an** orange? **any** orange**s**?	**any** sugar?

- We use *a / an* with singular countable nouns. *a / an* = one.
- We use *some* in ➕ with plural countable nouns and with uncountable nouns.
- We use *any* in ➖ and ❓ with plural countable nouns and with uncountable nouns.

🔍 **some in ❓**
We use *some* in ❓ to ask for and offer things.
*Can I have **some** sugar, please? Would you like **some** coffee?*

9B quantifiers

uncountable (singular)	short answers	full answers 🔊 9.8
How **much** sugar do you eat?	A lot. A little. Not much. None.	I eat **a lot of** sugar. I eat **a little** sugar. I **don't** eat **much** sugar. I **don't** eat **any** sugar.
countable (plural)		
How **many** cookies do you eat?	A lot. A few. Not many. None.	I eat **a lot of** cookies. I eat **a few** cookies. I **don't** eat **many** cookies. I **don't** eat **any** cookies.

🔍 **a lot of and lots of**
A lot of and *lots of* mean the same thing, e.g., *He eats a lot of cheese / lots of cheese.*

- We use *How much…?* with uncountable nouns and *How many…?* with plural countable nouns.
- We use:
  a lot (of) with countable and uncountable nouns for a **big quantity**.
  a little / not…much with uncountable nouns for a **small quantity**.
  a few / not…many with countable plural nouns for a **small quantity**.
  not…any (*none* in short answers) for **zero quantity**.

a lot of and *much / many*

- In ➕ sentences, we usually use *a lot of*.
- In ➖ sentences and ❓, we usually use *much* and *many*.
  *I don't drink **much** water. Do you drink **much** coffee?*
- It is also possible to use *a lot of* in ➖ and ❓.
  *I don't eat **a lot of** vegetables. Do you drink **a lot of** coffee?*

9C comparative adjectives

A whale is **louder than** a lion.   🔊 9.18
Canada is **bigger than** the US.
K2 is **more difficult** to climb **than** Mount Everest.
My new job is **better than** my old one.
The traffic is always **worse** in the evening.

- We use comparative adjectives + *than* to compare two things, people, etc.

adjective	comparative	spelling
old nice	older nicer	one-syllable adjectives: + -er (or -r if the adjective ends in e)
big hot	bigger hotter	adjectives ending one vowel + one consonant: double consonant + -er
dry healthy	drier healthier	one- or two-syllable adjectives ending consonant + y: ~~y~~ -ier
tired	more tired	one-syllable adjectives ending -ed: *more* + adjective
famous expensive	more famous more expensive	two- or more syllable adjectives: *more* + adjective
good bad far	better worse farther / further	irregular

9A

a Write *a*, *an*, or *some* + a food or drink word.

some bread
1 _____
2 _____
3 _____
4 _____
5 _____
6 _____
7 _____
8 _____

b Complete the conversation with *a*, *an*, *some*, or *any*.

A What can we make for your brother and his girlfriend?
B Let's make <u>a</u> pizza.
A Good idea. Are there ¹_____ tomatoes?
B Yes. And there are ²_____ mushrooms, too.
A Great!
B Oh no! There isn't ³_____ cheese!
A Oh. Wait a minute. I bought ⁴_____ steak yesterday. Are there ⁵_____ potatoes?
B Yes, there are.
A Good. So we can have steak and French fries. Do we have ⁶_____ fruit?
B I think we have ⁷_____ oranges. Yes, and there's ⁸_____ apple and ⁹_____ bananas, too.
A OK. You can make ¹⁰_____ fruit salad for dessert.
B OK. Let's start cooking.

← p.71

9B

a Complete the questions with *How much* or *How many*.

<u>How much</u> sugar do you put in your tea?
1 _____ butter do you use for this cake?
2 _____ cans of soda did she drink?
3 _____ oil do I need?
4 _____ chocolates were in that box?
5 _____ rice do you want?
6 _____ coffee does he drink?
7 _____ bottles of water did you buy?
8 _____ cans of tuna do we have?
9 _____ orange juice is there in that carton?
10 _____ cookies did you eat?

b Circle the correct word or phrase.

I don't put *much* / *many* salt on my food.
1 We don't eat *a lot of* / *a lot* cookies.
2 A How much chocolate do you eat? B *A little.* / *A few.*
3 My husband doesn't drink *much* / *many* coffee.
4 A How much fruit did you buy?
   B *A lot.* / *A lot of.*
5 We eat *a lot of* / *much* fish. We love it!
6 A Do your children drink any milk?
   B No, *not much* / *not many*.
7 Donna ate her hamburger, but she didn't eat *much* / *many* French fries.
8 A How many vegetables do you eat?
   B *Any.* / *None.* I don't like them.
9 I have a cup of tea and *a few* / *a little* cereal for breakfast.
10 A Do you eat *much* / *many* meat?
    B No, I don't eat *no* / *any* meat. I'm a vegetarian.

← p.72

9C

a Write the comparative form of the adjectives.

big   bigger
1 high   _____
2 dirty   _____
3 important _____
4 late   _____
5 low   _____
6 bored   _____
7 wet   _____
8 modern   _____
9 comfortable _____
10 happy   _____

b Complete with a comparative adjective + *than*.

My sister is <u>younger than</u> me. She's only 18. (young)
1 The farmer's market is _____ the supermarket for vegetables. (cheap)
2 Italian is _____ for Spanish students _____ it is for English students. (easy)
3 I always feel _____ in the afternoon _____ in the morning. (tired)
4 This restaurant is _____ when it first opened. (busy)
5 Come in the summer. The weather is _____ in the spring. (good)
6 I love science. I find it _____ history. (interesting)
7 Cusco is _____ from the ocean _____ Lima. (far)
8 I'm _____ my brother. He's very tall. (short)
9 The economic situation is _____ it was last year. (bad)
10 Skiing is _____ I thought it was. (difficult)

← p.75

Go online to review the grammar for each lesson

10 GRAMMAR BANK

10A superlative adjectives

It's **the oldest** bridge in the world. 🔊 10.4
It's **the most popular** shopping mall in the US.
She's **the best** student in the class.
Monday is **the worst** day of the week.

- We use *the* + superlative adjective to say which is *the* (*biggest*, etc.) in a group.
- After superlatives, we use *in* (not *of*) + places, e.g., *the longest road **in** the world, the tallest building **in** New York*.

adjective	comparative	superlative	spelling
cold high	colder higher	the coldest the highest	one-syllable adjectives: + *-est*
big hot	bigger hotter	the biggest the hottest	adjectives ending one vowel + one consonant: double consonant + *-est*
dry sunny	drier sunnier	the driest the sunniest	one- or two-syllable adjectives ending consonant + *y*: + *-iest*
bored stressed	more bored more stressed	the most bored the most stressed	one-syllable adjectives ending *-ed*: *the most* + adjective
dangerous	more dangerous	the most dangerous	two- or more syllable adjectives: *the most* + adjective
good bad far	better worse farther/further	the best the worst the farthest/furthest	irregular

10B *be going to* (plans), future time expressions

I'm **going to take** a vacation next month. 🔊 10.9
I'm **not going to study** English.
Are you **going to fly** to Paris?

- We use *be going to* + verb (base form) to talk about future plans.
- We often use future time expressions with *going to*, e.g., *tomorrow, next week, next month, next year*, etc.

[+]

full form	contraction		
I am You are He / She / It is We are They are	I'm You're He / She / It's We're They're	going to	take a vacation next summer. study English tonight.

[–]

full form	contraction		
I am not You are not He / She / It is not We are not They are not	I'm not You aren't He / She / It isn't We aren't They aren't	going to	take a vacation next summer. study English tonight.

[?] [✓] [✗]

Am I Are you Is he / she / it Are we Are they	going to	take a vacation next summer? study English tonight?	Yes,	I am. you are. he / she / it is. we are. they are.	No,	I'm not. you aren't. he / she / it isn't. we aren't. they aren't.

10C *be going to* (predictions)

- We can use *be going to* + verb (base form) to make predictions (= to say what you think or can see is going to happen in the future).

I think it's **going to rain**. 🔊 10.20
You're **going to be** very happy.
I'm sure they're **going to win**.

10A

a Write the opposite.

the smallest	*the biggest*
1 the coldest	_____
2 the most expensive	_____
3 the best	_____
4 the most difficult	_____
5 the driest	_____
6 the shortest	_____
7 the nearest	_____
8 the cleanest	_____

b Complete the sentences with a superlative adjective.

The tigers are *the most dangerous* animals in the zoo. (dangerous)
1. Our house is _____ house on the street. (big)
2. For me, Saturday is _____ day of the week. (good)
3. My bedroom is _____ room in our house. (small)
4. Sit here – it's _____ chair in the room. (comfortable)
5. My neighbors upstairs are _____ people in the world. (noisy)
6. My boss is _____ person I know. (stressed)
7. Sophie is _____ student in our English class. (young)
8. _____ building in my town is the museum. (beautiful)

← p.78

10B

a Complete the sentences with the correct form of *be going to* and the verb in parentheses.

She doesn't have a car. She's *going to go* by train. (go)
1. We need a vacation. We _____ a hotel near the beach. (book)
2. Tomorrow is Saturday. I _____ in bed until 10:00! (stay)
3. My sister _____ medicine. She wants to be a doctor. (study)
4. Laura and David _____ married soon. (get)
5. Jack's office is very busy right now. He _____ late tonight. (work)
6. My son _____ to college – he wants to get a job. (not go)
7. We _____ any museums because the kids think they're boring. (not visit)

b Complete the sentences with *be going to* + a verb.

not buy   call   not come   get
have   live   ~~sleep~~   watch

I'm at a friend's house. I*'m going to sleep* on her sofa.
1. I need to talk to my mom. I _____ her tonight.
2. What _____ we _____ for dinner this evening?
3. My mother isn't feeling very well, so she _____ to the concert with us.
4. There's a lot of snow! How _____ you _____ to work?
5. They love their old car. They _____ a new one.
6. *The Force Awakens* is on TV tonight. _____ you _____ it?

← p.80

10C

a Write predictions for the pictures.

be   get   have   make   ~~play~~   send

He's going to play tennis.
1. _____ dinner.
2. _____ a nice day.
3. _____ the bus.
4. _____ an omelet.
5. _____ an email.

b Complete the predictions with *be going to* and a verb.

be   buy   not finish   forget   have (x2)   not like
not pass   sleep   ~~snow~~   win

It's very cold. Do you think it*'s going to snow*?
1. You're driving too fast! We _____ an accident!
2. She isn't a very good student. She _____ the exam.
3. Their new album is great! A lot of people _____ it!
4. I have a lot of homework. I _____ it tonight.
5. They're playing very well. I think they _____ the game.
6. Look at the time. We _____ late.
7. Oh no, it's a horror movie. I know I _____ it.
8. He didn't write down her address. He _____ it.
9. The baby's very tired. She _____ well tonight.
10. Tokyo is a wonderful city. You _____ a great time there.

← p.83

Go online to review the grammar for each lesson

143

11 GRAMMAR BANK

11A adverbs (manner and modifiers)

adverbs of manner

1. She wants to live **independently**. 🔊 11.1
   Her children always speak **politely**.
   She eats very **quickly**.
2. I work **hard**.
   We speak English **well**.

- We use adverbs of manner to say <u>how</u> people do things.
- Adverbs usually go after the verb or verb phrase.
  I speak English **well**. **NOT** ~~I speak well English.~~
1. We usually form adverbs by adding *-ly* to adjectives.
2. Some adverbs are irregular. They can be the same as the adjective, e.g., *fast*, *hard*, or a different word, e.g., *well*.

adjective	adverb	spelling
slow	slowly	
quick	quickly	+ *-ly*
bad	badly	
careful	carefully	
healthy	healthily	consonant + y: ~~y~~ + *-ily*
easy	easily	
possible	possibly	le → *-ly*
good	well	
fast	fast	irregular
hard	hard	

- Remember the difference between adjectives and adverbs.
  I'm a **careful** driver. (*careful* is an adjective. It describes the noun, *driver*.)
  I drive **carefully**. (*carefully* is an adverb. It describes the verb, *drive*.)

very, really, etc.

It isn't **very** expensive. 🔊 11.2
She drives **incredibly** fast.
They speak **really** slowly.

- We use the adverbs *very*, *really*, etc., to modify adjectives or other adverbs.
- They always go <u>before</u> the adjective or adverb.

🔍 **Words ending in *-ly***
Be careful. Some words that end in *-ly* aren't adverbs, e.g., *friendly* (= adjective).
He's a **friendly** person.

11B verb + infinitive

1. I **want to travel** for six months. 🔊 11.6
   She **decided to go** to Australia.
   You **need to practice** every day.
   When did you **learn to play** the guitar?
2. **Would** you **like to go** to Africa?
   I **wouldn't like to be** famous.

🔍 **would like and like**
I'**d like** to dance. = I want to dance.
I **like** dancing. = I enjoy it; I like it in general.

1. Many verbs are often followed by another verb in the infinitive. These include *want*, *need*, *learn*, *promise*, *decide*, *plan*, *choose*, *try*, *remember*, *forget*, and *hope*.
2. *I would like to* = *I want to* (now or in the future).
   Would like is also followed by the infinitive.
- **Contractions:** '*d* = *would*. *wouldn't* = *would not*.
- We can also use *Would you like…?* to offer, e.g., *Would you like a drink?*
- *would like* is the same for all persons.

11C definite article

1. *the* 🔊 11.12
   Can you close **the window**, please?
   Can you check their address on **the internet**?
   It's **the best** restaurant I know.
2. *no article*
   Men are usually more interested in sports than **women**.
   She's **my mother's cousin**. That's **Tom's chair**!
   What time did you **have breakfast**?
   Jim goes **to school by bus**.
   Karen's studying physics **in college**.

🔍 ***a / an* or *the*?**
We often use *a* the first time we mention a person or thing. The next time we use *the* because it is now clear what we are talking about, e.g., *Let's have **a** pizza*. ***The** pizzas are very good here.*

1. We use *the*:
- when it is clear what we are talking about,
  e.g., *Close **the** window.* = the window that is open.
- when there is only one of something, e.g., *the internet*, *the sun*, etc.
- before superlative adjectives, e.g., *the biggest*, *the best*, etc.
2. We don't usually use *the*:
- when we talk about people or things in general.
  Men are more interested in sports than **women**. (general)
  BUT **The women** in this class work harder than **the men**. (specific)
- before possessive *'s*.
  She's my mother's cousin. **NOT** ~~She's the my mother's cousin.~~
- with:
  meals: *have breakfast, lunch, dinner*, etc.
  by + transportation: *go by car, travel by train*, etc.
  general places: *work, school, college, bed, home*.

11A

a Adjective or adverb? Circle the correct form.

People drive very *dangerous* / *(dangerously)*.
1. He wrote down her email *careful* / *carefully*.
2. My neighbor's children aren't very *polite* / *politely*.
3. My niece plays the piano *beautiful* / *beautifully*.
4. Fast food is very *unhealthy* / *unhealthily*.
5. Old people often walk very *slow* / *slowly*.
6. I bought a *real* / *really* cheap bag at the sale.
7. My friend sings very *good* / *well*.
8. My sister speaks Spanish *perfect* / *perfectly*.
9. We wear *casual* / *casually* clothes to work.
10. The view from the top is *incredible* / *incredibly* beautiful.

b Complete the sentences with adverbs from these adjectives.

bad   careful   easy   fast   good   hard   healthy   ~~perfect~~   quiet

The trains in Sweden run *perfectly* even when it snows.
1. Can you talk _____, please? I'm trying to sleep.
2. Don't drive _____ when it's raining.
3. I don't like being in the ocean because I can't swim very _____.
4. She sat down _____ because the chair only had three legs.
5. We're working _____ because we need to finish the job.
6. Professional soccer players usually eat very _____.
7. We played _____ in the semi-final and we lost 5–1.
8. She was the best student in the class and she passed the exam _____.

← p.87

11B

a Complete the sentences with the infinitive form of the verb from the list.

be   buy   call   ~~climb~~   drive   get married   go
have   leave   see   stay

Sam loves Africa. He wants *to climb* Mount Kilimanjaro.
1. I learned _____ a car when I was 17.
2. Our refrigerator is broken. We need _____ a new one.
3. I wouldn't like _____ famous. I'm happy the way I am now.
4. He promised _____ his girlfriend when he got home.
5. The weather was terrible. We decided _____ at home.
6. The boss would like _____ you in his office.
7. They're planning _____. They're looking for a venue.
8. I hope _____ time to see the sights when I'm in Seoul next week.
9. Would you like _____ on a safari?
10. I'm really enjoying the party. I don't want _____.

b Circle the correct form.

I hate *fly* / *(flying)* so I usually travel by train.
1. Would you like *to have* / *have* dinner with me tonight?
2. My grandmother learned *to speak* / *speaking* Spanish when she was 60!
3. I'd like *to travel* / *traveling* around Asia.
4. I like *relax* / *relaxing* on the weekend.
5. Do you want *to play* / *playing* soccer?
6. He's hoping *to get* / *getting* the results of his test next week.
7. Most people hate *to go* / *going* to the dentist.
8. I love *to read* / *reading* detective stories.
9. It's cold. You need *to wear* / *wearing* a coat.
10. My mom doesn't mind *to cook* / *cooking*.

← p.89

11C

a Circle the correct word or phrase.

How much time do you spend on *internet* / *(the internet)*?
1. My brother is *in college* / *in the college* studying math.
2. I love traveling *by train* / *by the train*.
3. We're going to visit my aunt *on weekend* / *on the weekend*.
4. Let's stay *at home* / *at the home* tonight. I don't want to go out.
5. I love reading *novels* / *the novels*.
6. Yolanda is *best* / *the best* student in our class.
7. I love clear nights when you can see *moon* / *the moon*.
8. That's *the man* / *a man* I told you about yesterday.
9. Can you open *a door* / *the door* for me, please?
10. He had *breakfast* / *the breakfast* late this morning.

b Complete with *the* or *–*.

It's the longest river in *the* world.
1. What time do you finish _____ work?
2. I don't like _____ people who talk loudly at the movies.
3. _____ children behaved very badly yesterday.
4. Lorena doesn't like _____ dogs.
5. Where do you usually have _____ lunch during the week?
6. _____ sun came out, so we went for a walk.
7. Can you pass _____ salt, please?
8. My brother chose _____ most expensive ice cream.
9. Last year, we went on vacation by _____ car.
10. Is James in _____ office today? He wasn't in yesterday.

← p.91

Go online to review the grammar for each lesson

12 GRAMMAR BANK

12A present perfect

1. **A Have you seen** the new Matt Damon movie? 🔊 12.2
   B Yes, **I have**.
   She hasn't read any books in English.
2. **Have you ever read** a Russian novel?
   I've never worked in an office.
3. **Have you finished** the exercise?
   Your parents have arrived. They're in the living room.

1. We use the present perfect when we talk or ask about events in the past, but when we don't say or ask when.
2. We often use the present perfect with *ever* (= at any time in your life) and *never* (= at no time in your life).
3. We also use the present perfect to talk about recent events, e.g., *I've finished my homework.*

+

full form of *have*	contraction	past participle of main verb
I have	I've	
You have	You've	
He / She / It has	He / She / It's	**seen** that movie.
We have	We've	
They have	They've	

−

full form of *have*	contraction	past participle of main verb
I / You / We / They have not	haven't	**seen** that movie.
He / She / It has not	hasn't	

? ✓ ✗

?	✓	✗
Have I / you / we / they **Has** he / she / it	**seen** that movie?	Yes, I / you / we / they **have**. Yes, he / she / it **has**.	No, I / you / we / they **haven't**. No, he / she / it **hasn't**.

- To make the present perfect, we use *have / has* + the past participle of the verb.
- *'s = has* in present perfect.

base form	simple past	past participle
like	liked	liked
want	wanted	wanted

- Past participles of regular verbs are the same as the simple past.

base form	simple past	past participle
read /rid/	read /rɛd/	read /rɛd/
see	saw	seen

- Past participles of irregular verbs are sometimes the same as the simple past, e.g., *read* /rɛd/ but sometimes different, e.g., *seen*.
  Look at the list of irregular past participles on p.165.

12B present perfect or simple past?

A Have you been to that new Italian restaurant? 🔊 12.8
B Yes, **I have**.
A When did you go there?
B I went last weekend.
A Who **did you go** with?
B I went with some people from work.

- We often use the **present perfect** to ask / tell somebody about a past action for the first time. We don't ask / say when the action happened.
  Have you been to that new Italian restaurant?
- Then we use the **simple past** to ask / talk about the details.
  "When did you go there?" "I went last weekend."
- We use the simple past **NOT** the present perfect with *when* and past time expressions, e.g., *yesterday, last week*.
  When did you see the movie? **NOT** *When have you seen the movie?*
  I saw it last week. **NOT** *I've seen it last week.*

been or gone?

A Have you ever **been** to Japan? 🔊 12.9
B Yes, I've **been** to Tokyo three times.
A My sister has **gone** to Japan to study Japanese.

- *been* and *gone* have different meanings. *been* is the past participle of *be*, and *gone* is the past participle of *go*.
- In the present perfect, we use *been to* (**NOT** *gone to* **OR** *been in*) to say that somebody has visited a place.
  I've been to Tokyo three times.
  Have you been to the new Japanese restaurant on Pine Street?
- We use *gone to* when somebody goes to a place and is still there.
  My parents have gone to the US for their vacation. They're having a great time.
- Compare:
  Nick has been to Paris. = He visited Paris and came back at some time in the past.
  Nick has gone to Paris. = He went to Paris and he is in Paris now.

12A

a Write the sentences with contractions.

I have seen the movie. *I've seen the movie.*
1. She has not read the book. _____
2. You have not finished your ice cream! _____
3. We have heard the news. _____
4. He has arrived at the airport. _____
5. They have not asked for the check. _____
6. We have not seen him before. _____
7. It has stopped raining. _____

b Write + and − sentences and ? in the present perfect. Use contractions where possible.

+ I / see a famous actor. *I've seen a famous actor.*
1. + I / change my email address _____
2. − my boyfriend / work abroad _____
3. ? you / decide what to do _____
4. − they / pass the exam _____
5. ? he / accept the invitation _____
6. + she / study three languages _____
7. − the train / arrive _____
8. ? the children / clean their room _____
9. − my girlfriend / called me _____
10. + my father / help me a lot _____

c Write a sentence in the present perfect for each picture. Use the verbs in the list.

ask ~~clean~~ not finish paint pass see

He's cleaned the floor.
1. _____ a good movie.
2. _____ his driver's test.
3. _____ her book.
4. _____ the wall.
5. _____ a difficult question.

→ p.94

12B

a Circle the correct form.

(Have you ever seen) / Did you ever see a Japanese movie?
1. I *haven't finished* / *didn't finish* this book. I'm on page 210.
2. My boyfriend *has given* / *gave* me a ring for my last birthday.
3. They've *bought* / *bought* a new house last month.
4. *Have you ever danced* / *Did you ever dance* the tango?
5. My friends *have gone* / *went* to a party last weekend.

b Circle the correct verb, *been* or *gone*.

Let's go to the Peking Duck. I've never (been) / gone there.
1. The secretary isn't here. She's *been* / *gone* out for lunch.
2. I've never *been* / *gone* to the US.
3. My neighbors aren't at home. They've *been* / *gone* on vacation.
4. Have you ever *been* / *gone* to China?
5. We have lots of food. I've *been* / *gone* to the supermarket.

c Put the verbs in parentheses in the present perfect or simple past.

A *Have* you ever *been* to Thailand? (be)
B No, but I *went* to South Korea last year. (go)
A ¹_____ you ever _____ any countries in South America? (visit)
B Yes, I have. I ²_____ to Brazil a few years ago. (go)
A ³Who _____ you _____ with? (go)
B My boyfriend. It was a work trip and his company ⁴_____ for everything. (pay)
A How wonderful! ⁵_____ you there for long? (be)
B No, we ⁶_____ only there for five days. (be)
A ⁷Where _____ you _____? (stay)
B We ⁸_____ a suite in a five-star hotel. It was beautiful! (have)
A ⁹_____ the company _____ you on any other trips recently? (invite)
B No. My boyfriend ¹⁰_____ working there a year later, so that was our only trip. (stop)

→ p.96

Go online to review the grammar for each lesson

Days and numbers

VOCABULARY BANK

1 DAYS OF THE WEEK

a Complete the days of the week with the letters.

W   Fr   S   Th   T   M   S

<u>M</u> onday /ˈmʌndeɪ/
____ uesday /ˈtuzdeɪ/
____ ednesday /ˈwɛnzdeɪ/
____ ursday /ˈθərzdeɪ/
____ iday /ˈfraɪdeɪ/
____ aturday /ˈsætərdeɪ/
____ unday /ˈsʌndeɪ/

b 🔊 1.11 Listen and check.

c 🔊 1.12 Listen and repeat the **bold** phrases.
  the <u>week</u>end (= Saturday and Sunday)
  a <u>week</u>day (= Monday–Friday)
  What day is it to<u>day</u>?   It's <u>Fri</u>day.
  Have a good <u>week</u>end.   You too.
  See you <u>la</u>ter. See you to<u>mo</u>rrow. See you on <u>Mon</u>day.

ACTIVATION Cover the days. Say them in order.

> 🔍 **Capital letters**
> Days of the week begin with a capital letter.
> Tuesday **NOT** ~~tuesday~~

2 NUMBERS 0–20

a Match the words and numbers.

twelve   twenty   eleven   three   eighteen
five   fifteen   seven

0 <u>ze</u>ro /ˈzɪroʊ/
1 one /wʌn/
2 two /tu/
3 <u>three</u>____ /θri/
4 four /fɔr/
5 _____ /faɪv/
6 six /sɪks/
7 _____ /ˈsɛvn/
8 eight /eɪt/
9 nine /naɪn/
10 ten /tɛn/
11 _____ /ɪˈlɛvn/
12 _____ /twɛlv/
13 thir<u>teen</u> /θərˈtin/
14 four<u>teen</u> /fɔrˈtin/
15 _____ /fɪfˈtin/
16 six<u>teen</u> /ˌsɪksˈtin/
17 seven<u>teen</u> /sɛvnˈtin/
18 _____ /eɪˈtin/
19 nine<u>teen</u> /ˌnaɪnˈtin/
20 _____ /ˈtwɛnti/

b 🔊 1.13 Listen and check.

ACTIVATION Cover the words. Say the numbers.

> 🔍 **Phone numbers**
> 794-1938 = seven nine four, one nine three eight
> 44 = four four **OR** double four
> 0 = zero **OR** oh /oʊ/

3 NUMBERS 21–100

a Write the numbers.

<u>21</u>   <u>twen</u>ty-one /ˌtwɛnti ˈwʌn/
_____ <u>thir</u>ty /ˈθərti/
_____ <u>thir</u>ty-five /ˈθərti ˈfaɪv/
_____ <u>for</u>ty /ˈfɔrti/
_____ <u>for</u>ty-three /ˈfɔrti ˈθri/
_____ <u>fif</u>ty /ˈfɪfti/
_____ <u>fif</u>ty-nine /ˌfɪfti ˈnaɪn/
_____ <u>six</u>ty /ˈsɪksti/
_____ <u>six</u>ty-seven /ˌsɪksti ˈsɛvn/
_____ <u>seven</u>ty /ˈsɛvnti/
_____ <u>seven</u>ty-two /ˈsɛvənti tu/
_____ <u>eigh</u>ty /ˈeɪti/
_____ <u>eigh</u>ty-eight /ˈeɪti ˈeɪt/
_____ <u>nine</u>ty /ˈnaɪnti/
_____ <u>nine</u>ty-four /ˈnaɪnti fɔr/
_____ a <u>hun</u>dred /ə ˈhʌndrəd/

b 🔊 1.27 Listen and check.

> 🔍 **Pronunciation**
> 13 and 30, 14 and 40, etc., are similar, but the stress is different, e.g., thir|<u>teen</u>, <u>thir</u>|ty, four|<u>teen</u>, <u>for</u>|ty, etc.

ACTIVATION Cover the words. Say the numbers.

← p.9

4 HIGH NUMBERS

a Write the missing numbers or words.

<u>105</u>   a / one hundred and five
_____ two hundred
350   three hundred and _____
875   eight hundred _____ seventy-five
1,000   a / one <u>thou</u>sand /ˈθaʊz(ə)nd/
_____ one thousand five hundred
2,012   two thousand and _____
5,420   five thousand four _____ and twenty
_____ twenty-five thousand
100,000   a / one hundred _____
1,000,000 a / one <u>mil</u>lion /ˈmɪlyən/
2,300,000 two million _____ hundred thousand

b 🔊 9.14 Listen and check.

ACTIVATION Cover the words. Say the numbers.

← p.74

← p.7

Countries

VOCABULARY BANK

1 CONTINENTS

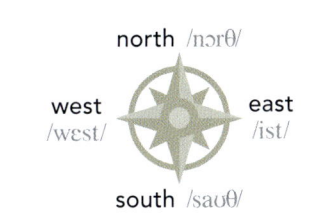

north /nɔrθ/
west /wɛst/
east /ist/
south /saʊθ/

a Match the words and continents 1–6.

Continent	Adjective
☐ Africa /ˈæfrɪkə/	☐ African /ˈæfrɪkən/
☐ Asia /ˈeɪʒə/	☐ Asian /ˈeɪʒn/
☐ Australia /ɔˈstreɪlyə/	☐ Australian /ɔˈstreɪlyən/
☐ Europe /ˈyʊrəp/	☐ European /yʊrəˈpiən/
1 North America /nɔrθ əˈmɛrɪkə/	☐ North American /nɔrθ əˈmɛrɪkən/
☐ South America /saʊθ əˈmɛrɪkə/	☐ South American /saʊθ əˈmɛrɪkən/

b 🔊 1.18 Listen and check.

c Cover the words and look at the map. Can you remember the continents and their adjectives?

> 🔍 **Capital letters**
> Use CAPITAL letters for continents, countries, nationalities, and languages, e.g., *Spanish* **NOT** *spanish*.

2 COUNTRIES AND NATIONALITIES

a 🔊 1.19 Match the countries and flags. Then listen and check.

Country /ˈkʌntri/   **Nationality adjective**

☐ England /ˈɪŋglənd/   ☐ English /ˈɪŋglɪʃ/
☐ Ireland /ˈaɪərlənd/   ☐ Irish /ˈaɪrɪʃ/
1 Spain /speɪn/   ☐ Spanish /ˈspænɪʃ/
☐ Turkey /ˈtərki/   ☐ Turkish /ˈtərkɪʃ/

☐ Germany /ˈdʒərməni/   ☐ German /ˈdʒərmən/
☐ Mexico /ˈmɛksɪkoʊ/   ☐ Mexican /ˈmɛksɪkən/
☐ Morocco /məˈrɑkoʊ/   ☐ Moroccan /məˈrɑkən/
☐ the United States (or the US) ☐ American /əˈmɛrɪkən/

☐ Argentina /ɑrdʒənˈtinə/   ☐ Argentinian /ɑrdʒənˈtɪniən/
☐ Brazil /brəˈzɪl/   ☐ Brazilian /brəˈzɪlyən/
☐ Canada /ˈkænədə/   ☐ Canadian /kəˈneɪdiən/
☐ Egypt /ˈidʒɪpt/   ☐ Egyptian /iˈdʒɪpʃn/
☐ Peru /pəˈru/   ☐ Peruvian /pəˈruːviən/
☐ Russia /ˈrʌʃə/   ☐ Russian /ˈrʌʃn/

☐ China /ˈtʃaɪnə/   ☐ Chinese /ˌtʃaɪˈniz/
☐ Japan /dʒəˈpæn/   ☐ Japanese /dʒæpəˈniz/
☐ Vietnam /viɛtˈnæm/ ☐ Vietnamese /viɛtnəˈmiz/

☐ the Czech Republic /ˌtʃɛk rɪˈpʌblɪk/ ☐ Czech /tʃɛk/
☐ France /fræns/   ☐ French /frɛn(t)ʃ/
☐ Thailand /ˈtaɪlænd/   ☐ Thai /taɪ/

b Cover the words and look at the flags. Can you remember the countries and nationalities?

ACTIVATION Choose six countries. Say the continent.

Canada is in North America.

⬅ p.8

💬 **Go online** to review the vocabulary for each lesson

149

Classroom language

VOCABULARY BANK

a Match the phrases and pictures.

The teacher says

- ☐ Open your books, please.
- ☐ Go to page 84.
- ☐ Do exercise a.
- ☐ Read the text.
- 1 Look at the board.
- ☐ Close the door.
- ☐ Work in pairs (or groups).
- ☐ Answer the questions.
- ☐ Listen and repeat.
- ☐ Stand up.
- ☐ Sit down.
- ☐ Turn off your phone.
- ☐ Please stop talking!

b 🔊 1.33 Listen and check.

> 🔍 **Please**
> Use **please** at the beginning or end of a phrase to be polite.
> *Please come here.* **OR** *Come here, please.*

c Match the phrases and pictures.

You say

- ☐ Sorry, can you repeat that, please?
- 14 Sorry I'm late.
- ☐ I don't understand.
- ☐ Can I have a copy, please?
- ☐ How do you spell it?
- ☐ I don't know.
- ☐ How do you say *gato* in English?
- ☐ Can you help me, please?
- ☐ What page is it?

d 🔊 1.34 Listen and check.

e Cover the sentences and questions and look at the pictures. Say the sentences and questions.

ACTIVATION Try to use the **You say** language in your next English lesson.

⬅ p.10

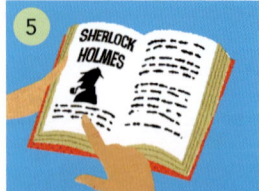

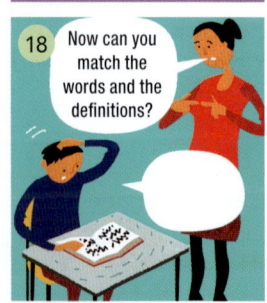

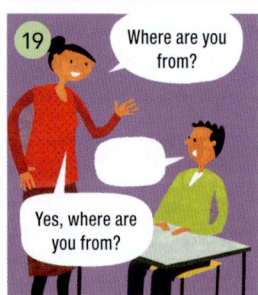

Things

VOCABULARY BANK

a   Match the words and photos.

- ☐ a bag /bæg/
- ☐ a calendar /ˈkæləndər/
- ☐ a change purse /tʃeɪndʒ pərs/
- ☐ a charger /ˈtʃɑrdʒər/
- 1 a coin /kɔɪn/
- ☐ a credit card /ˈkrɛdət kɑrd/ (or debit card)
- ☐ a dictionary /ˈdɪkʃəˌnɛri/
- ☐ a file / a binder /faɪl/ /ˈbaɪndər/
- ☐ glasses /ˈglæsəz/
- ☐ headphones /ˈhɛdfoʊnz/
- ☐ an ID card /aɪˈdi kɑrd/
- ☐ a key /ki/
- ☐ a lamp /læmp/
- ☐ a laptop /ˈlæptɑp/
- ☐ a magazine /ˌmægəˈzin/
- ☐ a newspaper /ˈnuzˌpeɪpər/
- ☐ a notebook /ˈnoʊtbʊk/
- ☐ a pen /pɛn/
- ☐ a pencil /ˈpɛnsl/
- ☐ a (cell) phone /foʊn/
- ☐ a photo /ˈfoʊtoʊ/
- ☐ a piece of paper /pis əv ˈpeɪpər/
- ☐ scissors /ˈsɪzərz/
- ☐ sunglasses /ˈsʌnˌglæsəz/
- ☐ a tablet /ˈtæblət/
- ☐ a ticket /ˈtɪkɪt/
- ☐ a tissue /ˈtɪʃu/
- ☐ an umbrella /ʌmˈbrɛlə/
- ☐ a wallet /ˈwɑlət/
- ☐ a watch /wɑtʃ/

b   🔊 2.1 Listen and check.

> 🔍 **Plural nouns**
> Some words for things are always plural, e.g., *glasses*, *headphones*, *scissors*. Don't use *a* / *an* with plural nouns. **NOT** a glasses, a headphones.

ACTIVATION Cover the words and look at the photos. In pairs, ask and answer.

What is it?   *It's a watch.*
What are they?   *They're glasses.*

← p.15

Go online to review the vocabulary for each lesson

Adjectives

VOCABULARY BANK

a Match the words and pictures.

- [ ] <u>beau</u>tiful /ˈbyutəfl/   <u>ug</u>ly /ˈʌgli/
- [ ] big /bɪg/   small /smɔl/
- [ ] cheap /tʃip/   ex<u>pen</u>sive /ɪkˈspɛnsɪv/
- [ ] clean /klin/   <u>dir</u>ty /ˈdərti/
- [ ] <u>ea</u>sy /ˈizi/   <u>di</u>fficult /ˈdɪfɪˌkʌlt/
- [ ] fast /fæst/   slow /sloʊ/
- [ ] full /fʊl/   <u>em</u>pty /ˈɛm(p)ti/
- [1] good /gʊd/   bad /bæd/
- [ ] high /haɪ/   low /loʊ/
- [ ] hot /hɑt/   cold /koʊld/
- [ ] light /laɪt/   dark /dɑrk/
- [ ] long /lɔŋ/   short /ʃɔrt/
- [ ] old /oʊld/   new /nu/
- [ ] old /oʊld/   young /yʌŋ/
- [ ] rich /rɪtʃ/   poor /pɔr/
- [ ] right /raɪt/   left /lɛft/
- [ ] right /raɪt/   wrong /rɔŋ/
- [ ] safe /seɪf/   <u>dan</u>gerous /ˈdeɪndʒ(ə)rəs/
- [ ] the same /seɪm/   <u>di</u>fferent /ˈdɪf(ə)rənt/
- [ ] strong /strɔŋ/   weak /wik/
- [ ] tall /tɔl/   short /ʃɔrt/

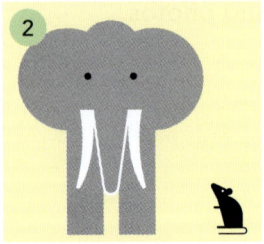

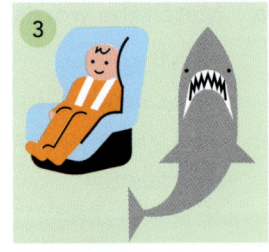

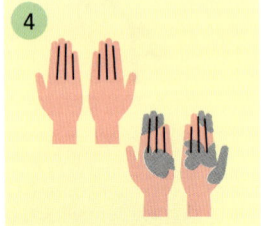

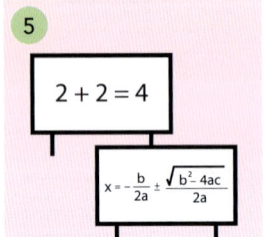

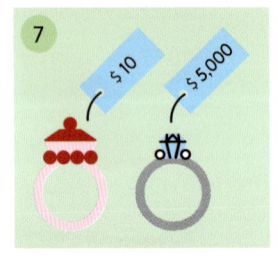

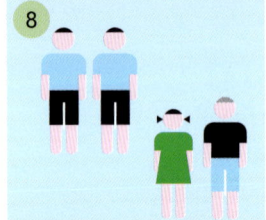

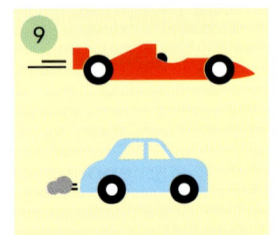

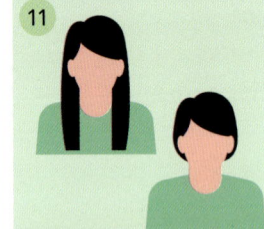

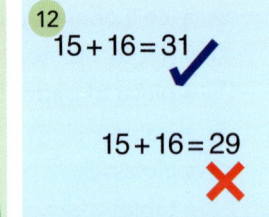

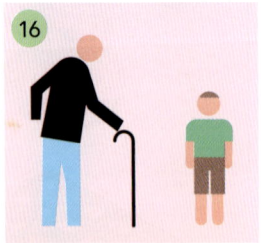

b 🔊 2.7 Listen and check.

c Test your partner. **A** say an adjective and **B** say the opposite.

> 🔍 **Modifiers: very / really**
> We often use modifiers before adjectives.
> A Ferrari is **very / really** fast.

ACTIVATION Look at the things in the list. Say two adjectives for each one. Use modifiers.

| a Ferrari   Mount Everest   Bill Gates |
| the *Mona Lisa*   the Pyramids   Africa |
| your town or city |

a Ferrari (It's really fast and very expensive.

> 🔍 **Opinion adjectives**
> **good:** nice /naɪs/, great /greɪt/, fan<u>tas</u>tic /fænˈtæstɪk/
> **bad:** <u>aw</u>ful /ˈɔfl/, <u>te</u>rrible /ˈtɛrəb(ə)l/

← p.16

Verb phrases

VOCABULARY BANK

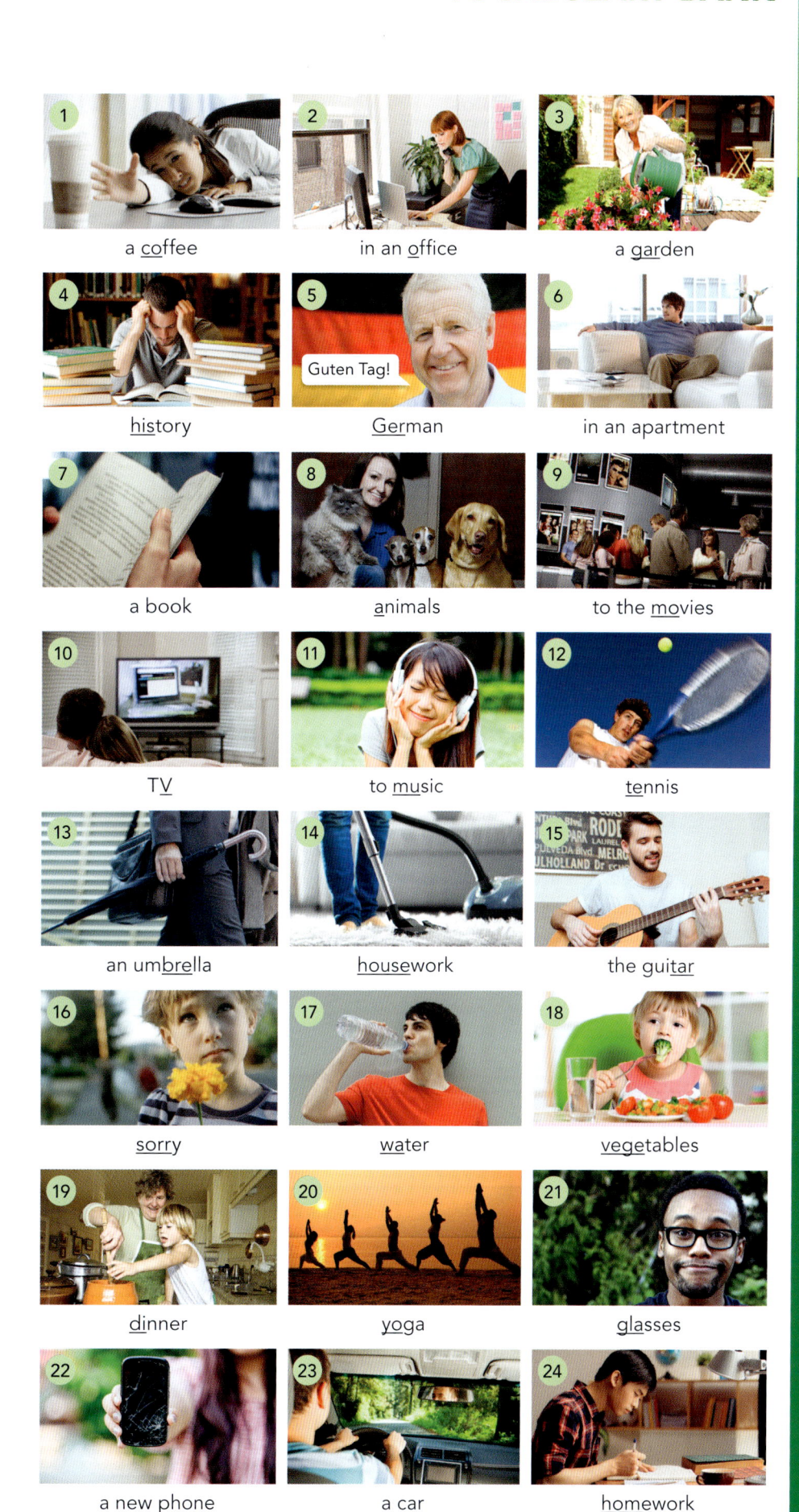

a   Match the verbs and photos.

- [ ] cook /kʊk/
- [ ] do /du/
- [ ] drink /drɪŋk/
- [ ] drive /draɪv/
- [ ] eat /it/
- [ ] go /goʊ/
- [ ] have /hæv/
- [ ] like /laɪk/
- [ ] listen /ˈlɪsn/
- [ ] live /lɪv/
- [ ] need /nid/
- [ ] play /pleɪ/
- [ ] read /rid/
- [ ] say /seɪ/
- [ ] speak /spik/
- [ ] study /ˈstʌdi/
- [ ] take /teɪk/
- [1] want /wɑnt/
- [ ] watch /wɑtʃ/
- [ ] wear /wɛr/
- [ ] work /wərk/

b 3.2 Listen and check.

ACTIVATION Cover the verbs and look at the photos. Test yourself or a partner.

← p.22

1 a coffee
2 in an office
3 a garden
4 history
5 German
6 in an apartment
7 a book
8 animals
9 to the movies
10 TV
11 to music
12 tennis
13 an umbrella
14 housework
15 the guitar
16 sorry
17 water
18 vegetables
19 dinner
20 yoga
21 glasses
22 a new phone
23 a car
24 homework

Go online to review the vocabulary for each lesson

153

Jobs

VOCABULARY BANK

a   Match the words and photos.

- an a<u>cc</u>ountant /əˈkaʊntnt/
- an a<u>c</u>tor /ˈæktər/
- an a<u>d</u>ministrator /ədˈmɪnəstreɪtər/
- 1 an a<u>r</u>chitect /ˈɑrkətɛkt/
- a <u>ch</u>ef /ʃɛf/ (or cook)
- a <u>cl</u>eaner /ˈklinər/
- a con<u>s</u>truction worker /kənˈstrʌkʃn ˈwərkər/
- a <u>d</u>entist /ˈdɛntɪst/
- a <u>d</u>octor /ˈdɑktər/
- an engi<u>n</u>eer /ɛndʒəˈnɪr/
- a <u>fa</u>ctory <u>wo</u>rker /ˈfæktəri ˈwərkər/
- a flight at<u>t</u>endant /ˈflaɪt əˈtɛndənt/
- a <u>g</u>uide /gaɪd/
- a hair <u>s</u>tylist /hɛr ˈstaɪlɪst/
- a <u>j</u>ournalist /ˈdʒɜrnəlɪst/
- a <u>l</u>awyer /ˈlɔyər/
- a (bank) <u>ma</u>nager /ˈmænɪdʒər/
- a <u>m</u>odel /ˈmɑdl/
- a mu<u>s</u>ician /myuˈzɪʃn/
- a <u>n</u>urse /nɜrs/
- a <u>p</u>ilot /ˈpaɪlət/
- a po<u>li</u>ce <u>o</u>fficer /pəˈlis ˈɑfəsər/
  (or po<u>li</u>ceman, po<u>li</u>cewoman)
- a re<u>c</u>eptionist /rɪˈsɛpʃənɪst/
- a <u>sa</u>lesperson /ˈseɪlzpərsn/
- a <u>so</u>ccer <u>pla</u>yer /ˈsɑkər ˈpleɪər/
- a <u>s</u>oldier /ˈsoʊldʒər/
- a <u>ta</u>xi <u>dri</u>ver /ˈtæksi ˈdraɪvər/
- a <u>t</u>eacher /ˈtitʃər/
- a <u>v</u>et /vɛt/
- a <u>wai</u>ter /ˈweɪtər/ / a <u>wai</u>tress /ˈweɪtrəs/

> 🔍 **a / an + jobs**
> We use a / an + job words.
> She's a model. **NOT** She's model.

b   🔊 3.10 Listen and check.

c   🔊 3.11 Listen and repeat the sentences. What do *you* do?

ACTIVATION   Cover the jobs and look at the photos. In pairs, say what the people do.

She's a journalist.   *He's an engineer.*

← p.25

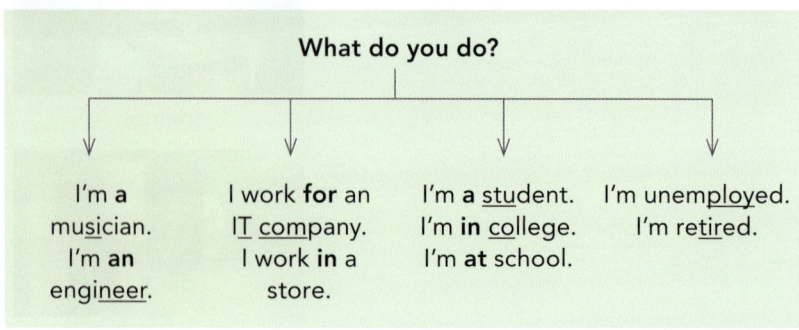

What do you do?

- I'm **a** mu<u>si</u>cian.
  I'm **an** engi<u>n</u>eer.
- I work **for** an IT company.
  I work **in** a store.
- I'm **a** <u>s</u>tudent.
  I'm **in** <u>c</u>ollege.
  I'm **at** school.
- I'm unem<u>p</u>loyed.
  I'm re<u>ti</u>red.

The family

VOCABULARY BANK

a Look at the two family trees. Number the people in relation to Richard.

1 <u>fa</u>ther /ˈfɑðər/
2 <u>mo</u>ther /ˈmʌðər/
3 <u>bro</u>ther /ˈbrʌðər/
4 <u>sis</u>ter /ˈsɪstər/
5 <u>daugh</u>ter /ˈdɔtər/
6 son /sʌn/
7 <u>grand</u>father /ˈgrænfɑðər/
8 <u>grand</u>mother /ˈgrænmʌðər/
9 aunt /ænt/
10 <u>un</u>cle /ˈʌŋkl/
11 <u>ne</u>phew /ˈnɛfyu/
12 niece /nis/
13 <u>cou</u>sin /ˈkʌzn/
14 wife /waɪf/

b Complete 1–5 with *children*, *couple*, *grandparents*, *parents*, or *parents-in-law*.

1 my father and my mother
 = my _____ /ˈpɛrənts/
2 my wife's mother and father
 = my _____ /ˈpɛrənt ɪn lɔ/
3 my grandfather and my grandmother
 = my _____ /ˈgrænpɛrənts/
4 my son and my daughter
 = my _____ /ˈtʃɪldrən/
5 a husband and wife
 = a (married) _____ /ˈkʌpl/

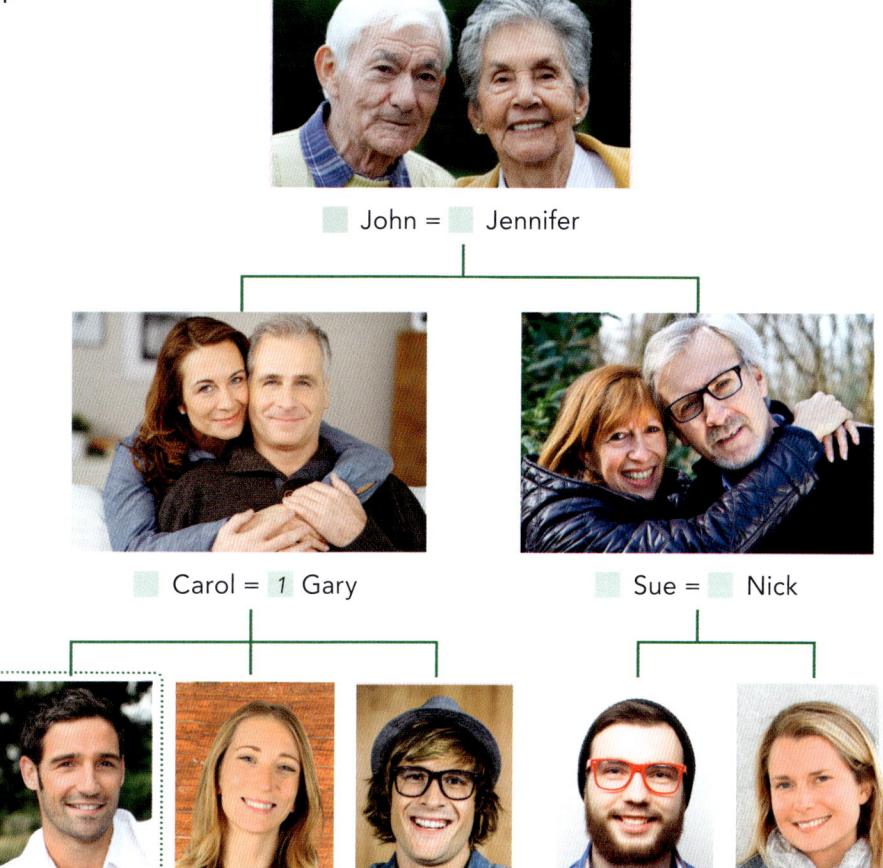

c ▶ 4.3 Listen and check your answers to **a** and **b**.

> 🔍 **More family words**
> my wife's mother = my <u>mother-in-law</u>
> my husband's sister = my <u>sister-in-law</u>
> my mother's new husband = my <u>step</u>father
> my father's new wife = my <u>step</u>mother
> the person I am in a relationship with
> = my <u>part</u>ner

ACTIVATION Cover the words. In pairs, ask and answer.

Who's Jennifer?
  She's Richard's grandmother.

Who are Sue and Nick?
  They're Richard's aunt and uncle.

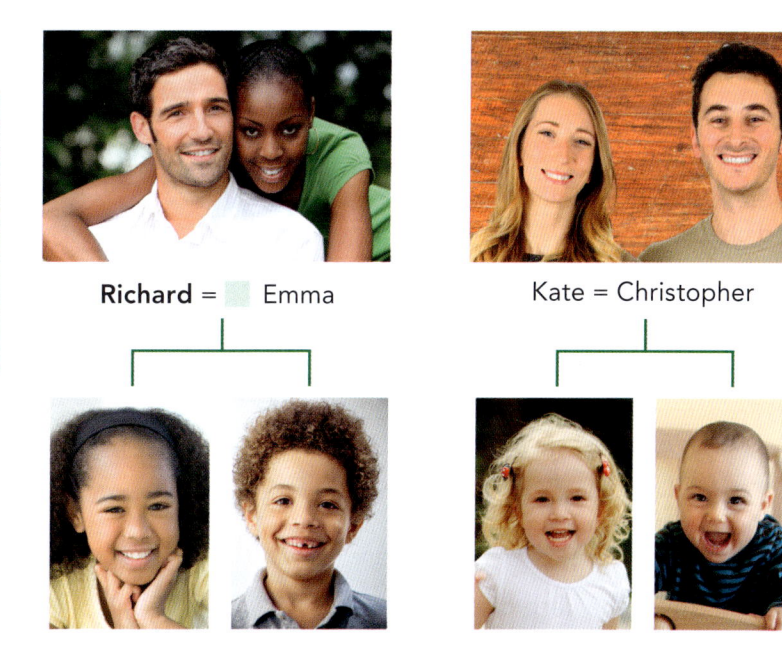

⬅ p.31

John = Jennifer

Carol = 1 Gary   Sue = Nick

Richard   Kate   Steven   Hugh   Sarah

Richard = Emma   Kate = Christopher

Chloe   Jake   Ruby   Oliver

Daily routine

VOCABULARY BANK

a Match the verb phrases and pictures.

Busy Belinda

- [ ] take a <u>sh</u>ower
- [ ] have a <u>c</u>offee
- [ ] do the <u>house</u>work
- [ ] <u>st</u>art work at 8:30
- [ ] <u>f</u>inish work at 6:30
- [ ] get dressed
- [1] wake up at 7:00
- [ ] have lunch at work
- [ ] go <u>sh</u>opping
- [ ] go to bed
- [ ] have <u>p</u>izza for <u>d</u>inner
- [ ] get home late
- [ ] go to work by bus
- [ ] put on <u>m</u>a<u>k</u>e-up
- [ ] check <u>e</u>mails
- [ ] get to work

Chill Charlie

- [ ] go to <u>Sp</u>ani<u>sh cl</u>asses
- [17] get up at 8:00
- [ ] have <u>break</u>fast
- [ ] shave
- [ ] go home <u>e</u>arly
- [ ] walk to work
- [ ] rel<u>ax</u>
- [ ] take the dog for a walk
- [ ] sleep for eight hours
- [ ] make dinner
- [ ] take a bath
- [ ] see friends

b ▶ 4.8 Look at the pictures. Listen and check.

> 🔍 **have**
> 1 For family and possessions, e.g., *I have three children. He has a big house.*
> 2 For activities, e.g., *I have lunch at 1:30. She has breakfast in the morning.*
> 3 For food and drink, e.g., *have a coffee, have a sandwich.*

ACTIVATION Cover the verb phrases. **A** describe Belinda's day. Then **B** describe Charlie's day.

← p.32

Time

VOCABULARY BANK

1 TELLING THE TIME

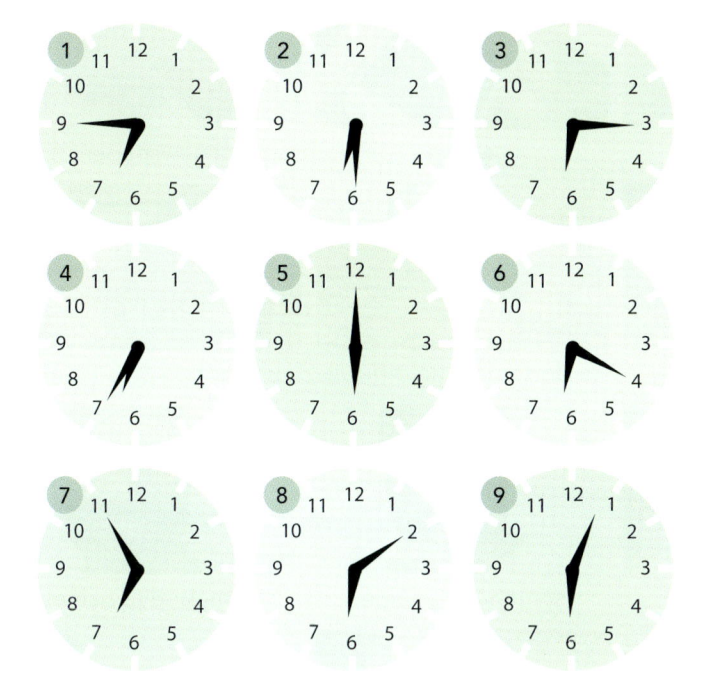

a Match the clocks and phrases.

☐ It's six fifteen. / It's (a) quarter after six.
☐ It's six o'clock.
1 It's six forty-five. / It's (a) quarter to seven.
☐ It's six ten. / It's ten after six.
☐ It's six fifty-five. / It's five to seven.
☐ It's six thirty-five. / It's twenty-five to seven.
☐ It's six-thirty. / It's half past six.
☐ It's three minutes after six.
☐ It's six twenty. It's twenty after six.

b 🔊 3.26 Listen and check.

> 🔍 **Time**
> You can ask for the time in two ways:
> *What time is it?* **OR** *What's the time?*
>
> For times that are not multiples of five, we use *minutes*, e.g., 6:03 = *It's three minutes after six.*
>
> When you can't be exact, use *about*:
> "What time do you get up?"
> "At **about** 7:00."

ACTIVATION Cover the phrases and look at the clocks. Ask and answer with a partner.

What time is it? / What's the time?) (*It's…*

⬅ p.28

2 EXPRESSIONS OF FREQUENCY

a Complete the expressions.

How often do you see your friends?
1 every /ˈɛvri/ *day*   M, T, W, Th, F, S, S
2 every w_____   week 1, week 2, week 3, etc.
3 every m_____   January, February, March, etc.
4 every y_____   e.g., 2017, 2018, 2019, etc.
5 once /wʌns/ a _____   e.g., only on Mondays
6 twice /twaɪs/ a _____   e.g., on Mondays and Wednesdays
7 three times a _____   e.g., on Mondays, Wednesdays, and Fridays
8 four times a _____   e.g., in January, April, July, and October

b 🔊 4.17 Listen and check.

ACTIVATION Cover the left-hand column. Test yourself.

3 ADVERBS OF FREQUENCY

a What do the highlighted words mean? Match sentences 1–6 to a–f.

1 *b* I **always** /ˈɔlweɪz/ get up at 7:00 during the week.
2 ☐ I **often** /ˈɔfn/ go to the movies after work.
3 ☐ I **usually** /ˈyuʒuəli/ finish work at 6:00.
4 ☐ I **sometimes** /ˈsʌmtaɪmz/ meet a friend for lunch.
5 ☐ I **hardly ever** /ˈhɑrdli ˈɛvər/ go to the theater.
6 ☐ I **never** /ˈnɛvər/ have coffee.

a About seven or eight times a month.
b ~~I start work at 8:00 every day.~~
c But on Fridays we stop at 3:00.
d I don't like it.
e Only once or twice a year.
f About once or twice a month.

b 🔊 4.18 Listen and check.

c 🔊 4.19 Listen and repeat the highlighted adverbs of frequency.

> 🔍 **normally**
> *Normally* /ˈnɔrməli/ is the same as *usually*.
> *I normally get up early.* = *I usually get up early.*

ACTIVATION Cover sentences 1–6 and look at a–f. Can you remember the sentences?

⬅ p.34

> 🔵 **Go online** to review the vocabulary for each lesson

157

More verb phrases

VOCABULARY BANK

a Match the verbs and photos.

- [ ] buy /baɪ/
- [ ] call /kɔl/
- [1] dance /dæns/
- [ ] draw /drɔ/
- [ ] find /faɪnd/
- [ ] for<u>get</u> /fərˈgɛt/
- [ ] give /gɪv/
- [ ] hear /hɪr/
- [ ] help /hɛlp/
- [ ] leave /liv/
- [ ] look for /lʊk fɔr/
- [ ] meet /mit/
- [ ] paint /peɪnt/
- [ ] re<u>mem</u>ber /rɪˈmɛmbər/
- [ ] run /rʌn/
- [ ] see /si/
- [ ] send /sɛnd/
- [ ] sing /sɪŋ/
- [ ] swim /swɪm/
- [ ] take /teɪk/
- [ ] talk /tɔk/
- [ ] tell /tɛl/
- [ ] try /traɪ/
- [ ] use /yuz/
- [ ] wait for /weɪt fɔr/

b 🔊 5.1 Listen and check.

ACTIVATION Cover the verbs and look at the photos. Test yourself or a partner.

⬅ p.38

1 the tango
2 a taxi
3 a newspaper
4 in the ocean
5 to do something difficult
6 your bag on a train
7 a parking space
8 somebody's name
9 somebody's name
10 somebody a secret
11 somebody flowers
12 to a friend
13 a song
14 a noise
15 a photo
16 somebody
17 the internet
18 a text message
19 your keys
20 a friend
21 a picture
22 a bus
23 a race
24 a picture
25 a movie

158

The weather and dates

VOCABULARY BANK

1 THE WEATHER

a Complete the chart with words from the list.

cloudy /ˈklaʊdi/   cold /koʊld/   foggy /ˈfɔgi/
hot /hɑt/   raining /ˈreɪnɪŋ/   snowing /ˈsnoʊɪŋ/
sunny /ˈsʌni/   windy /ˈwɪndi/

What's the weather like?

☀	It's ¹ _sunny_.	25→	It's ⁵ _____.
95°	It's ² _____.	☁ (foggy)	It's ⁶ _____.
☁	It's ³ _____.	15°	It's ⁷ _____.
🌧	It's ⁴ _____.	❄	It's ⁸ _____.

b 🔊 5.17 Listen and check.

> **Other adjectives for weather**
> warm /wɔrm/ = not very hot (opp. cool)
> wet = raining (opp. dry)
>
> **Nouns and adjectives**
> Noun: sun, cloud, wind, fog
> Adjective: sun**ny**, cloud**y**, wind**y**, fog**gy**

c Cover the sentences in the chart and look at the pictures. Ask and answer with a partner.

What's the weather like? *It's sunny.*

d 🔊 5.18 Match the seasons and pictures. Then listen and check.

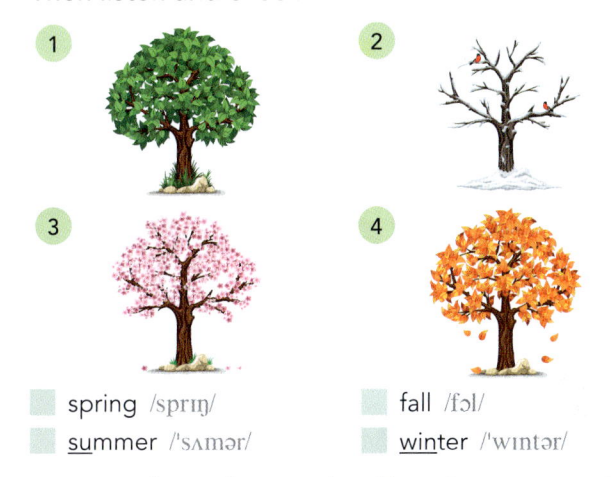

1 2
3 4

☐ spring /sprɪŋ/   ☐ fall /fɔl/
☐ summer /ˈsʌmər/   ☐ winter /ˈwɪntər/

ACTIVATION What's the weather like where you are? What season is it?

↩ p.42

2 ORDINAL NUMBERS AND THE DATE

a Complete the numbers and words.

1st	first /fərst/
2nd	second /ˈsɛkənd/
3rd	third /θərd/
4th	fourth /fɔrθ/
_5th_	fifth /fɪfθ/
6th	_____ /sɪksθ/
7th	_____ /ˈsɛvnθ/
_____	eighth /eɪtθ/
_____	ninth /naɪnθ/
10th	_____ /tɛnθ/
11th	_____ /ɪˈlɛvnθ/
_____	twelfth /twɛlvθ/
13th	_____ /θərˈtinθ/
14th	_____ /fɔrˈtinθ/
_____	twentieth /ˈtwɛntiəθ/
21st	_____ /ˈtwɛnti fərst/
_____	twenty-second /ˈtwɛnti ˈsɛkənd/
23rd	_____ /ˈtwɛnti θərd/
_____	twenty-fourth /ˈtwɛnti fɔrθ/
30th	_____ /ˈθərtiəθ/
_____	thirty-first /ˈθərti fərst/

b 🔊 6.10 Listen and check.

c Look at how we write and say the date.

> **Writing and saying the date**
> We write   We say
> March 22nd   March twenty-second or
>   **the twenty-second of** March
> 1/12   January twelfth or
>   **the twelfth of** January
>
> **Prepositions with years, months, and dates**
> Use *in* + years, e.g.,   The Los Angeles Olympics are **in** 2028.
> Use *in* + months, e.g., My birthday's **in** February.
> Use *on* + dates, e.g.,   The meeting is **on** Friday, September 5th.
>
> **Saying years**
> 1807 eighteen "oh" seven
> 1936 nineteen thirty-six
> 2008 two thousand eight
> (for years 2000–2010)
> 2011 two thousand eleven OR twenty eleven

ACTIVATION What's the date today?
What's the date tomorrow?

↩ p.48

Go online to review the vocabulary for each lesson

159

go, have, get

VOCABULARY BANK

a Match the verb phrases and photos.

go

- [ ] by bus /bʌs/ (or by car /kɑr/, by plane /pleɪn/)
- [1] for a walk /wɔk/
- [ ] home (from school) /hoʊm/
- [ ] out (on Friday night) /aʊt/
- [ ] shopping /ˈʃɑpɪŋ/
- [ ] to a restaurant /ˈrɛstərənt/
- [ ] to bed (late) /bɛd/
- [ ] to church /tʃərtʃ/ (or to mosque /mɑsk/, to temple /ˈtɛmpl/, etc.)
- [ ] to the beach /bitʃ/
- [ ] back (to work) /bæk/
- [ ] on vacation /veɪˈkeɪʃn/

have

- [ ] a car /kɑr/ (or a bike /baɪk/)
- [ ] long hair /lɔŋ hɛr/
- [ ] breakfast /ˈbrɛkfəst/ (or lunch /lʌntʃ/, dinner /ˈdɪnər/)
- [ ] a drink /drɪŋk/
- [ ] a good time /gʊd taɪm/
- [ ] a sandwich /ˈsændwɪtʃ/
- [ ] a sister /ˈsɪstər/ (or a brother /ˈbrʌðər/)

get

- [ ] a newspaper /ˈnuzpeɪpər/ (= buy or obtain)
- [ ] a taxi /ˈtæksi/ (= take)
- [ ] an email /ˈimeɪl/ (= receive)
- [ ] dressed /drɛst/
- [ ] home /hoʊm/ (= arrive)
- [ ] to the airport /ˈɛrpɔrt/ (= arrive)
- [ ] up /ʌp/ (early, late)

b 🔊 7.16 Listen and check.

c Cover the verb phrases and look at the photos. Test yourself or a partner.

ACTIVATION Take turns saying five things you did yesterday and five things you did last week with *went*, *had*, or *got*.

> Yesterday, I got up early. I had breakfast in a café. I went shopping...

↩ p.59

The house

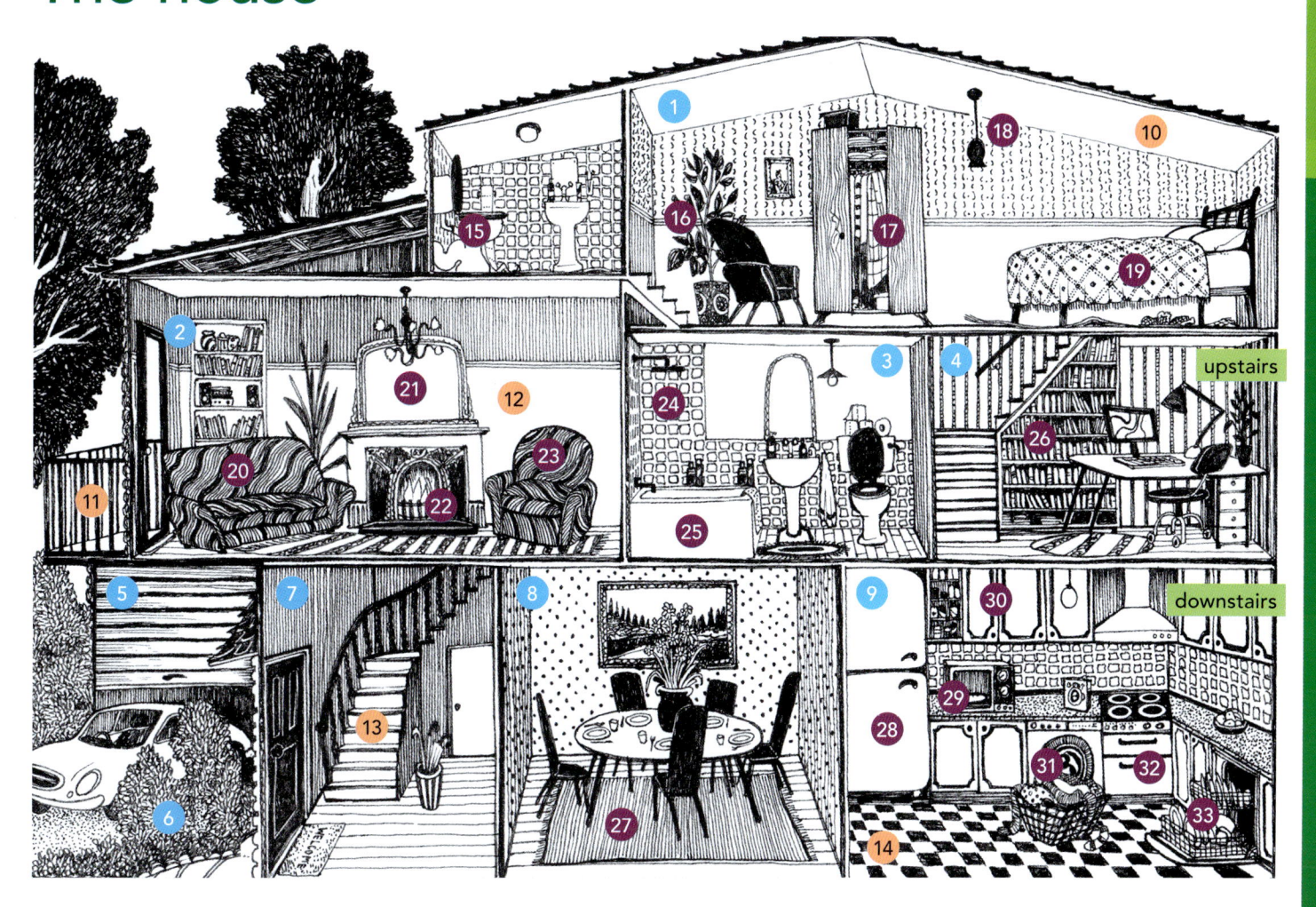

VOCABULARY BANK

upstairs

downstairs

1 ROOMS

Match the words and pictures 1–9.

- ☐ a <u>bath</u>room /ˈbæθrum/
- 1 a <u>bed</u>room /ˈbɛdrum/
- ☐ a <u>dining</u> room /ˈdaɪnɪŋ rum/
- ☐ a <u>gar</u>age /gəˈrɑdʒ/
- ☐ a <u>hall</u> /hɔl/
- ☐ a <u>kit</u>chen /ˈkɪtʃən/
- ☐ a <u>living</u> room /ˈlɪvɪŋ rum/
- ☐ a <u>stud</u>y / an <u>off</u>ice /ˈstʌdi/ /ˈɔfəs/
- ☐ a <u>yard</u> /yɑrd/

2 PARTS OF A HOUSE

Match the words and pictures 10–14.

- ☐ a <u>bal</u>cony /ˈbælkəni/
- ☐ a <u>ceil</u>ing /ˈsilɪŋ/
- ☐ a <u>floor</u> /flɔr/
- ☐ <u>stairs</u> /stɛrz/
- ☐ a <u>wall</u> /wɔl/

3 THINGS IN A ROOM

a Match the words and pictures 15–33.

- ☐ an <u>arm</u>chair /ˈɑrmtʃər/
- ☐ a <u>bath</u>tub /ˈbæθtʌb/
- ☐ a <u>bed</u> /bɛd/
- ☐ a <u>cup</u>board /ˈkʌbərd/
- ☐ a <u>dish</u>washer /ˈdɪʃwɑʃər/
- ☐ a <u>fire</u>place /ˈfaɪərpleɪs/
- ☐ a <u>light</u> /laɪt/
- ☐ a <u>mic</u>rowave /ˈmaɪkrəweɪv/
- ☐ a <u>mir</u>ror /ˈmɪrər/
- ☐ a <u>plant</u> /plænt/
- ☐ a re<u>frig</u>erator / a <u>fridge</u> /rɪˈfrɪdʒəreɪtər/ /frɪdʒ/
- ☐ a <u>rug</u> /rʌg/
- ☐ a <u>shelf</u> (shelves) /ʃɛlf/
- ☐ a <u>show</u>er /ˈʃaʊə/
- ☐ a <u>so</u>fa / a <u>couch</u> /ˈsoʊfə/ /kaʊtʃ/
- ☐ a <u>stove</u> /stoʊv/
- ☐ a <u>toi</u>let /ˈtɔɪlət/
- ☐ a <u>ward</u>robe /ˈwɔrdroʊb/
- ☐ a <u>wash</u>ing ma<u>chine</u> /ˈwɑʃɪŋ məˈʃin/

b 🔊 8.10 Listen and check 1–3.

> 🔍 **Heat and central air conditioning**
> *Heat* is a system that makes a house warm.
> *Central air conditioning* is a system that makes a house cool.

ACTIVATION Cover the words and look at the pictures. Test yourself or a partner.

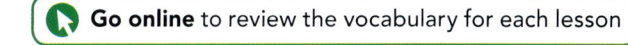

⬅ p.64   Go online to review the vocabulary for each lesson   161

Prepositions

VOCABULARY BANK

1 PLACE

a Match the words and pictures.

- ☐ in /ɪn/ (the wardrobe)
- ☐ in front of /ɪn frʌnt əv/ (the table)
- ☐ on /ɑn/ (the chair)
- ☐ un<u>der</u> /ˈʌndər/ (the bed)
- **1** be<u>hind</u> /bɪˈhaɪnd/ (the sofa)
- ☐ be<u>tween</u> /bɪˈtwin/ (the windows)
- ☐ across from /əˈkrɔs frəm/ (the woman)
- ☐ next to /nɛkst tu/ (the armchair)
- ☐ <u>o</u>ver /ˈoʊvər/ (the mirror)

b 🔊 8.22 Listen and check.

ACTIVATION In pairs, point and ask and answer about the pictures.

Where's the ghost? *He's under the bed.*

> 🔍 **above and below**
> above /əˈbʌv/ is similar to over.
> below /bɪˈloʊ/ is similar to under.

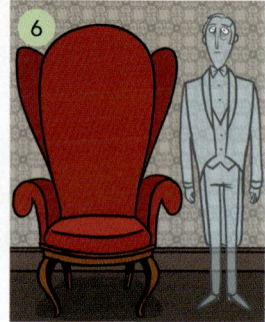

2 MOVEMENT

a Match the words and pictures.

- ☐ from /frəm/ (the bedroom)
  to /tu/ (the bathroom)
- ☐ <u>in</u>to /ˈɪntu/ (the wardrobe)
- ☐ out of /aʊt əv/ (the wardrobe)
- ☐ through /θru/ (the window)
- ☐ up /ʌp/ (the stairs)
- ☐ down /daʊn/ (the stairs)

b 🔊 8.23 Listen and check.

ACTIVATION In pairs, point and ask and answer about the pictures.

Where's the ghost going? *He's going up the stairs.*

⬅ p.67

Food and drink

VOCABULARY BANK

a Match the words and photos.

Breakfast /ˈbrɛkfəst/

- bread /brɛd/
- butter /ˈbʌtər/
- cereal /ˈsɪriəl/
- 1 cheese /tʃiz/
- coffee /ˈkɑfi/
- eggs /ɛgz/
- jam /dʒæm/
- (orange) juice /dʒus/
- milk /mɪlk/
- sugar /ˈʃʊgər/
- tea /ti/
- toast /toʊst/

Lunch /lʌntʃ/ **or dinner** /ˈdɪnər/

- fish /fɪʃ/ e.g., salmon, tuna
- herbs /ərbz/
- meat /mit/ e.g., chicken, sausages, steak
- (olive) oil /ɔɪl/
- pasta /ˈpɑstə/
- rice /raɪs/
- salad /ˈsæləd/
- seafood /ˈsifud/
- spices /ˈspaɪsɪz/

Vegetables /ˈvɛdʒtəblz/

- carrots /ˈkærəts/
- French fries /frɛntʃ fraɪz/
- lettuce /ˈlɛtəs/
- mushrooms /ˈmʌʃrumz/
- onions /ˈʌnyənz/
- peas /piz/
- peppers /ˈpɛpərz/
- potatoes /pəˈteɪtoʊz/
- tomatoes /təˈmeɪtoʊz/

Fruit /frut/

- apples /ˈæplz/
- bananas /bəˈnænəz/
- oranges /ˈɔrɪndʒɪz/
- a pineapple /ˈpaɪnæpl/
- strawberries /ˈstrɔbɛriz/

Desserts /dɪˈzərts/

- cake /keɪk/
- fruit salad /frut ˈsæləd/
- ice cream /aɪs ˈkrim/

Snacks /snæks/

- candy /ˈkændi/
- chocolate /ˈtʃɒklət/
- cookies /ˈkʊkiz/
- nuts /nʌts/
- potato chips /pəˈteɪtoʊ tʃɪps/
- a sandwich /ˈsændwɪtʃ/

b 🔊 9.1 Listen and check.

ACTIVATION Cover the words and look at the photos. Test yourself or a partner.

↻ p.70

Go online to review the vocabulary for each lesson

163

Places and buildings

VOCABULARY BANK

a Match the words and photos.

- a church /tʃərtʃ/
- a department store /dɪˈpɑrtmənt stɔr/
- a hospital /ˈhɑspɪtl/
- a market /ˈmɑrkət/
- a park /pɑrk/
- pharmacy /ˈfɑrməsi/
- a police station /pəˈlis ˈsteɪʃn/
- a post office /poʊst ˈɔfəs/
- a shopping mall /ˈʃɑpɪŋ mɔl/
- a supermarket /ˈsupərˌmɑrkət/
- 1 a town hall /taʊn hɔl/

- an art gallery /ɑrt ɡæləri/
- a castle /ˈkæsl/
- a museum /myuˈziəm/
- a theater /ˈθiətər/
- a zoo /zu/

- a bridge /brɪdʒ/
- a river /ˈrɪvər/
- a road /roʊd/
- a square /skwɛr/
- a street /strit/

- a bus station /ˈbʌs steɪʃn/
- a parking lot /ˈpɑrkɪŋ lɑt/
- a train station /treɪn ˈsteɪʃn/

> 🔍 **Other places of worship (= religious buildings)**
> a cathedral /kəˈθidrəl/
> a mosque /mɑsk/
> a synagogue /ˈsɪnəɡɑɡ/
> a temple /ˈtɛmpl/

b 🔊 10.2 Listen and check.

c Cover the words and look at the photos. Test yourself or a partner.

ACTIVATION Ask and answer about places with a partner.

> Is there a _____ near where you live / near this school?

← p.78

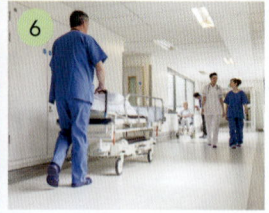

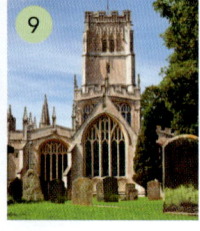

Irregular verbs

Present	Simple past	Past participle
be /bi/	was /wəz/ were /wər/	been /bin/
become /bɪˈkʌm/	became /bɪˈkeɪm/	become
begin /bɪˈgɪn/	began /bɪˈgæn/	begun /bɪˈgʌn/
break /breɪk/	broke /broʊk/	broken /ˈbroʊkən/
bring /brɪŋ/	brought /brɔt/	brought
build /bɪld/	built /bɪlt/	built
buy /baɪ/	bought /bɔt/	bought
can /kæn/	could /kʊd/	—
catch /kætʃ/	caught /kɔt/	caught
come /kʌm/	came /keɪm/	come
cost /kɔst/	cost	cost
do /du/	did /dɪd/	done /dʌn/
drink /drɪŋk/	drank /dræŋk/	drunk /drʌŋk/
drive /draɪv/	drove /droʊv/	driven /ˈdrɪvn/
eat /it/	ate /eɪt/	eaten /ˈitn/
fall /fɔl/	fell /fɛl/	fallen /ˈfɔlən/
feel /fil/	felt /fɛlt/	felt
find /faɪnd/	found /faʊnd/	found
fly /flaɪ/	flew /flu/	flown /floʊn/
forget /fərˈgɛt/	forgot /fərˈgɑt/	forgotten /fərˈgɑtn/
get /gɛt/	got /gɑt/	gotten /ˈgɑtn/
give /gɪv/	gave /geɪv/	given /ˈgɪvn/
go /goʊ/	went /wɛnt/	gone /gɑn/
have /hæv/	had /hæd/	had
hear /hɪr/	heard /hərd/	heard
know /noʊ/	knew /nu/	known /noʊn/
leave /liv/	left /lɛft/	left
lose /luz/	lost /lɔst/	lost
make /meɪk/	made /meɪd/	made
meet /mit/	met /mɛt/	met
pay /peɪ/	paid /peɪd/	paid
put /pʊt/	put	put
read /rid/	read /rɛd/	read /rɛd/
run /rʌn/	ran /ræn/	run
say /seɪ/	said /sɛd/	said
see /si/	saw /sɔ/	seen /sin/
send /sɛnd/	sent /sɛnt/	sent
sing /sɪŋ/	sang /sæŋ/	sung /sʌŋ/
sit /sɪt/	sat /sæt/	sat
sleep /slip/	slept /slɛpt/	slept
speak /spik/	spoke /spoʊk/	spoken /ˈspoʊkən/
spend /spɛnd/	spent /spɛnt/	spent
stand /stænd/	stood /stʊd/	stood
swim /swɪm/	swam /swæm/	swum /swʌm/
teach /titʃ/	taught /tɔt/	taught
take /teɪk/	took /tʊk/	taken /ˈteɪkən/
tell /tɛl/	told /toʊld/	told
think /θɪŋk/	thought /θɔt/	thought
understand /ʌndərˈstænd/	understood /ʌndərˈstʊd/	understood
wake /weɪk/	woke /woʊk/	woken /ˈwoʊkən/
wear /wɛr/	wore /wɔr/	worn /wɔrn/
win /wɪn/	won /wʌn/	won
write /raɪt/	wrote /roʊt/	written /ˈrɪtn/

Vowel sounds

SOUND BANK

		usual spelling	! but also
iː	tree	ee meet three ea speak eat e me we	people police key niece
ɪ	fish	i his this win six big swim	English women busy
ɪr	ear	eer cheer engineer ere here we're ear dear hear	
æ	cat	a thanks dance black Japan have tablet	
ɛ	egg	e yes help ten pet very red	friend weather breakfast any said
ɛr	chair	air airport stairs pair hair are square careful	their there wear
ɑ	clock	o hot stop doctor job not box	father watch want
ɔ	saw	al talk small aw saw draw	water bought fought
ɔr	horse	or sport door short	four board
u	boot	oo school food u* June use ew new flew	do fruit juice shoe

		usual spelling	! but also
ʊ	bull	u full put oo good book look cook	could would woman
ʊr	tourist	A very unusual sound. euro Europe sure plural	
ʌ	up	u bus lunch ugly run lucky cut	come brother son does young
ə	computer	Many different spellings. /ə/ is always unstressed. umbrella America famous second ago	
ɜr	bird	er her verb ir first third ur nurse turn	learn work world word
aʊ	owl	ou out thousand house count ow how down	
oʊ	phone	o* old home close don't oa road toast	slow low
ɑr	car	ar party charger start far	
eɪ	train	a* name make ai rain paint ay play day gray	break steak great eight they
ɔɪ	boy	oi coin noise toilet oy enjoy unemployed	
aɪ	bike	i* nine twice y my why igh high night	buy

* especially before consonant + *e*

☐ vowels   ☐ vowels followed by /r/   ☐ diphthongs

Consonant sounds

SOUND BANK

		usual spelling		! but also
	parrot	p pp	pilot Peru paper sleep apple happy	
	bag	b bb	be butter table number job hobby	
	key	c k ck	credit card actor kitchen like black back	archictect school
	girl	g gg	green get argue big eggs bigger	
	flower	f ph ff	Friday fifteen wife photo alphabet office coffee	
	vase	v	very eleven live travel river love	of
	tie	t tt	tea take student sit letter bottle	liked dressed
	dog	d dd	dance understand bad read address middle	played tired
	snake	s ss ce/ci	sister stops stress actress police nice city	
	zebra	z s, se	zero zoo Brazil music please dogs watches	
	shower	sh ti (+ vowel)	shopping shoes Spanish fish station information	sugar sure
	television	si (+ on)	decision occasion	usually garage
	thumb	th	think thirty throw bathroom fourth tenth	
	mother	th	the these then that other with	
	chess	ch tch t (+ ure)	cheap children church watch match picture adventure	
	jazz	j dge	January jacket July enjoy bridge fridge	German manager
	leg	l, le ll	like little plane girl small spelling	
	right	r rr	rice rich problem try sorry terrible	write wrong
	witch	w wh	window wait Wednesday twenty why when	one once
	yacht	y before u	yellow yesterday young yes use university music	
	monkey	m mm	man Monday money swim summer swimming	
	nose	n nn	no never nine ran dinner thinner	know
	singer	ng	England language song thing long going	think bank
	house	h	happy hungry hotel hall head behind	who whose

☐ voiced   ☐ unvoiced

Go online to watch the Sound Bank videos

OXFORD
UNIVERSITY PRESS

198 Madison Avenue
New York, NY 10016 USA

Great Clarendon Street, Oxford, OX2 6DP, United Kingdom

Oxford University Press is a department of the University of Oxford. It furthers the University's objective of excellence in research, scholarship, and education by publishing worldwide. Oxford is a registered trade mark of Oxford University Press in the UK and in certain other countries

© Oxford University Press 2021

The moral rights of the author have been asserted

First published in 2021

2025

11

No unauthorized photocopying

All rights reserved. No part of this publication may be reproduced, stored in a retrieval system, or transmitted, in any form or by any means, without the prior permission in writing of Oxford University Press, or as expressly permitted by law, by licence or under terms agreed with the appropriate reprographics rights organization. Enquiries concerning reproduction outside the scope of the above should be sent to the ELT Rights Department, Oxford University Press, at the address above

You must not circulate this work in any other form and you must impose this same condition on any acquirer

Links to third party websites are provided by Oxford in good faith and for information only. Oxford disclaims any responsibility for the materials contained in any third party website referenced in this work

ISBN: 978 0 19 490616 6 Student Book with Online Practice Pack
ISBN: 978 0 19 490617 3 Student Book Component
ISBN: 978 0 19 490615 9 Student Online Practice

Printed in China

This book is printed on paper from certified and well-managed sources

ACKNOWLEDGMENTS

The authors would like to thank all the teachers and students around the world whose feedback has helped us to shape American English File.

The authors would also like to thank: all those at Oxford University Press (both in Oxford and around the world) and the design team who have contributed their skills and ideas to producing this course.

Finally very special thanks from Clive to Maria Angeles, Lucia, and Eric, and from Christina to Cristina, for all their support and encouragement. Christina would also like to thank her children Joaquin, Marco, and Krysia for their constant inspiration.

The publisher and authors would also like to thank the following for their invaluable feedback on the materials: Jane Hudson, Brian Brennan, Isabel Orgillés Trol, Beatriz Martin, Philip Drury, Rachael Smith, Robert Anderson, Maria Vanessa Ferroni, Freia Layfield, Cristina Cogollos, Lesley Poulaud, Magdalena Muszyńska, Dagmara Lata, Marcin Zaród, Sam Millin, Sylwia Kossakowska-Pisarek, Pavlína Zoss, Ruth Valentová, Elif Barbaros, Hamide Cakir, Zahra Bilides, Polina Kuharenko, Ellen Van Raemdonck, Eva Misky, Gyula Kiss, Marisa Lobato, Wagner Roberto Silva dos Santos, Thalysor Nobrega, Sarah Giles, Biagio Iaquinta, Amory Lee Ewerdt, Roberto Sanchez, Wayne Rimmer, Mowbray Bates, Aideen Lyons Murphy, Ola Skolimowska, Karla Mikešová, Marta Zanzi

The Publisher and Authors are very grateful to the following who have provided information, personal stories, and/or photographs: Marjan Jahangiri and Darius Latham-Koenig for 'Busy lives' p.32/33; Charlotte Campbell p.51 (interview); Joaquin Cogollos for the story 'It's written in the cards' p.82/83; Jack Horton, p.87 (interview); Sir Ian McKellen, p.98/99 (interview); Cristina Cogollos, p.114 'My Favorite Day')

The authors and publisher are grateful to those who have given permission to reproduce the following extracts and adaptations of copyright material: p.23 Adapted extract from 'What foreigners who live here really think of the British way of life' by James Gillespie. http://www.express.co.uk/news/uk/425830/What-foreigners-who-live-here-really-think-of-the-Britishway-of-life. Daily Express Online/N&S Syndication. Reproduced by permission. p.24 Adapted extract from 'Shift work: Learning to love our offbeat schedules' by Jessica E Hall, from Offbeat Home & Life (http://offbeathome.com). Reproduced by permission of the publisher and the author. p.30 Adapted extract from 'Doug Pitt: Not easy to know but 'the guy who will step in'' by Steve Pokin, November 8 2014, www.newsleader.com. Reproduced by permission of Springfield News-Leader/USA TODAY Network. p.32 Extract from 'How I make it work: Marjan Jahangiri' by Ruby Warrington, 3 July 2011. www.thesundaytimes.co.uk. Reproduced by permission of News Syndication. p.37 Extract from 'A Life in the Day: the superstar DJ David Guetta' by Danny Stott, 24 May 2015, www.thesundaytimes.co.uk. Reproduced by permission of News Syndication. p.53 Adapted extract from 'Perfect wake up songs: science determines top 20 songs to help you get up in the morning', November 4 2015, from http://www.hngn.com. Reproduced by permission of Headlines and Global News. p.56 Adapted extract from 'Couple flown to Grenada in the Caribbean and not Granada in Spain lose $34,000 lawsuit against British Airways for ticket mix up' by James Nye from www.dailymail.co.uk, 27 August 2014. Reproduced by permission. p.58 Extract from 'Celebrating New Year's Eve in Reykjavik' by Jennifer Dombrowski. © 2016 Jennifer Dombrowski, Luxe Adventure Traveler. All rights reserved. p.59 Adapted Extract from 'New Year's Eve 2011 – NYE Gig Story'. Reproduced by permission of The Disco Studio. The Disco Studio is a retailer of DJ Equipment and related accessories. p.59 Adapted extract from 'New Year's Eve on Copacabana is awesome' by Marcelo Souza, January 18 2015, www.traveltranquilo.com/new-years-eve/. Reproduced by permission of Marcelo Souza de Araujo. p.69 Adapted extract from 'How the Modern Detective Novel Was Born' by Martin Edwards, May 29 2015,

www.publishersweekly.com/pw/by-topic. Republished by permission of Publisher's Weekly, permission conveyed through Copyright Clearance Center, Inc. p.70 Adapted extract from 'Why I Eat The Same Thing Every Single Day' by Nathan Wiebe, www.mindbodygreen.com, 20 June 2015. Copyright mindbodygreen LLC. Reproduced by permission. p.79 Adapted extract from 'She Learns to Cross Streets in Ho Chi Minh City, Vietnam' by Evelyn Hannon, www.journeywoman.com. Reproduced by permission of the author. p.80 Adapted extract from '5:1, Continent Run Summarised' by Gunnar Garfors, www.garfors.com, 20 June 2012. Reproduced by permission of the author. p.81 Adapted extract from http://www.responsibletravel.com/copy/planning-a-trip-but-dont-know-where-to-start. Reproduced by permission of www.responsibletravel.com. p.88 Definition of 'Bucket List' from www.oxfordlearnersdictionaries.com/definition/english. Reproduced by permission of Oxford University Press. p.88 Adapted extract from 'About me' by Stefka Poessel, https://foodandphotosrtw.com. Reproduced by permission of the author. p.88 Adapted extract from '101 Bucket List Ideas for 2015 you can do (almost) everywhere' by Stefka Poessel, https://foodandphotosrtw.com. Reproduced by permission of the author. p.88 Adapted extract from 'Remember life before the internet?' By Marie-Claire Dorking, from http://www.marieclaire.co.uk/blogs/548460/remember-life-before-the-internet.html. Reproduced by permission of Time Inc UK.

Sources: www.cosmopolitan.com/food-cocktails/; www.dailymail.co.uk; www.tripadvisor.com; www.nydailynews.com; www.hostelworld.com; www.theguardian.com; http://thoughtcatalog.com/michael-koh

The publisher would like to thank the following for their kind permission to reproduce photographs: Cover: Hobbit/Shutterstock. 123RF pp.39 (pens and pencils/belchonock), 155 (smiling man/Wavebreak Media Ltd); Alamy Stock Photo pp.9 (Japanese Fans/Allstar), 22 (Notting Hill carnival/LondonPhotos), 23 (tacos), 23 (world map/Lifestyle pictures), 24 (Vancouver police squad patrol car vehicle downtown BC Canada/Radharc Images), 30 (Doug Pitt/epa European pressphoto agency b.v.), 30 (Gyllenhaal siblings/Allstar Picture Library), 35 (festival, Greece/Peter Eastland), 35 (elderly Okinawan woman/Chris Willson), 35 (fruit shop/age fotostock), 42 (heavy snow/Don Tonge), 42 (London marathon/Avpics), 43 (urban spring/Jan Dagnall), 43 (Chicago Marathon/Tribune Content Agency LLC), 48 (sad snowman on field/Johner Images), 51 (headphones/Jiri Hera), 62 (businessman/Image Source), 63 (Bateman's house/ parkerphotography), 63 (elderly lady/ClassicStock), 64 (Bateman's house/Tony Watson) 71 (Thanksgiving dinner/foodfolio), 72 (apple juice/Mediablitzimages), 72 (pineapple chunks/ScotStock), 72 (honey/Paul Airs), 72 (dark chocolate/gbimages), 72 (sparkling water/Jan Dagnall), 78 (Madera Mexico/Alexander Cimbal), 85 (Hôtel Lagunita, Mexico/Hemis), 86 (Brooklyn Bridge/Washington Imaging), 90 (Blue Tooth/Pakpoom Phummee), 91 (cassette player/Frankie Angel), 91 (Yellow pages/Jamie Mann) 91 (Thomas Guide Map/ Drive Images) 96 (friends at cafe/Ammentorp Photography), 98 (Ian McKellen, Gandalf/AF archive), 99 (Ian McKellen, X-Men/AF archive), 106 (Langham Hotel/Nick Moore), 115 (Infield/Robert Landau), 115 (Venice Beach, Simon Dannhauer), 116 (Living Room/Blend Images), 117 (Maine B&B/Joseph Reid), 151 (folder/Richard Heyes), 151 (wallet/L A Heusinkveld), 151 (tissue paper/Photo Alto sas), 151 (Driver's License), 151 (paper/Geoffrey Kidd), 153 (man relaxing/Upper Cut Images), 154 (receptionist/Ace Stock Ltd), 154 (TV reporter/dmac), 154 (taxi driver/fStop Images GmbH), 154 (tour guide speaker/T.M.O.Pictures), 154 (Charlie Adam/Ahmad Faizal Yahya), 154 (shaking hands/Wavebreak Media ltd), 154 (cellist player/redsnapper), 154 (Lawyer/ Andriy Popov), 154 (Police Woman/Ira Berger), 158 (man singing/Image Source), 158 (drawing/Shepic), 160 (boy on stairs/Image Source), 160 (boy eating breakfast/Image Source), 160 (news vendor/Roger Bamber), 160 (terminal 3, Heathrow/Kumar Sriskandan), 160 (woman hailing Taxi/Eric Carr), 163 (uncooked meat/Juan Mayano), 164 (Hyde Park/Pawel Libera Images), 164 (beauty department/Robert Stainforth), 164 (market/Homer Sykes), 164 (church/incamerastock), 164 (theatre/Kirsty McLaren), 164 (New York City, MoMA/Patrick Batchelder), 164 (Dalyan River/Dorling Kindersley ltd), 164 (Itchen toll bridge/Motoring Picture Library), 164 (City Hall/Mark Summerfield), 164 (Pharmacy/Wavebreak Media), 164 (Post Office/Allen Creative), 164 (Urban Street/Ellen Isaacs), p.54 Van Gough painting/Fogg Art Museum, Harvard Art Museums, p. 54 USA/Bequest from the Collection of Maurice Wertheim, Class 1906); Caters News Agency Ltd p.85 (underground hotel room/Caters News Agency); Children and The Arts p.55 (Adele for Face of Britain/Children and The Arts); Christina Latham-Koenig pp.31 (Tom/Christina Latham-Koenig), 31 (Celia and children/Christina Latham-Koenig), 31 (Miriam and family/Christina Latham Koenig), 32 (Marjan Jahangiri operating/Christina Latham-Koenig), 33 (Darius Latham-Koenig/Christina Latham-Koenig), 71 (lettuce/Christina Latham-Koenig), 87 (Jack Horton/Christina Latham-Koenig); Erlebniswelt Muotathal GmbH p.85 (Hüttenhilfe Husky-Lodge/erlebniswelt muotathal GmbH p.85 (Hüttenhilfe Husky-Lodge/erlebniswelt muotathal GmbH); Getty Images pp.9 (Australian tennis fan/Marianna Massey) 11 (Shakira/Paul Archuleta), 14 (Virginia Woolf/Hulton Archive), 14 (male portrait/Robbie Jack - Corbis), 21 (Coney Island/Andy Ryan), 30 (celebrity couple/Josiah Kamau), 30 (WillSmith & son Trey/ Steve Granitz /Wire Images) 30 (Mary-Kate Olsen and Olivier Sarkozy/James Devaney), 34 (girl using laptop/Alicia Frost), 34 (girl using computer/Teresa Lett), 35 (builder portrait/Gianluca Colla), 37 (DJ performing/Gabriel Olsen), 42 (outdoor theatre/VisitBritain/Eric Nathan), 43 (Chicago_Millenium Park/Jumping Rocks), 43 (Chicago Art Institute/Patty C-Smith), 50 (piano player/ Lawrence Manning), 53 (Woman jumping/Ari Wasabi), 55 (Kurt Vonnegut portrait/Ron Galella), 55 (Billy Dee Williams/ABC Photo Archives), 55 (Adele portrait/Dave Hogan), 58 (fireworks display/Giulio Bisio Photo), 59 (firework display/Samba Photo), 63 (female portrait/H. Armstrong Roberts), 63 (business portrait/Verity Jane Smith), 63 (retro secretary/Alija), 71 (Shakshuka/Alena Gamm/EyeEm), 73 (scale/ jonathansloane), 75 (Quiz Night/Jeff Greenberg), 87 (food market/DreamPictures/Shannon Faulk), 102 (female portrait/Peeter Viisimaa), 102 (male portrait/Nicolas McComber), 102 (Argentian woman/Ajr Images), 102 (rooftop portrait/Oliver Rossi), 102 (Bruno Mars/Jason LaVeris), 102 (Daniel Craig/Jason LaVeris), 102 (Jay-Z/Todd Plitt), 102 (Cate Blanchett/Samir Hussein), 102 (Helen Mirren/Gary Gershoff), 102 (Leonardo DiCaprio/Todd Plitt), 102 (Alecia Moore/Gregg DeGuire), 102 (Dakota Johnson/Karwai Tang), 153 (reaching for coffee/Jose Luis Pelaez Inc), 153 (businesswoman/ Image Source), 153 (cat and dogs/Malcolm MacGregor), 153 (tennis player/David J Spurdens/Digital Vision), 153 (businesspeople/Chris Ryan), 153 (child with flower/Cheyenne Montgomery), 153 (man drinking water/Westend61), 153 (cooking with grandma/Karina Mansfield), 153 (young man/Fyza Hashim), 154 (architect/Tetra Images), 154 (dentist/Benelux/Corbis/VCG), 154 (army soldier/Gravity Images), 154 (haircut/Frank Gaglione), 154 (teacher/Getty Images), 154 (builder/Rick Gomez), 154 (engineer/Andrew Brookes), 154 (catwalk/ Stefan Gosatti), 154 (pilot/AAGAMIA), 154 (actor rehearsing/Dougal Waters), 155 (young boy/Kidstock), 158 (happy man/Fancy/Veer/Corbis), 158 (thoughtful man/Fancy/Veer/Corbis), 158 (mansearching/Fuse), 158 (whispering/Fuse), 158 (unattended backpack/ Archdpoet), 158 (helping/Tara Moore), 158 (woman hugging/Image Source RF/DreamPictures), 158 (painter/Marc Romanelli), 158 (queuing in fancy dress/JW LTD), 160 (couple reading menu/OMG), 160 (beach relaxation/M Swiet Productions), 164 (Police Officer/ csfotoimages); Guardian News & Media Ltd p.14 (Virginia Woolf writers room/Guardian News & Media Ltd 2016/Eamonn McCabe); Guardian News & Media Guardian News & Media Ltd p.14 (Ian Rankin writers room/Guardian News & Media Ltd 2016/Eamonn McCabe); Gunnar Garfors p.80 (Gunnar Garfors); Indiana Museum p.55 (Kurt Vonnegut/From the collection of the Indiana State Museum and Historic Sites); Leonie Morse p.32 (Marjan Jahangiri/Leonie Morse); Nathan Weibe p.70 (Nathan Weibe); News Syndication p.56 (Adam Armstrong and girlfriend India/News Syndication/Jim Clarke (The Sun,05 June 2011); Oxford University Press pp.8 (Czech Republic flag/EyeWire), 15 (biro pen/Dennis Kitchen Studio, Inc), 15 (wallet/Peter Viney), 15 (open dictionary/Catherine Johnson/OUP), 16 (American flag/Photodisc), 71 (chicken salad/Cathie Johnson/OUP),16 (American flag/Photodisc), 71 (chicken salad/Sarah Bench), 72 (water bottle/Mark Mason), 78 (the river Nile/erichon), 114 (student/fancy), 115 (healthy salad/ Alena Hauryilk/Shutterstock/Oxford University Press), 149 (Scottish flag/Oxford University Press), 149 (English flag/Oxford University Press), 149 (Irish flag/OxfordUniversity Press), 149 (Spanish flag/Graphi-Ogre), 149 (Poland flag/ Graphi-Ogre), 149 (Turkish flag/Graphi-Ogre), 149 (Mexican flag/Graphi-Ogre), 149 (American flag/Graphi-Ogre), 149 (German flag/Graphi-Ogre), 149 (Brazilian flag/Graphi-Ogre), 149 (Egypt flag/Graphi-Ogre)149 (Argentina flag/Graphi-Ogre), 149 (Russian flag/Graphi-Ogre), 149 (Japanese flag/Graphi-Ogre), 149 (China flag/Graphi-Ogre), 149 (French flag/Graphi-Ogre), 149 (Czech Republic flag/Graphi-Ogre), 149 (Moroccan Flag/OUP), 149 (Canadian Flag/OUP), 149 (Peruvian Flag/OUP), 149 (Vietnamese Flag/OUP), 149 (Thai Flag/OUP), 153 (German man/Image Source), 151 (coin/Catherine Johnson/OUP), 151 (phone charger/Catherine Johnson/OUP), 151 (newspaper/Alamy/OUP), 153 (movie ticket queue/image100), 153 (couple watching television/Corbis), 154 (chef/Photolibrary), 154 (car production line/Monty Rakusen), 154 (waiter/Corbis), 154 (airline stewardess/image100), 158 (listening/Image Source), 160 (travel friends/ Ann Haritonenko), 164 (country highway/Digital Vision), 164 (supermarket shopping/Photographers Choice), 164 (dinosaur exhibit/BananaStock); Responsible Travel p.81 (Justin Francis/Responsible Travel founder/www.responsibletravel.com); Rex Shutterstock pp.16 (the White House/ REX/Shutterstock), 30 (female celebrities/Henry Lamb/Photowire/BEImages/BEI), 99 (Macbeth performance/REX/Shutterstock); SCALA Group SPA p.55 (Billy Dee Williams Self Portrait 1993/National Portrait Gallery/Smithsonian Institution/Art Resource 2016/SCALA, Florence); Shutterstock pp.8 (3D earth illustration/Mmaxer), 8 (Morroccan flag/N.Vector Design), 8 (Vietnamese Flag/Sarunyu_foto), 8 (English flag/Maxx-Studio), 8 (Brazilian flag/Baloncici), 8 (Argentian flag/railway fx), 8 (Egyptian flag/Tomasz Guzowski), 8 (Peruvia flag/Gladder), 9 (Brazilian Fans/Mango),11 (video call/Mila Supinskaya Glashchenko), 11 (male teacher/Monkey Business Images), 15 (yellow umbrella/rtem), 15 (closed umbrellas/tale), 15 (wristwatch/Ian 2010), 15 (two wristwatches/Pavel Mirchuk), 16 (American football player/Brocreative), 16 (New York taxis/Bufflerump), 16 (KFC food/ fotorawin), 16 (fries/mubus7), 16 (Levis jeans/Thinglass), 16 (hot dog/ Africa Studio), 17 (Lower Manhattan skyline/mandritoiu),19 (left turn sign/defpicture), 19 (no mobiles sign/nikolae), 19 (no photography sign/darsi), 21 (Rockefeller building/ Sean Pavone), 21 (Central Park/Gimas), 22(woman in Autumn/Martin Novak), 23 (Thai Scenery/ESB Professional), 24 (day to night/tcharts), 24 (office/Monkey Business Images), 25 (professions/g stockstudio), 28 (croissant/Tanapat Phuengpak), 28 (coffee/Maxsol), 28 (chocolate brownie/margouillat photo), 30 (bow tie/Olga Popova), 30 (wristwatch/ Iablonskyi Mykola), 30 (handbag/Katrin Kot), 30 (glasses/STILLFX), 30 (ring/PhotoNAN), 31 (commuters/William Perugini), 32 (stethoscope/5 second studio), 33 (drums/furtseff), 33 (clock/PaulPaladin), 33 (bookshelf/connel), 39 (electric guitar/mekcar), 39 (camera/Tatiana Popova), 39 (trainers/Denis Rozhnovsky), 43 (Chicago River Walk/Page Light Studios), 44 (jeans/Nisakorn Neera), 44 (t-shirt/Olga Kovalenko), 44 (leather shoes/ Lucy Liu), 44 (green jumper/Alexander Kalina), 44 (shirt/Karkas), 44 (skirt/istanbul_image_video), 44 (blazer jacket/Karkas), 44 (trousers/Karkas), 45 (t-shirt/Africa Studio), 45 (leather jacket/dora modly-paris), 45 (jeans/Early Spring), 49 (Summer beach vacation/Marcel Jancovic), 50 (accordion player/Goran Bogicevic), 50 (guitar player/Igor Stepovik), 50 (girl plays violin/astudio), 50 (guitar player/pikselstock), 50 (drumplayer/Africa Studio), 50 (keyboard player/IngoSStar), 50 (trumpet player/Mr Twister), 50 (saxophone player/Africa Studio), 56 (starfish/ZoranOrcik), 56 (hat/Rustle), 56 (Boeing 747/Chris Parypa Photography), 58 (woman by elevator/wowsty), 59 (music DJ/Vladimir Hodac), 62 (greenwallpaper/Nadezhda Bolotina), 62 (open old book on white background/ Jiri Hera), 63 (cover board texture/fluke water), 63 (detective/Ysbrand Cosijn), 64 (Oil painting landscape/Fresh Stock), 66 (abstract figure/Joe Techapanupreeda), 66 (key/Bjoern Wylezich), 66 (Roosevelt Hotel/Andry Bayda), 67 (bathroom/gifted), 67 (hotel hallway/Alexey Zaytsev), 70 (clipboard/Mega Pixel), 70 (sandwich/Vankad), 72 (valentine sweets/AN NGUYEN), 72 (chips/Keith Homan), 72 (Coca Cola/M. Unal Ozmen), 72 (egg/Evgeny Karandaev), 72 (apple/S-F), 72 (Walkers crisps/urbanbuzz), 72 (olive oil/valigloo), 72 (sliced bread/kwanchai.c), 72 (teaspoon/azure1), 72 (teaspoon and sugar/Juris Surainis), 72 (Oreo cookies/Steven Senne),73 (chip flat/Sara Winter), 78 (New York station/Felix Lipov), 78 (Port Mann Bridge/Daniel Avram), 78 (Vietnam street/View Apart), 78 (Burj Khalifa/Rastos), 79 (motorbikes, Vietnam/xuanhuongho), 80 (wood/ Local Studio), 82 (beige background/Svetlana Dikhtyareva), 86 (turkey sandwich/Studio Touch), 88 (jungle/AustralianCamera), 89 (sky/Roman Sigaev), 91 (recycling set/Filip Fuxa), 91 (carbon paper/YoonSpy), 91 (fax machine/immfocus studio), 101 (pizza/Stepanek Photography), 101 (male portrait/eurobanks), 101 (middle aged couple/goodluz), 101 (woman using laptop/Monkey Business Images), 101 (Japanese student/KPG_Payless), 101 (male portrait/Serenethos), 102 (Thai man/I am Way), 102 (female portrait/AJR_photo), 104 (baked beans/marco mayer), 104 (herbal tea/Davydenko Yuliia), 113 (stylish woman/A. and I. Kruk), 115 (Los Angeles/Chones), 115 (leather boots/Devin_Pavel), 116 (room/Smoxx), 151 (laptop/ifong), 151 (desk lamp/BalancePhoto), 151 (notebook/Everything), 151 (diary/V_ctoria), 151 (family portrait/Monkey Business Images), 151 (smart phone/scyther5), 151 (satchel/BEAUTYofLIFE), 151 (blank paper/Garsya), 151 (headphones/Igor Lateci), 151 (iPad/Alexey Boldin), 151 (tickets/M. Stasy), 153 (yoga/Nadya Lukic), 153 (gardening/Kinga), 153 (busy student/wavebreakmedia), 153 (book reading/arisara), 153 (teen listens to music/leungchopan), 153 (vacuuming/Africa Studio), 153 (man plays guitar/Dean Drobot), 153 (girl eats vegetables/Oksana Kuzmina), 153 (treadmills/wavebreakmedia), 153 (broken phone/Take Photo), 153 (man driving car/Sergey Novikov), 153 (student studying/Dragon Images), 154 (dentist/HedgeHog94), 154 (Asian Nurse/Stephen/Coburn), 154 (doctor/ michaeljung), 154 (cleaners/Iakov Filimonov), 154 (female employee/withGod), 154 (businessman/Andrey_Popov), 154 (male vet/SpeedKingz), 154 (saleswoman/racorn), 155 (elderly couple/Andresr), 155 (middle aged couple/racorn), 155 (senior couple/lsantilli), 155 (male portrait/Phovoir), 155 (young couple/cate_89), 155 (male portrait/Raisa Kanareva), 155 (woman/goodluz), 155 (mixed race couple/Phovoir), 155 (young girl/Monkey Business Images), 155 (toddler/Elena Stepanova), 155 (smiling baby/pavla), 158 (tango dancing/Karelian), 158 (booking a taxi/Denys Prykhodov), 158 (buying a newspaper/l i g h t p o e t), 158 (girl swimming/Imagentle), 158 (man reading instructions/Monkey Business Images), 158 (aerial parking view/Chesky), 158 (girl receives flowers/VGstockstudio), 158 (friends drinking coffee/wavebreakmedia), 158 (couple taking selfie/victorsaboya), 158 (Google search/), 158 (using smart phone/EpicStockMedia), 158 (marathon/David Acosta Alley), 158 (cinema audience/BlueSkyImage), 159 (four seasons vector/Pagina), 160 (Kids at school/Lopolo), 160 (female on bus/ Supavadee butradee), 160 (coffee shop/Monkey Business Images), 160 (brother & sister/ Monkey Business Images), 160 (walking in the park/Aleksandar Mijatovic), 160 (businessman/lipik), 160 (church crowd/Nando Machado), 160 (girl shopping/EpicStockMedia), 160 (blonde girl/photoff), 160 (teens dancing/Pressmaster), 160 (man drinking coke/Kues), 160 (man holding car keys/pikselstock), 160 (eating sandwich/ pixelheadphoto digitalskillet), 160 (email menu/khaythka), 160 (girl buttoning shirt/Borysevych.com), 160 (morning routine/Pranee Chaiyadam), 160 (key and lock/Brian A Jackson), 164 (shopping mall/esterpoon), 164 (animal zoo/Thitisan), 164 (Bodiam Castle/Tony Baggett) 164 (old square, Prague/MarinaDa), 164 (hospital/ Spotmatik Ltd), 164 (train Station/ Songquan Deng), 164 (bus station/ TonyV3112), 164 (parking lot/Lina Mo).

Pronunciation chart artwork by: Ellis Nadler

Illustrations by: Victoria Antolini/Wolphins: p.46/7; Laura Barnard: pp.60, 80; Lisa Beta/Illustration Web: pp.18,19; Paul Boston/Meiklejohn: pp.10, 103 (desks), 108 (desks), 150; Jan Bowman: pp.26, 27; Bill Brown/Illustration Division: pp.103 (scenes), 109 (scenes), 142, 143, 147, 156, 162; Peter Bull: pp.8 (maps), 60, 149; Stephen Collins: pp.40/1, 105, 110, 131, 133, 134, 135, 138, 141; Hannah Davies/Illustration: p.82/83; Mark Duffin: p.67; Rohan Eason/Illustration Eeb: p.161; Ivan Gillett/NB Illustration: pp.6, 7, 38, 39; Satoshi Hashimoto: p.140; Pauline Reeve/Bright: p.74; Joe Todd Stanton: p.45 (shirts); Anders Wenngren/Illustration Division: pp.18 (icons), 49 (icons), 68 (icons), 90, 97, 152; Paul Young/Artist Partners: p.67.

Commissioned photography by: Gareth Boden pp.64, 65; MM Studios pp.6, 7, 15, 24, 38, 69, 90, 151, 163.

The manufacturer's authorised representative in the EU for product safety is Oxford University Press España S.A. of El Parque Empresarial San Fernando de Henares, Avenida de Castilla, 2 – 28830 Madrid (www.oup.es/en or product.safety@oup.com).OUP España S.A. also acts as importer into Spain of products made by the manufacturer.